THE GREAT BOOK OF
TRACTORS

THE GREAT BOOK OF
TRACTORS

Peter Henshaw

THUNDER BAY
P·R·E·S·S

San Diego, California

Thunder Bay Press
An imprint of the Advantage Publishers Group
5880 Oberlin Drive, San Diego, CA 92121-4794
www.thunderbaybooks.com

All notations of errors or omissions should be addressed
to Thunder Bay Press, editorial department, at the above
address. All other correspondence (author inquiries,
permissions) concerning the content of this book should
be addressed to Salamander Books Ltd., The Chrysalis
Building, Bramley Road, London W10 6SP, United
Kingdom.

Library of Congress Cataloging-in-Publication Data

Henshaw, Peter, 1962-
    The great book of tractors / Peter Henshaw.
    p. cm.
    ISBN 1-59223-305-8
    1. Farm tractors—United States—History. I. Title.

TL233.6.F37H46 2004
629.225'2'0973--dc22   2004047936

Printed in China
1 2 3 4 5 08 07 06 05 04

Credits
Project Editor: Katherine Edelston
Designer: Cara Hamilton
Production: Don Campaniello
Reproduction: ClassicScan Pte. Ltd.

CONTENTS

The 1900s–1910s:
THE PIONEERS

Today we take tractors for granted. But only a few generations ago they didn't exist, and farm work depended on muscle—both horse and human. Rural life in those days is now often remembered as a peaceful idyll—the reality was harsh, with lots of hard, physical work, constantly at the mercy of the weather. It was hard work for little reward, too, both in terms of wages and productivity. An experienced plowman with two or three horses might work an acre a day, maybe 1.5 acres in light soils. Today, a 120 horsepower (hp) tractor, by no means the biggest, can plow 2–3 acres per hour.

This great leap in productivity has transformed the rural landscape. In developed countries only 2–3 percent of the population now actually works in agriculture and most people live in towns and cities. The engine was the industrial revolution which drove that cultural transformation, made possible only by the mechanization of farming. A whole range of machinery was improved year by year, but the tractor—that mobile work horse—has always been the key player.

The modern tractor did not spring out of the air fully formed. Like most technological advances, it was an improvement on something else. Steam power was well established in British farms by the mid-nineteenth century. Stationary steam engines had long been used in mines and factories, but now they were being used for threshing or, as in the U.S., cane crushing. The problem, apart from their huge expense, was simply that once an engine had been installed, it could then not be moved.

The answer was blindingly simple. Mount a smaller steam engine onto a wheeled chassis and it could be towed by horses from farm to farm. This enabled farmers to share the expense and the engine could do more than one job on each farm. By 1851, there were an estimated 8,000 portable steam engines working on British farms. And these engines were developing rapidly. The Royal Agricultural Society of England conducted annual tests and found that efficiency was improving year by year. In 1849, the best portable engine burned 11.5 lb. of coal per horsepower hour. Six years later, it did the same work on just 3.7 lb. of coal.

Many companies that went on to build tractors, such as J. I. Case, started out making portable steamers. In fact, Case was to be a notable pioneer right through these early days. But in several ways, portable steam engines were limited—for one thing, they had to be small and light enough to be towed by a team of horses. They were also restricted to stationary work—farmers still relied on draft animals for jobs like harvesting and plowing. So the next obvious step was to build a steamer that powered itself along, and the steam traction engine was born. These were mobile and powerful, but in many cases, particularly in Europe, were simply too heavy for field work. John Fowler of England had the answer, in cable plowing. Two traction engines were used, one parked at each end

RIGHT: *Many modern tractor manufacturers started out by working with steam power, as with this Case traction engine. Case was a pioneer in the early days.*

LEFT: *Charles Hart and Charles Parr were pioneers, building their first internal combustion engine tractor in 1902. It was oil-cooled and rated at 30 hp.*

more development potential. The internal combustion gasoline engine, on the other hand, was right at the beginning of its life. More compact and powerful than steam, it promised to be ideal where steam was too heavy or expensive. By the 1880s, the four-stroke gasoline motor was developing fast, and proprietary engines were available off the shelf, in Europe and the U.S.

In fact, the U.S., which hadn't had the benefit of Europe's head start in steam power, took the lead in applying the gasoline engines to agriculture. John Charter's company, the Charter Gasoline Engine Co., was already hard at work building such motors in Sterling, Illinois. It's generally accepted that when, in 1889, John Charter mounted one of his own gasoline single-cylinder engines onto a Rumely traction engine, he was building the world's first gasoline tractor. After demonstrations on various farms in South Dakota, powering a threshing machine, the company found itself with orders for five or six replicas.

The tractor industry was born, but competition wasn't long in coming, and within three years a further three gasoline tractors appeared. Like the Charter, all were

of the field, and the plow was pulled to and fro between them by steel cable.

Steam, of course, was now a highly developed technology, having been in use for over a hundred years, but had little

RIGHT: *Note the high-mounted kerosene tank on this very early Waterloo Boy. Gasoline came later, and diesel much later still.*

BELOW: *The heart of the Waterloo was a horizontal twin-cylinder engine. This layout would form the basis of John Deere machines for forty years.*

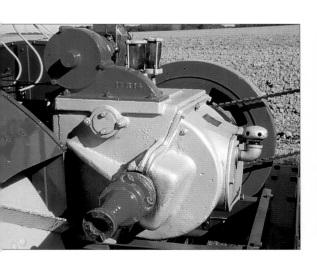

little more than big steam traction engines with gasoline motors bolted in. Like their steam predecessors, they were heavy, lumbering beasts, more suited to stationary work than direct plowing or harvesting.

The Capital tractor, built by the Dissinger brothers in Wrightsville, Pennsylvania, was one such. Using an engine built under license from Otto of Germany (inventor of the four-stroke principle), it was designed for threshing. The Capital came to nothing, but the Dissingers returned to tractors a decade later, with more success. Perhaps more significant was the first Case tractor. J. I. Case was already well established as a maker of steam engines, and bought in a Patterson 20 hp motor to power its first gasoline machine. It was a bold move for a company devoted to steam, but the project was soon abandoned. Those early gasoline engines were unreliable compared to steam, and it would be another twenty years before Case had another go with gasoline.

John Froelich got further with his 1892 tractor. He was a busy man, doing contract work threshing and drilling wells, as well as running a steam-powered feed mill. Using a gasoline engine to power a drill probably gave Froelich the idea to apply it to a tractor. So he bought a massive single-cylinder Van Duzen engine, fitting it to a wooden chassis of his own design with running gear supplied by the Robinson

BELOW: *A homely farm boy image helped to sell the Waterloo Boy, but it didn't prevent the takeover of the company by John Deere & Co., whose own tractor experiments were making slow progress.*

ABOVE: *Most early tractors were straight replacements for the big steam traction engines—it was another few years before lighter, cheaper tractors caught on.*

BOTTOM: *Case was already well-established in agricultural machinery when the first tractors came along, but didn't produce its own until 1912.*

steam engine company. It was primitive, with gravity-fed fuel and exposed gear drive, but Froelich's machine worked. He took it on a demonstration threshing tour of South Dakota, working just over fifty days and threshing 62,000 bushels. Unlike a traditional traction engine, it stood the driver on a platform right at the front, providing the driver with an unobstructed view, while a reverse gear helped with positioning.

Word got around, and a group of Iowa businessmen contacted Froelich, keen to invest in a new idea that patently worked. A deal was done, and in 1893 the Waterloo Gasoline Traction Engine Company was born, with Froelich as president. The idea was to put his machine into production and sell it to eager farmers. In the event, only four were ever built and just two were sold, both of which were returned with mechanical faults! The tractors were dropped and John Froelich left, but not before designing a new stationary engine, which Waterloo Gasoline went on to build

successfully. In any case, its tractor heritage was not forgotten. In 1912, Waterloo returned with the Waterloo Boy, which was soon bought up by John Deere & Co.

Huber dipped a toe into the early tractor market before thinking better of it, but returned in later years, just like Waterloo and J. I. Case. A well-established maker of steam traction engines, in 1898 Huber took over the Van Duzen company, which by then had already designed its own tractor. Under Huber, this went into production, and a batch of thirty were built, which underlines what a limited market it was then—those thirty tractors probably made Huber the biggest manufacturer of its time!

But the world was changing, and new entrants were embarking on more regular production. It wasn't mass production yet—Henry Ford's tractor was still years away—but the early 1900s saw increasing numbers of tractors produced as reliability improved and demand grew. Charles Hart and Charles Parr were a good example. They built their first tractor in 1902, powered by their own 30 hp twin-cylinder engine. It

ABOVE: *The Rumely Oil Pull had a great big, heavy flywheel, which was needed to smooth out the power pulses from the two massive pistons.*

BELOW: *Although it was sometimes mistaken for a steam traction engine, thanks to its distinctive cooling tower, the Oil Pull used new technology.*

was oil-cooled, with a large rectangular cooling tower mounted on the front—this would become a trademark of Hart-Parr tractors for twenty years. They were massive machines, designed for the wide open wheat prairies of the U.S. and Canada. The largest weighed 26 tons and was rated at 100 hp at the flywheel. Advance Rumely tractors followed similar lines. They too were oil-cooled, with a big front-mounted cooling tower, and, like the early Hart-Parrs, looked much more like steam traction engines than any gasoline machine.

But just like those traction engines, these were too big and expensive for the average farmer. What they needed was a straight replacement for the farm horse, something more the size of a small car—lightweight and affordable. The pioneer tractor of this type came not from the U.S. but Britain. Daniel Albone, of Hertfordshire in the south of England, was a small-scale bicycle

manufacturer. He also had a very inventive mind, building his own car in 1898 and his first tractor three years later. The little 8 hp three-wheeled Ivel tractor was a great success, designed to put most of its meager weight over the driving wheels, for better traction. Within five years, it was being exported to eighteen countries, and the ever-inventive Albone designed a fire engine and military ambulance based on the same chassis. Arguably, Dan Albone's machine was the world's very first small, lightweight tractor.

ABOVE RIGHT: *Not steam traction or gasoline-powered. "Oil Pull" derived from the fuel it ran on—the big Rumely could actually use almost any type of liquid fuel.*

RIGHT: *The top of the Oil Pull's cooling tower. A cooling updraft was created by the simple method of pumping in the hot exhaust gases.*

ABOVE: *The Little Bull's driver could not see which way the front wheel was pointing, so a large arrow did the job for him.*

Innovation was also proceeding elsewhere in Europe. In 1907, the French Gousi tractor offered an early form of power takeoff (PTO), to power trailed implements. PTOs would not become widely available for another decade and a half. The same year, Deutz of Germany built a plowing tractor, the first bidirectional machine, in that the driver could face in either direction.

Meanwhile, in the U.S., there was a fresh attempt to produce a low-cost alternative to the tractor that most farmers could afford—the motor plow. These were more like ride-

BELOW: *The advanced Twin City 16-30 of 1918 gave a hint of things to come, with its lower-slung bodywork that hid all mechanical parts.*

on cultivators than true tractors, with a front-mounted small engine driving the front wheels. The driver sat at the back, over a smaller pair of wheels, though on some cheaper motor plows he didn't even have a seat, but walked along behind, just as he had done in the old days! As a further appeal to traditionalists, some of these were controlled by reins rather than a steering wheel and levers.

The most successful motor plow was the Moline Universal, introduced in 1914 with a 12 hp twin-cylinder motor, later updated with four cylinders and electric starting. Moline's Universal D was actually the first tractor that didn't need hand cranking. There were several advantages to the motor plow layout: having the engine mounted

over the driving wheels made for good traction; at the back, the driver had a good view of the implement for row-crop work; and of course they were far cheaper than a conventional tractor. But as it turned out, not cheap enough—within a few years, the motor plows were driven away by a formidable new competitor.

All this time, a revolution had been brewing. The motor plows—and before them, Dan Albone's English Ivel—had shown that a tractor could be lightweight and affordable. But they were too small for many U.S. farmers. More crucially, none of them was mass produced, so they weren't as cheap as they could have been.

Allis-Chalmers's motor plow, the 6-12, cost $850 when it was launched in 1919.

ABOVE: *Henry Ford himself drives one of his many prototype tractors.*

The key to driving down prices was mass production, which no one had yet applied to a tractor. With hindsight, there was just one man who could—Henry Ford. Ford was in a unique position. In the motor-making business since 1903, he had pioneered the world's first mass-produced car just five years later, the Model T. The T's simplicity and astonishingly low price made it a huge success. More to the point for our story, Henry was a farmer's son who knew how hard nonmechanized farming was. It seems inevitable now that he would use the lessons he had learned in the car business to produce a "Model T tractor," one that all farmers could afford.

Henry didn't rush into it. He produced his first experimental tractor in 1907 and is said to have expressed interest in the idea a couple of years earlier. With Model T profits starting to flow in, and hence no pressure to rush into production, Ford could take his time to get the tractor right. He apparently built fifty prototypes over the next ten years, all of which were tested in the field. To cut costs to the bone, all were small, simple machines that used as many car components as possible.

When it finally went into production in 1917, the Fordson Model F was revealed as a neat little 20 hp tractor. Although simple in the extreme, it was more like a miniature full-size tractor than a motor plow: complete with a liquid-cooled four-cylinder engine of 251 cu. in., three-speed enclosed transmission with reverse, and frameless construction. The latter abandoned the traditional chassis, using the engine and transmission as stressed members, thus saving weight and cost. But above all, the Fordson Model F was cheap—at $750 in 1918, it was cheaper than the

Allis-Chalmers motor plow, and within four years the price had been slashed even further to only $395.

It sold by the thousands. Countless farmers who would never have considered a tractor before, went out and bought a Fordson. This one tractor did more to mechanize U.S. farms than any other —at one point, three-quarters of all tractors sold in the U.S. were Fordsons. In Britain, too, the Model F was very popular, particularly in the First World War, when it played a vital role in food production. By the time production ended in 1928, nearly 750,000 Fordsons had been churned out, and its place in history was assured. The tractor industry, not to mention farming, would never be the same again.

IVEL
[1903]

IVEL

Power: 20 hp @ 850 rpm
(initially 8 hp)
Weight: 3,638 lb.
Engine:
Water-cooled, twin-cylinder
Transmission: Single-speed
Clutch: Cone type

BELOW: *The Ivel was almost certainly the first small, lightweight tractor, and it worked. Albone patented it as an "agricultural motor."*

The U.S. may have won the race to build the first gasoline tractor, but in 1901 Daniel Albone began building what was arguably the first small, lightweight machine. Albone was a racing cyclist and inveterate inventor. He produced bicycles (including the first-ever ladies' frame), tandems, motorcycles, and also a tractor.

In 1902 he patented what he called the "agricultural motor," which he named the Ivel after a river near his home—the term "tractor" hadn't yet been thought of! But this was no paper patent. The Ivel tractor actually existed and went into production at Albone's factory the year after his patent

was filed. Unlike the earliest U.S. tractors, based on the dimensions of existing steam or oil tractors, the Ivel was small and lightweight. With 20 hp at 850 rpm, it was a tricycle design which weighed just 3,638 lb. Albone had a flair for marketing as well as invention—he worked on exports, and promoted the Ivel as a fire engine and also as military ambulance. Sadly, he died in 1906, only five years into production, and without his driving force, his company went into receivership in 1920. But the Ivel remains one of the very earliest tractors powered by an Otto cycle gasoline engine, and certainly the first on a small scale.

EAGLE 20-35
[1906]

"**Y**ou take no chances when you buy an Eagle tractor . . . tested and tried out in every condition of field and belt work . . . it will do your work at a big saving over horse cost, and therefore will pay you a profit . . . Built right, works right and is priced right." Never undersold, the Eagle was also a pioneering machine—the Eagle Manufacturing Company had been building farm equipment for many decades, but jumped into the new tractor market in 1906 with its twin-cylinder 20-35. Several models were offered over the early years: a 12-22, 13-25, and 16-30, plus the big 20-35 pictured here.

Not until 1930 did Eagle offer the six-cylinder 6A. In the meantime, its faithful twin got the full public relations treatment. "You get superior engine qualities—the famous Eagle two-cylinder engine with three-bearing crankshaft, cylinders cast in pairs, valve-in-head action which gives more power and cleaner combustion . . . Perfex radiator insures thorough cooling even in hottest weather. Double drive insures perfect traction under all conditions . . . Simple in construction . . . any man can run it and keep it in repair without help . . . Eagle—The Tractor that Takes the Guesswork Out of Farming!"

The specifications here refer to the 1921 16-30—although built eighteen years after the 20-35 pictured, it stayed faithful to the same basic twin-cylinder format.

EAGLE 16-30 (1921)

Engine: Water-cooled, twin cylinder
Bore x stroke: 8.0 x 8.0 in.
Capacity: 802 cu. in.
Drawbar Power: 20 hp @ 500 rpm
Transmission: Two-speed
Weight: 7,210 lb.

BELOW: *Although the first Eagle tractor produced was viewed by many as pioneering, their machines began to look increasingly outdated in the 1920s. But the company did good business with early models such as this 20-35 seen here. This model was the largest they made.*

TWIN CITY 60-90
[1913]

Before Minneapolis-Moline was established, there was Twin City. The Minneapolis Threshing Machine Company, the Moline Plow Company, and the Minneapolis Steel & Machinery Company merged in 1929 to form Minneapolis-Moline. The Minneapolis Steel & Machinery Company was established in 1902 and began producing its own tractors in 1910 under the "Twin City" name. They formed the nucleus of the new company's lineup and provided its tractor heritage. They came from Minneapolis, Minnesota, a veritable nursery for new tractor manufacturers. Early Twin Citys were not innovative, but they were big, owing as much to steam engines as gasoline. They were usually bought by big farms, as they could recoup their high initial cost through plowing vast acreages, or powering large threshers.

So the 60-90 of 1913 (it actually started out as a 60-110 but was downgraded in its first year) was a 14-ton monster that looked exactly like the steam traction engines it competed with. Even the giant 100-gallon fuel tank looked like a truncated steam boiler! The difference was in the six-cylinder gasoline engine, with similarly massive dimensions. Each piston measured over seven inches across and rumbled up and down a stroke of nine inches, which gave a capacity of over 2,200 cu. in.

It might not have made the 110 hp originally promised, but with a genuine 90 hp at the belt, the 60-90 had no problem powering the largest thresher. It could also be found plowing, or even helping to build roads. A single forward gear gave a speed of 2 mph and a large canopy served to protect the engine, which otherwise was open to the elements. The 60-90 was still listed up until 1920, though not many were made—all but the largest farms were put off by its $4,000 price tag. Fortunately, Minneapolis Steel & Machinery also had contracts to build tractors for Bull and J. I. Case. (The specifications below refer to the later 1915 model 60-90.)

LEFT: *With its six big cylinders and a genuine 90 hp, the Twin City 60-90 was one of the most powerful tractors you could buy in 1913.*

TWIN CITY 60-90 (1915)

Engine: Water-cooled, six-cylinder
Bore x stroke: 7.25 x 9.0 in.
Capacity: 2,230 cu. in.
PTO Power: 90 hp
Drawbar Power: 60 hp
Transmission: Single-speed
Weight: 28,000 lb.

MOGUL 8-16
[1914]

Modern tractor companies survive by merger. In 1902, McCormick Harvesting Machine and the Deering Harvester Company did the same, joining with three smaller partners to form International Harvester, and one of the giants of the industry was born.

But these things don't always work out as planned. Before the merger, Deering and McCormick were bitter rivals. After the merger they remained so. Two separate dealer networks were kept up, sometimes in the same town. The McCormick men refused to sell what they saw as a rebadged Deering, and vice versa.

So International found itself compelled to produce two distinct models, one for each network of dealers. Titan tractors were sold by Deering dealers, and the Mogul could be found in the McCormick showroom on the other side of town. But this rivalry may have actually speeded tractor development, as the competition to build a better machine was as intense as ever.

The Mogul was a simple tractor, but advanced for its time. Its single-cylinder engine was hopper cooled, but a closed cooling system was soon added, plus a two-speed transmission. But just three years later it was made to look decidedly old-fashioned by its replacement, now sold as an International, not a Mogul. This had a modern four-cylinder engine, running at the high speed of 1,000 rpm. The new International machine had a three-speed transmission and at 3,660 lb. was significantly lighter than its predecessor. It also featured a power takeoff, a production

first for a U.S. tractor, and really the first in the world to be commercially successful. And the engine and radiator were enclosed by sheet metal, and not exposed to the air.

Oddly, despite all these pioneering features, the 8-16 was quite old-fashioned in other ways. It still used a riveted separate chassis, and the exposed chain and sprocket final drive looked rather crude next to an enclosed shaft and gear drive. But this little 8-16, the very first to wear the International badge, consolidated the company as a major manufacturer.

LEFT & BELOW: *Not the original Mogul, but this is its 8-16 replacement, now badged as an International and more modern in every way. It was lighter than its predecessor and it also featured a power takeoff.*

INTERNATIONAL 8-16

Engine: Water-cooled, four-cylinder
Bore x stroke: 4.25 x 5.0 in.
Capacity: 284 cu. in.
PTO Power: 18.5 hp @ 1,000 rpm
Drawbar Power: 11.0 hp
Transmission: Three-speed
Speeds: 1.8–4.1 mph
Weight: 3,660 lb.

WATERLOO BOY MODEL R
[1914]

If the name is unfamiliar, you'll surely recognize the color scheme. The Waterloo Boy came in John Deere green and yellow because, from 1918, that's who made it. John Deere didn't design the Waterloo Boy, but instead bought the Waterloo Gas Engine Company lock, stock, and tractor.

Deere's own tractor experiments were making slow progress, but the Waterloo was an established design and ready to sell.

It was quite unlike many other tractors, with its twin-cylinder overhead valve engine mounted horizontally in the frame. This layout evidently impressed John Deere, as the company stuck with this design right up until 1960!

The original twin-cylinder Waterloo Boy went into production in 1912, but several design changes were made before the Model R of 1914 appeared, with a 333 cu. in. version of the twin-cylinder engine, which produced 25 belt hp and 12 drawbar hp at 750 rpm. There were a further thirteen variations on the Model R theme before the Model N took over in 1917. Available right through to 1924 (by which time it was sadly outdated) the Model N boasted a larger, more powerful engine. It also added a two-speed transmission (the R was a single-speed), which led to an easy way to recognize the difference between the two—the N had a huge drive gear for each rear wheel, nearly as big as the wheel itself. Or look for the radiator—it's mounted on the right hand side of the frame on Model Rs, the opposite side on Ns. Compared to some of its smaller, lighter rivals, the Waterloo Boy looked a little clumsy and old-fashioned. But for Deere its existence was crucial—it gave the company a toehold in the tractor market and led directly to the twin-cylinder format that underpinned John Deere machines for the next forty years.

LEFT: *There may well have been no John Deere tractors were it not for the Waterloo Boy. John Deere's own tractor experiments were proceeding too slowly but the Waterloo was tried, tested, and ready to sell.*

WATERLOO BOY MODEL N
(1917)

Engine Type: Water-cooled, twin-cylinder ohv

Bore x stroke: 5.5 x 7.0 in.

Capacity: 333 cu. in.

Fuel: Kerosene

PTO Power: 25 hp @ 750 rpm

Drawbar Power: 12 hp @ 750 rpm

Transmission: Two-speed

MOLINE UNIVERSAL
[1915]

Strictly speaking, the Moline Universal wasn't a tractor at all—officially it was a "Motor Plow." Shortly before the Fordson revolutionized the tractor business, these strange devices had a few years of popularity, especially in the U.S. They were a basic, low-cost alternative to the conventional tractor, with a simpler design and smaller engine. But despite this they had their advantages. The Moline Plow Company built a prototype motorized plow in 1913, but this was soon scrapped.

Instead of persevering with its own design, Moline adopted the John Deere school of tractor marketing—it bought an existing design as a shortcut into the business. In Moline's case, this was the Universal Tractor Company, which it took over in 1915. Universal's motor plow had been launched the year before with a horizontally opposed twin-cylinder engine. Now built by Moline, it was updated with a more powerful four-cylinder engine of 18 hp, and became the leading motor plow in the U.S.

Instead of the conventional tractor's rear-wheel drive and small closely spaced front wheels, the Universal took the opposite layout. Two big front wheels did the driving, with the engine mounted between them, and two smaller wheels at the rear. With the motor mounted right over the driving wheels, traction was good. Like most motor plows, this made for heavy steering, but horse-drawn implements could be adapted to fit relatively easily. It even came with electric starting.

But despite its popularity and obvious advantages, the Moline Universal motor plow was out of production by the end of 1923. Why? Well, apart from the postwar farming depression, it was the old story—you could buy a Fordson for a fraction of the price.

LEFT: *Moline's Universal was the most successful motor plow and very popular—until the Fordson appeared a few years later.*

MOLINE UNIVERSAL
MODEL D (1920)

Engine: Water-cooled, four-cylinder
Bore x stroke: 3.5 x 5.0 in.
Capacity: 192 cu. in.
PTO Power: 27.5 hp @ 1,800 rpm
Drawbar Power: 17.4 hp @ 1,800 rpm
Transmission: Single-speed
Speed: 3.6 mph
Fuel Consumption: 8.15 hp/hr
  per gallon
Weight: 3,590 lb.

TITAN 10-20
[1915]

Thirteen years after they merged, McCormick and Deering—who had become known as International Harvester—were still hardly on speaking terms. So while McCormick dealers were given the Mogul 8-16 to sell, the Deering network had the Titan. For the most part, Moguls were designed and built at International Harvester's Chicago factory, using throttle-governed engines, while Titans were powered by Famous power units and came from Milwaukee. Fortunately, both the 8-16 Mogul of 1914 and 10-20 Titan (which appeared in 1915) were successful.

As a modern machine, the Titan's twin-cylinder engine started on gas, running on kerosene once warmed up. If it ever pinked (preignited) under load, water injection cooled down the combustion. There was no radiator as such; instead, a 35-gallon water tank simply cooled the coolant via its own radiated heat.

The Mogul and Titan were so successful that in 1917 International Harvester suspended production of its big tractors to concentrate on these small ones. Relatively light and affordable, these machines were far more useful to the average farmer than the large, outdated machines derived from the steam engine.

This move certainly worked well for International, which sold over 17,000 Titans in 1918 alone. Some 3,500 were also exported to Britain during the First World War, which, along with the Fordson, was hugely significant in introducing British farmers to the inherent advantages of a modern tractor.

LEFT: *The Titan was hugely successful and, along with the Mogul, was the first big-selling small tractor.*

BELOW: *Note the International Harvester badge on the front of this Titan—but as far as Deering dealers were concerned, it was a Titan pure and simple. McCormick dealers had the Mogul 8-16 instead.*

TITAN 10-20	
Engine:	Water-cooled, two-cylinder
Bore x stroke:	6.25 x 8.0 in.
Capacity:	490 cu. in.
Drawbar Power:	10 hp
Belt Power:	20 hp
Transmission:	Two-speed
Speeds:	2.0 & 2.75 mph
Weight:	6,138 lb.

SAUNDERSON MODEL G
[1916]

Dan Albone (see Ivel, page 14) wasn't the only British tractor pioneer. H. P. Saunderson from Bedford in the southeast of England, was equally inventive, and seemed to have a similar flair for publicity. As a young man, he had traveled to Canada, returning home in 1890 with a keen interest in mechanized farming. At first, he just imported Massey-Harris machinery, but began producing vehicles himself from around 1903. Three- and four-wheeled models were available, such as the four-wheel, single-cylinder Model L. These were dual-purpose machines, with their load beds over the rear wheels aimed as much at load carrying as field work.

Sales were low until Saunderson began making pure farm tractors, the Universal series in general and the Model G (as pictured here) in particular. The Model G was a more conventional machine than earlier Saundersons, some of which were designed to fit within the shafts of horse-drawn machinery. The arrival of the Model G in 1916 coincided with Britain's wartime boom in tractor demand, and for a short time, it was Britain's best-selling tractor. Also, unlike many of its prewar rivals, it did survive after 1918, alongside newer tractors like the Austin. A French version of the Saunderson was also built under the Scemia name. Sadly, the company didn't survive the tractor slump of the 1920s.

And Mr. Saunderson's flair for publicity? To demonstrate the all-around abilities of the Universal, in 1906 he invited the press to a day out with a difference. First they watched a Universal pull binders to harvest a wheat crop; then the same tractor powered a thresher; then a grinder to turn the grain into flour. While a baker got on with using the flour to bake bread, the tractor plowed up the field and planted it for next year's crop. Five hours from harvesting, the impressed journalists were eating the freshly baked bread—and all with one tractor. (Specifications are given below for the later Model L Saunderson.)

LEFT: *Was this the British Fordson? Saundersons weren't mass produced on a Fordson scale, but production was certainly big enough to make this Britain's best-selling tractor for a while.*

SAUNDERSON MODEL L

Engine: Air-cooled, single-cylinder
Bore x stroke: 6.5 x 10.0 in.
Capacity: 332 cu. in.
Transmission: Two-speed
PTO Power: 30 hp
Load Capacity: 2 tons

MASSEY-HARRIS NO2
[1916]

Based in Canada, Daniel Massey and Alanson Harris were both makers of mowers and binders. They merged in 1891 to form one of the best-known names in the business—Massey-Harris. Although keen to expand their product line, it would take a further ten years before the Massey-Harris company began using gasoline engines to power their machines.

Their first moves into the tractor market were tentative as well. Like so many other pioneers in the industry, Massey-Harris didn't jump straight in with its own tractor. From 1915 the company was distributing the Minneapolis-built Big Bull, though this was not a success. But by this time, Massey-Harris had already commissioned one Dent Parrett to design a machine specifically for them. This was the first Massey-Harris badged tractor, and was produced up until 1923. It came in three sizes: the 12-25 hp No1, 12-22 hp No2 (pictured here), and 15-28 hp No3.

All three were simple machines, which were basically just a steel frame with a Buda four-cylinder engine mounted crossways, driving through a two-speed plus reverse gearbox, and the chief distinction between the first two was that the No2 had enclosed rear wheel gears. Despite using the same 287 cu. in. Buda engine as the No1, the No2 was derated from 25 hp at the belt to 22, though with the same 12 drawbar hp. Either model could run on gasoline or kerosene, as would the larger No3, which used a 397 cu. in. Buda engine.

Unfortunately, Mr. Parrett had designed these machines before 1914, and the fast pace of tractor technology soon made the Massey-Harris tractors look crude, expensive, and decidedly old-fashioned. The usual question was being asked by their customers: Why buy one of these when a Fordson was so much cheaper? The company eventually decided to abandon the Parratt tractors in 1923, but better was to come.

LEFT: *Early Massey-Harris tractors were based on a Parrett design that was already outmoded—but more advanced Massey-Harrises were to follow.*

MASSEY-HARRIS NO2

Engine: Water-cooled, four-cylinder
Bore x stroke: 4.25 x 5.5 in.
Capacity: 287 cu. in.
PTO Power: 22 hp @ 1,000 rpm
Drawbar Power: 12 hp
Transmission: Two-speed
Speeds: 1.75 & 2.4 mph
Weight: 5,200 lb.

FORDSON MODEL F
[1917]

Henry Ford came from farming stock. Hardly surprising then, that after building a cheap, mass-produced car that thousands could afford to buy, the Model T, he decided to try and do the same for the tractor. With the Fordson Model F tractor he certainly succeeded.

The Model F was simpler, lighter, and easier to understand than any rival, not to mention cheaper. For his tractor, Henry applied exactly the same mass-production techniques that had already served him so well—the Fordson was designed from the start to be made in huge numbers as cheaply as possible. In 1918 it was sold for just $750. Within four years, the price had been cut to $395, and later to just $230.

Henry Ford had been experimenting with tractors for ten years by the time the Model F went on sale—the first prototypes were little more than Model T cars minus bodywork and with tractor-type steel wheels, but the production tractor was quite different. It did away with a conventional chassis, using the engine and transmission as stressed members—that made it lighter than any rival, plus cheaper to make. This in turn gave it a better power to weight ratio from its simple 251 cu. in. four-cylinder engine, and easier handling.

All this at an affordable price spelled the end for some rival tractor manufacturers. For many, the 1920s farming recession was simply the final straw. But Henry just cut the price of the Fordson again, and mopped up the surplus demand. As a result, he sold three-quarters of a million Model Fs. So the Fordson's biggest achievement wasn't in its technical advances (though they were impressive enough), but that it persuaded a whole generation of small farmers to take the plunge and buy their first tractor. Maybe for that reason alone, the Model F is the most significant tractor ever made.

LEFT: *The Fordson Model F made tractor ownership a reality for thousands of small farmers. It was the very first really affordable tractor and it was destined to change tractor manufacturing forever.*

FORDSON MODEL F
KEROSENE

Engine: Water-cooled, four-cylinder
Bore x stroke: 4.0 x 5.0 in.
Capacity: 251 cu. in.
PTO Power: 18.1 hp @ 1,000 rpm
Drawbar Power: 9.34 hp
Transmission: Three-speed
Speeds: 1.3–6.8 mph
Fuel Consumption: 7.32 hp/hr per gallon
Weight: 2,710 lb.

SAMSON

[1917]

SAMSON MODEL M (1920)

Engine: Water-cooled, four-cylinder

Bore x stroke: 4.0 x 5.5 in.

Capacity: 276 cu. in.

PTO Power: 19 hp (rpm not available)

Drawbar Power: 11.5 hp

Transmission: Two-speed

Speeds: 2.3 & 3.2 mph

Fuel Consumption: 6.9 hp/hr per gallon

Weight: 3,300 lb.

BELOW: *Where Ford went, arch rival General Motors felt it had to follow—but its conventional four-wheel Samson tractor was not a great success, and production was ceased in the early 1920s.*

Henry Ford's determination to build a tractor struck a chord with his bitter rival, General Motors. GM couldn't afford to ignore any market that Henry appeared to be taking advantage of, so when it became clear that Ford was about to mass produce a cheap tractor, his rival had no choice but to follow suit.

But there was a crucial difference. For Henry Ford, the tractor was almost a labor of love. He had grown up on a farm, and knew what a difference an affordable tractor could make to the lives of small farmers. Of course, Henry was also a shrewd businessman, knowing that the U.S. tractor market was potentially huge enough for anyone able to make a machine cheap and reliable enough to exploit it, but

his heart was there too. General Motors had no such emotional attachment to the ideal of a cheap tractor. Nor had it time for the ten years of research and development which Henry had spent on his various prototypes. It needed a ready-made tractor in double-quick time and found it in the Samson, an established manufacturer from Stockton, California. They bought the company in February 1917, and had high hopes for its three-wheeled Sieve Grip machine. Unfortunately, this was no match for the Fordson, and the more conventional four-wheeled Samson M came too late to worry Ford. In any case, the parent company was in trouble by the early 1920s, anxious to rid itself of unprofitable sidelines. Samson was closed down in 1922.

CASE 10-20 CROSSMOTOR

[1917]

This was the tractor that set Case on their path to success. Its innovative Crossmotor, as the name suggested, mounted the four-cylinder engine across the frame, rather than longitudinally. This brought no real advantage, though it may have given better weight distribution. More to the point was that the cast chassis was far more rigid and strong than the more common riveted chassis. Over time, these would flex and bend, pulling the transmission gears out of alignment.

The four-cylinder engine came along by chance. Case had recently bought the Pierce Motor Company, which already made an overhead valve motor for its car.

This was redesigned for tractor use, with the cylinders and upper half of the crankcase cast in one—the cylinder head was removable though, and there were ports in the crankcase to allow the cleaning of coolant passages.

Uniquely among Case Crossmotors, the 10-20 was a three-wheeler, using only a single driven wheel (eliminating the need for a differential), though the second rear wheel could be clutched in for difficult going. It was followed by the more conventional 9-18, with four wheels and a steel-fabricated chassis, soon uprated to 10-18. Five thousand were sold in three years, wedding Case to the Crossmotor concept.

CASE 10-18	
Engine: Water-cooled, 4-cylinder	
Bore x stroke: 3.875 x 5.00 in.	
Capacity: 236 cu. in.	
PTO Power: 18.4 hp @ 1,050 rpm	
Drawbar Power: 11.2 hp @ 1,050 rpm	
Transmission: Two-speed	
Speeds: 2.25 & 3.5 mph	
Fuel Consumption: 6.25 hp/hr per gallon	
Weight: 3,760 lb.	

BELOW: *The 10-20 proved the Crossmotor concept. This is a later, four-wheeler Case Crossmotor.*

TWIN CITY 16-30
[1917]

The first Twin City tractors, built by the Minneapolis Steel & Machinery Company, were heavy, high horsepower beasts, intended to compete with steam traction engines. But the new 16-30, unveiled in 1917, was quite a departure from this concept.

In fact, it previewed a new trend in tractor design that looked forward to the layout of the modern tractor. Up until that point, most tractors had left the driver and engine exposed to the elements, but the 16-30 was low-slung and streamlined, enclosing the engine and part of the driver's platform in sheet metal. It was also much smaller than previous Twin City tractors, weighing in at a comparatively lightweight 7,800 lb. The four-cylinder engine—the company's own 588 cu. in. unit—was a miniature compared to ancestors like the giant 60-110. In appearance as well as design, the 16-30 made a big step forward toward the modern tractor layout, but it would be another decade before the low lines and enclosed bodywork became the acceptable industry standard.

As further evidence of the Minneapolis's more advanced thinking, an electric starter and lights could also be ordered, and there was a K-W high-tension magneto. Hyatt roller bearings were used throughout, a great improvement over the bronze plain bearings used previously. Unfortunately, the 16-30 also suffered from starting problems, and only 702 were ever built by the company. But this early setback didn't put Minneapolis off advanced tractors—two years after the 16-30 model it announced the little 12-20, an up-to-the-minute four-cylinder tractor with four valves per cylinder.

LEFT: *Swap the wheels, and you could be looking at a vintage racing car. The Twin City 16-30 pioneered this low-slung design, which, unusually for the time, enclosed the engine and part of the driver's platform in sheet metal. The sheet metal served to protect the engine from the elements, but unfortunately the driver was not afforded quite the same consideration!*

TWIN CITY 16-30

Engine: Water-cooled, four-cylinder
Bore x stroke: 5.0 x 7.5 in.
Capacity: 588 cu. in.
PTO Power: 30 hp
Drawbar Power: 16 hp
Transmission: Two-speed
Weight: 7,800 lb.
Optional Equipment:
  Electric starter and lights

EMERSON-BRANTINGHAM 12-20
[1918]

Emerson-Brantingham was yet another company that bought its way into the tractor industry. It was a sensible move, far quicker and less risky than producing its own design from scratch, in a new and unfamiliar technology. The company was actually a pioneer of the U.S. agricultural machinery industry—founder John H. Manny was an inventor who had produced a successful horse-drawn reaper in 1852. A couple of years later, financier Ralph Emerson joined the company followed by Charles Brantingham. In 1909 the company officially became Emerson-Brantingham.

In 1912, Emerson took over the Big Four Tractor Company of Minneapolis. Big Four's Model 30 was a typically huge machine for the time, with 30 hp at the drawbar, later uprated to 45 hp. But such big machines were fast losing popularity with farmers, especially with Henry Ford on the scene, and it was one reason why the Big Four company came up for sale relatively cheaply.

But Emerson also made smaller machines. The Model 20, introduced the year after Big Four came under the Emerson wing, was one such tractor. That was followed by the 12-20 in 1918, a thoroughly conventional four-cylinder machine with two-speed transmission and a low weight of 4,400 lb. It was also far more powerful than the official rating of 12-20 might suggest—at Nebraska, the tractor tested there mustered over 17 hp at the drawbar and 27 hp at the PTO! The 12-20 was then updated as the Model K in 1925. The Model Q, pictured here, came later.

Sadly, Emerson-Brantingham never really recovered from the 1920s farming depression, and the company was bought by J. I. Case in 1928. The new owners soon dropped the Emerson-Brantingham tractor lineup.

LEFT: *Exposed ring gear apart, the Emerson-Brantingham 12-20 was a neat, modern tractor—but unfortunately for them, not as neat, modern, or cheap as a Fordson.*

EMERSON-BRANTINGHAM 12-20 GASOLINE

Engine: Water-cooled, four-cylinder
Bore x stroke: 4.75 x 5.0 in.
Capacity: 354 cu. in.
PTO Power: 27 hp @ 900 rpm
Drawbar Power: 17.6 hp @ 900 rpm
Transmission: Two-speed
Speeds: 2.1–2.8 mph
Fuel Consumption: 7.32 hp/hr per gallon
Weight: 3,660 lb.

The 1920s:
HARD TIMES

The 1920s were tough times for tractor manufacturers, especially in the U.S. Firstly, the ultra-affordable Fordson was simply decimating the opposition—a proper tractor that was cheaper than a basic motor plow. Secondly, after a wartime boom in tractor demand, the 1920s saw the beginnings of a long slump in agriculture. Farmers faced with falling incomes were less and less inclined to risk money on a new tractor, or indeed anything else that wasn't absolutely essential. And even the low price of a Fordson was a big financial commitment for the smallest farmers.

So while in 1921 there were an estimated 186 tractor manufacturers in the U.S. alone, by the end of the decade most of those had gone out of business. Increasingly, the U.S. tractor industry was restricted to a four-way fight between the big boys: Fordson, International Harvester, J. I. Case, and John Deere. A second league included Allis-Chalmers (later to hit the big time), Hart-Parr/Oliver, Minneapolis-Moline, and lastly Massey-Harris.

Of course, some of those smaller manufacturers that fell by the wayside weren't mourned by many. There were 260 of them in 1917, but they didn't all make tractors. Some were just, in the words of *Farm Implement News*, "stock promotion schemes designed to relieve unsuspecting investors of their hard-earned dollars." It's telling that, of the few manufacturers who survived the 1920s and became major players, most, like Deere or Case, were solid, well-established companies, with a well-respected track record in the agricultural industry. Fordson and Hart-Parr were the honorable exceptions, and Henry Ford of course, had grown up on a farm.

Sadly, not all newcomers had this in-depth experience of what farmers needed. The U.S. tractor industry was expanding rapidly at the time, so it was attractive to investors of all sorts. But amongst the many new start-ups, some had no intention of making anything at all, just to unload bogus shares onto a receptive market. A cartoon of the time in *Farm Implement News* summed it all up. The cartoon showed the office of the "Skinum Tractor Company." The crooked promoter, puffing on a cigar, gloats over his inflated income from the sale of non-existent shares. Even some companies that did make tractors produced shoddy, poorly engineered machines that were of little practical use.

Something had to be done, and it came in the form of the Nebraska Tractor Tests— standardized, thorough tests of every machine that went on sale. Originally a state concern only, the Nebraska tests were so well regarded that they became a national, even international, standard by which tractors were judged. There had been tractor tests before in the United States, notably the Winnipeg Motor Contest, but none lasted more than a few years. The U.S. government also considered

RIGHT: *In the 1920s, big heavyweight machines like this International Harvester looked increasingly old-fashioned. With Fordson in the ascendance, this was the decade of the cheap, lightweight tractor.*

TOP: *The Happy Farmer met an unhappy end. This tractor was a brave attempt by the La Crosse implement company to enter the tractor business, but was short lived.*

ABOVE: *International's Farmall was a huge step forward, combining row-crop agility with enough power for belt work as well—the all-around tractor had arrived.*

standardized testing from around 1915, but its deliberations came to nothing.

The breakthrough came in 1918, when one Wilmot F. Crozier, who farmed in Polk County, Nebraska, found that his Ford tractor (not a Fordson) underperformed compared to the manufacturer's claims, while his Rumely Oil Pull actually produced more power than claimed! Mr. Crozier also sat in the Nebraska Legislature, and pushed through a bill to make tractor testing compulsory in the state. By the following summer, it was law—no tractor could be sold in Nebraska without first being tested at the state university. And if any unscrupulous manufacturers tried to cherry pick just the good bits of their test, the legislators had thought of that too—manufacturers had to quote the entire test results in any publicity or none at all.

The tests were exhaustive, taking up to a fortnight for every machine. Power at both the belt and drawbar (under various load conditions); fuel consumption in horsepower hours per gallon; engine and road speeds; and an accurate weight figure were all part of the Nebraska Tractor Test reports, which apart from a four-year break during the Second World War, have continued from March 1920 up to the present day.

So what with the farming recession, undercutting by Ford, and rigorous new tractor tests, the 1920s were difficult times for U.S. tractor manufacturers, even those that survived. Some made it through price cuts, others through technical innovation or concentrating on specialist markets, such as crawlers. The good news for all of them, though, was that the Fordson could not do everything, and some farmers were prepared to pay a premium for more powerful, more capable machines. The Farmall and the Twin City 17-28 for example, both cost twice as much as a Fordson, yet both sold by the trainload.

The Farmall could claim to be the most significant tractor of the decade. The brain child of International Harvester, it had been under development for seven years by the time it was finally unveiled in 1924. Pre-Fordson, IH was actually market leader, though its good-selling Mogul and Titan ranges were starting to look old-fashioned by the early 1920s. Various alternatives were explored, including a modern paraffin-fired steam tractor, though in the end they went for something more conventional—the Farmall.

But while it might look conventional, the Farmall was actually a new idea. Until then, tractors were either lightweight, low-powered machines for row-crop work (like motor plows), or much heavier and more powerful, for towing heavy implements or powering a thresher, but too cumbersome for treading between delicate crops. What many farmers wanted was a tractor with around 20 hp, but still agile enough to work row crops without damage. A tractor, in other words, that could do it all.

The Farmall, as its name suggested, was that machine. With excellent visibility and good ground clearance, it could tiptoe between rows without damaging the plants. The clearance also left space for fitting a mid-mounted implement, while its light weight minimized soil damage. It was agile, too, with a brake control which allowed the tractor to pivot around either rear wheel to make headland turns at the end of the field. But at the same time, it was sturdy and powerful enough for other jobs. It was a huge success, and rival manufacturers were soon unveiling their own do-it-all tractors.

Allis-Chalmers's response to all the challenges of the 1920s almost involved pulling out of the tractor market altogether.

But company boss General Otto Falk would have none of it, and instigated a severe cost-cutting program. The Allis 20-35 cost over $2,000 new in 1924—within a couple of years $500 had been slashed off the price, and by 1934 you could buy a new 20-35 for only $970! All this was achieved by making the 20-35 cheaper to produce, not just by

BELOW: *Twin City was the forerunner of Minneapolis-Moline, and this 17-28 sold well, thanks to light weight, great strength, and reliability.*

BOTTOM: *Revolution. Henry Ford's tractor dominated the 1920s, thanks to its low price and simple, straightforward design. It mechanized countless thousands of farms in the United States, Europe, and Russia.*

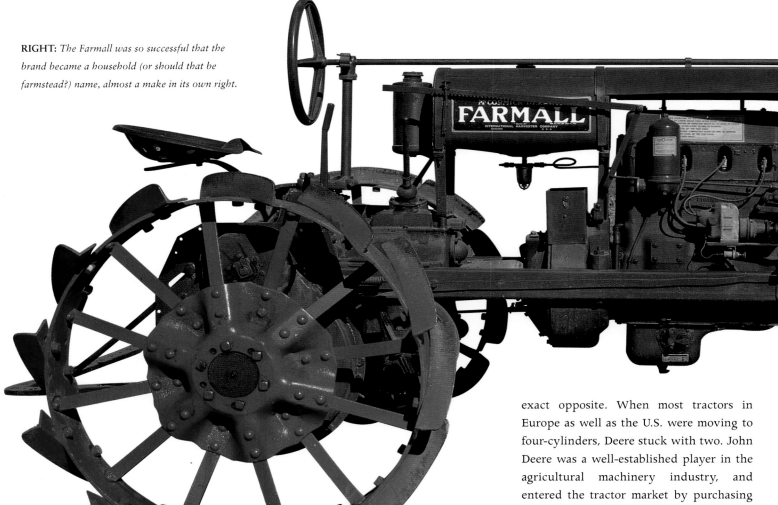

squeezing profit margins. Prompted by Ford and necessitated by a survival instinct, Allis-Chalmers was undergoing a crash course in production economics.

Tractor development was rapid at this time, so it's all the more remarkable that one basic design was in production for fifteen years. Minneapolis Steel & Machinery sold tractors under the Twin City brand, most of them heavy, conventional machines typical of the time. But in 1919 it made a great leap forward with the little 12-20 tractor. This was as advanced as the big old Twin Citys had been conventional, and its basic design would see the company through the difficult 1920s, through to 1929, when it became a leading member of the new Minneapolis-Moline concern.

The 12-20's four-cylinder engine had four valves per cylinder, and pressure lubrication by gear pump. It had a unit construction (frameless) chassis and enclosed oil bath transmission. It was also remarkably strong and promised a long life. A mere two speeds in the transmission was the only gap in its high-tech armory, though that was later resolved with the three-speed 21-32. In fact, a decade later Minneapolis-Moline would be the first manufacturer to standardize a five-speed transmission. The 17-28, 20-35, and 27-44 all stemmed from that original, innovative 12-20. Minneapolis had a lot to thank it for.

Twin City might have survived through innovation, but John Deere appeared to make it through the 1920s by doing the exact opposite. When most tractors in Europe as well as the U.S. were moving to four-cylinders, Deere stuck with two. John Deere was a well-established player in the agricultural machinery industry, and entered the tractor market by purchasing the Waterloo Boy concern.

By the early 1920s, the Waterloo Boy was looking very outdated—it had been designed back in 1912. John Deere's replacement was the Model D, and in some ways it was quite advanced—it used a frameless type of chassis pioneered by Fordson, and the transmission was fully enclosed. Alongside the modern parts, it retained an updated version of the horizontal twin-cylinder engine, but this apparently outdated unit turned into a major selling point. Low revving and torquey, it was ideal for low-speed work. Above all, it was simple and reliable, something which marked it out from some of its more complex rivals. Farmers appreciated these virtues and bought John Deeres, nicknamed "Johnny Poppers," by the thousands. So successful was the simple twin-cylinder format, that John Deere stuck with it for forty years. And why "Johnny Popper"? Simple, it was the distinctive exhaust note of that twin-cylinder engine.

Rugged simplicity, technical innovation, price cuts—there were plenty of ways to survive the Fordson revolution. Another was to specialize, and crawler tractors were an excellent example. The idea wasn't new—in Britain, it had been patented as early as the 1770s, and Richard Hornsby

ABOVE: *John Deere's Model D was the first in a long line of twin-cylinder tractors, the famous "Johnny Poppers."*

BELOW: *Twin City tractors of the 1920s impressed with their unit construction, advanced engines, and enclosed oil bath transmission.*

developed a crawler tractor around 1904. But it was two Americans who made a success of the concept. Benjamin Holt and Daniel Best were arch rivals, both California-based builders of steam traction engines, using massive wheels of up to six feet wide to prevent these heavy machines sinking into soft soil. Both ended up using the same solution—continuous crawler tracks, which would spread the machine's weight over a large area, but were more maneuverable than ultra-wide wheels. The two rivals finally merged in 1925 to form Caterpillar, a brand name owned by Holt, and very descriptive of the way these

tractors crawled along the ground. A new rationalized range chose the best of each line up, which included the big Best 30 and 60 crawlers, and Holt's smaller 2 Ton, 5 Ton, and 10 Ton. Caterpillar started out as the world's leading crawler manufacturer—it still is today. It wasn't alone, of course, and other specialist manufacturers, such as the Cleveland Motor Plow Co. (which built Cletracs) and the Monarch Tractor Co., also concentrated on crawlers. It wasn't until the 1930s that the mainstream tractor manufacturers followed their example and began building their own crawlers.

Meanwhile, Fordsons kept rolling off the production lines, keeping strictly to Henry Ford's simple one-model policy. The Fordson Model F continued to be a very basic, simple tractor, the only model available and with very few options—this was Henry's tried and trusted method of making his tractor as cheap as humanly possible. But that very policy allowed some

LEFT: *Despite the domination of Ford, John Deere, and others, there was room for smaller manufacturers to survive, such as this Co-op.*

BELOW: *The United States' two major crawler makers—Best and Holt—merged in 1925 to form Caterpillar. An industrial legend was born. This is one of the smallest Caterpillars, aimed at farmers.*

other manufacturers to survive, as we've seen, by specializing, innovating, or offering more choice than Ford did.

Perhaps if Henry Ford had committed himself more wholeheartedly to the tractor market—developing a range of larger Fordsons for example, or a crawler version —this wouldn't have been possible. But Ford, despite his agricultural background and passionate determination to mechanize U.S. farms, was not a full-time tractor man. He had a huge car business to worry about, and it was going through a critical phase. The long-running Model T was about to be replaced by the Model A, and Ford decided to clear his factory of every other product, to enable his company to concentrate on this new car.

So in 1928, production of the Fordson tractor was moved to Cork, in Ireland. It emerged a year later as the mildly updated N model, heavier and slightly more powerful than before. But that wasn't enough, and the Fordson began to lose market share. If Henry Ford wanted to stage a tractor comeback, he'd have to do something radical. In the 1930s, he did.

HUBER 15-30
[1921]

Huber, based in Marion, Ohio, was one of the first manufacturers to build a gas-powered tractor. Like many other tractor pioneers, Huber wasn't a new venture, but a well-established maker of steam traction engines. Its first internal combustion engine machine was unveiled in 1898, though it wasn't a new design. Instead, Huber simply bought in a proprietary Van Duzen engine and bolted it into one of its existing steam engine chassis and transmissions.

It was a success, and thirty were made in the first year, while Huber took over Van Duzen to ensure its engine supply. Actually, Huber would continue to buy in engines from outside the company right through to the 1930s, from manufacturers such as Mid West, Waukesha, and Stearns, among others. No matter who it bought engines from, Huber was to be a prominent part of the tractor industry for the next forty years, before switching over to construction machinery during the Second World War.

However, Huber did make a partial return to the tractor business in 1950, when it built the Global tractor on behalf of a marketing company.

LEFT: *The four-cylinder 15-30 was typical of early Hubers, and in fact every Huber tested at Nebraska was a four. The first, in May/June 1920 (one of the first tractors of any make to undergo a Nebraskan test), was a 12-25 Light Four. This produced 25.7 hp at the belt, running on kerosene, with a fuel efficiency of 5.77 hp/hr per gallon. There was 2,500 lb. of pull at the drawbar (which equated to 16.7 hp) at a speed of 2 mph. Respectable enough, but the Light Four tested had numerous problems: the water tank leaked and had to be replaced, the valves had to be reground, the magneto needed adjusting more than once, as did the governor, while a faulty carburetor was replaced. Seventeen years later, the last Huber to go through the Nebraskan test mill was a Model B, and this too proved troublesome—again, the valves had to be reground and the fuel tank needed attention. Still, the B was a modern-looking tractor, with an L-head Buda four-cylinder engine.*

HUBER 15-30

Engine: Water-cooled, four-cylinder
Bore x stroke: 4.5 x 6.0 in.
Capacity: 382 cu. in.
PTO Power: 44.7 hp @ 1,000 rpm
Drawbar Power: 26.9 hp
Transmission: Two-speed
Speeds: 2.7 & 4.2 mph
Fuel Consumption: 9.23 hp/hr
  per gallon
Weight: 6,090 lb.

LEFT: *Wheels, chassis, radiator, and engine—how much simpler could a tractor be? Full enclosure of the mechanical parts was just a few years away now.*

BELOW LEFT: *The steering linkage is clearly visible on this front view of the Huber, as is the Mid West power unit, transverse radiator, and fuel tank. A transverse-mounted radiator, set between the wheels, was far less vulnerable than one mounted right at the very front of the tractor.*

BELOW: *Ignore the "Huber" logo—the 15-30's four-cylinder engine was actually made by Mid West. Huber habitually bought in power units from other manufacturers, as did many of the smaller tractor makers who couldn't afford to tool up their own. The 382 cu. in. Mid West produced nearly 45 hp at the PTO, so Huber's 15-30 rating was extremely modest!*

JOHN DEERE D (UNSTYLED)

[1923]

John Deere owes its existence to this tractor. Well, almost. The company gained a toehold in the tractor business with the Waterloo Boy, but by the early 1920s, the Waterloo was sadly outdated. If the company was serious about staying in the tractor business, they needed to come up with something better. The Model D was just that, a thoroughly modern version of the Waterloo Boy that was an instant success and remained part of the John Deere lineup for an astonishing thirty years. That made it one of the longest-lived tractors of all time.

A cursory glance at the specifications might suggest that in the mid-1920s it was already looking dated. The transmission had only two speeds, and the engine was an update of the Waterloo Boy twin-cylinder, where most rivals now used four cylinders. But this simplicity turned out to be the Model D's strongest suit. It used fewer parts than any of its rivals, so there was therefore less that could go wrong. The slow revving engine would slog away from low speeds better than the "peaky" fours, so it really only needed that simple two-speed transmission.

Farmers liked the rugged simplicity of the "Johnny Popper," not to mention its reliability, and as a testament to this, 1,000 machines were sold in the first year of production. For John Deere, the Model D tractor was a true landmark machine. It was the first (apart from the unsuccessful Jain-Deere) to bear that famous name; it confirmed the classic twin-cylinder layout that was a Deere trademark for the next half-century; and of course, it underlined the fact that John Deere was here to stay.

BELOW: *Simplicity was the Model D's hallmark, and it was this, plus an innate reliability, that endeared it to generations of farmers, and enabled John Deere to carry on producing what was essentially a rather outmoded design for many years.*

LEFT: *The first real John Deere, the Model D, firmly established a mechanical layout that would see the company through to the early 1960s. Not that it was all-new—the twin-cylinder layout stemmed from the earlier Waterloo Boy.*

JOHN DEERE D

Engine: Water-cooled, twin-cylinder
Bore x stroke: 6.8 x 7.0 in.
Capacity: 508 cu. in.
PTO Power: 40 hp @ 900 rpm
Drawbar Power: 34.5 hp @ 900 rpm
Transmission: Three-speed
Speeds: 3.0–5.3 mph
Fuel Consumption: 10.1 hp/hr
  per gallon
Weight: 8,125 lb.

MCCORMICK-DEERING 10-20
[1923]

Remember the International 8-16, the first tractor to be sold by both McCormick and Deering dealers as an International? It was a great advance over the old Mogul 8-16, but its separate chassis and chain drive looked crude compared to the much cheaper Fordson. International hit back by offering a free plow with every new tractor, enabling it to clear its shipping yards of unsold stock, and then introduced a new machine.

The 15-30 (now badged a McCormick-Deering) of 1921 answered both those criticisms of the 8-16—it had gear final drive, properly enclosed in an oil bath, and a stressed (not riveted) chassis. Comparing this machine with its International predecessor shows just how quickly tractors were developing at this time: the old 15-30 weighed 8,700 lb., the new one nearly 3,000 lb. less; it was two feet shorter and cost almost half as much. Both tractors could do the same amount of work, but the new 15-30 needed less maintenance, and had a covered-in engine and transmission. International even put a lifetime guarantee on the ball-bearing crank. If the cylinders wore out, there were replaceable liners. It still cost more than a Fordson, but the promise of a long trouble-free life struck a chord with hardworking farmers—International sold over 128,000 15-30s in eight years.

The 10-20 (seen here) was a smaller version of the same thing, with all the same advances, but a 284 cu. in. four-cylinder engine in place of the 15-30's 381 cu. in. unit. And it was even more successful, albeit over a longer period. Over 216,000 machines were sold before production ceased in 1942.

LEFT: *Proving that life was possible post-Fordson, the McCormick-Deering 10-20 sold over 216,000 units in its long production run. International Harvester showed that modern design combined with toughness and a long life were still saleable commodities, even if they cost more than a Fordson. To underline its durability, there was a lifetime guarantee on the ball-bearing crankshaft. An oil-bath final drive completed the long-life specification.*

McCORMICK-DEERING 10-20

Engine: Water-cooled, four-cylinder
Bore x stroke: 4.25 x 5.0 in.
Capacity: 284 cu. in.
Drawbar Power: 10 hp
PTO Power: 20 hp
Transmission: Three-speed
Speeds: 2.0–4.0 mph
Weight: 3,945 lb.

FARMALL
[1924]

The 10-20 and 15-30 tractors were both respectably advanced for their time, but International had something far more revolutionary up its sleeve—the Farmall. The Farmall was a landmark design not just for International, but also for the entire tractor industry.

Why was it so revolutionary? Because it was the first genuine do-it-all tractor—hence the name. Until the Farmall's introduction, tractors fell into one of two categories: they were either small and light for cultivation, or heavier and more powerful for drawbar or belt work.

International had started work on the project back in 1916, and it's a measure of just how unique it was that the Farmall still took the market by storm when it was launched seven years later. With 16 hp at the drawbar and weighing 3,650 lb., it was hefty enough to pull a two-bottom plow, while 24 belt hp was enough to drive threshers and shredders. On the other hand, it was nimble, able to turn in its own length, while its high clearance and wide wheel spacing meant that it could drive between rows of cotton or corn without damaging any of the crops. In other words, a tractor that could do it all—and the Farmall certainly could.

But although IHC management had the foresight to pay for seven years of research and development, they didn't seem to realize at first just what an impact the new tractor was having. Production was actually held down for the first year or so, as they feared the Farmall would take sales from the superficially similar 10-20 (which had about the same power), so a mere 200 Farmalls were built in the first year of production. But then the floodgates of demand opened—over 4,000 Farmalls were sold in 1926, and ten times that in 1930. A new type of tractor had been born.

LEFT: *Compact and adaptable, the Farmall was a true do-it-all tractor, powerful enough for drawbar or belt work, yet light and nimble enough to work the crops without damaging them. It sounds like an obvious combination now, but in the 1920s most tractors could do one job or the other, but not both.*

FARMALL F20

Engine: Water-cooled, four-cylinder
Bore x stroke: 3.75 x 5.0 in.
Capacity: 220 cu. in.
Drawbar Power: 16 hp @ 1,200 rpm
PTO Power: 24 hp
Transmission: Four-speed
Speeds: 2.25–3.75 mph
Weight: 3,950 lb.

ALLIS-CHALMERS 20-35
[1924]

Allis-Chalmers was a relative latecomer to the tractor market, indeed to any sort of agricultural machinery. Its background lay in heavy engineering, though it was always on the lookout for new markets. After bankruptcy in 1912, the company was headed by General Otto Falk, and he determined that Allis-Chalmers's road to recovery lay in the growing tractor market.

There were a few blind alleys on that road, such as a monster half-track truck, and the little 6-12 motor plow, but Allis-Chalmers's new tractor division finally made the grade with the conventional 15-30 in 1918. Solid, straightforward, and reliable, it sold steadily, and word began to get around that Allis-Chalmers's engineering was dependable stuff. The 20-35 shown here was simply an update of the 15-30, announced in 1922 with more power from Allis-Chalmers's own 461 cu. in. four-cylinder engine. It was A-C's standard big tractor through the 1920s and 1930s, and farmers liked it.

The trouble was, there weren't enough of them—Fordson sold tens of thousands of Model Fs every year, while A-C sold only a few hundred 20-35s. There was a simple reason. At over $2,000, the 20-35 was too expensive. Sales dwindled to the point where George Gardner, then manager of A-C's Tractor Division, resigned his post and advised company boss General Falk to close the whole thing down.

With characteristic determination, Falk didn't. Instead, he promoted assistant manager Harry Merrit into the hot seat. Merrit was an energetic, hands-on operator, and he immediately began a serious cost-cutting exercise. That same year, the 20-35's price was slashed to $1,885. The following year it was cut again, to $1,495, and yet again the year after (1928) to $1,295. By 1934, it was being listed at $970, less than half the original price! Sales quickly rose, and A-C survived. (The specifications below refer to the 18-30, a mid-way model between the original 15-30 and later 20-35.)

LEFT: One of the earliest A-C tractors, the 20-35 was straightforward and reliable, though not cheap at over $2,000—drastic price cuts later boosted sales.

BELOW: Later 20-35s, such as this one, cost less than half the originals, and many more were sold as a result. This example has all the options fitted.

ALLIS-CHALMERS 18-30 (1921)

Engine: Water-cooled, four-cylinder
Capacity: 461 cu in.
PTO Power: 38.6 hp
Drawbar Power: 23.6 hp
Fuel Consumption: 9.81 hp/hr
  per gallon
Transmission: Two-speed
Speeds: 2.6 & 3.2 mph
Weight: 6,640 lb.

CLETRAC K20
[1926]

Crawlers, or tracklayers, had been selling in fairly limited numbers to farmers, both in Europe and the United States. They were heavier and more expensive than wheeled tractors, but nevertheless their use made sense where wheeled machines got bogged down, or where the wheels would cause far too much soil impaction. Even in today's market, rubber tracks are still a very popular choice for farmers needing high-horsepower tractors.

The Cleveland Tractor Company (hence, Cletrac) first built a motor plow in 1916, but soon moved on to light crawlers. Those first Cletracs were advertised as being "Geared to the ground" to emphasize their superior traction. Running continuous tracks over cogged wheels had been pioneered in the First World War by early military tanks, but in the 1920s, they rapidly gained in popularity for agricultural work. Like Caterpillar, Cletrac was a pioneer of diesel power, fitting a Hercules engine.

One of Cletrac's earliest offerings was the Model W 12-20, of which 17,000 were built between 1919 and 1932. A Model F followed in 1920, in four versions, including the small Hi-Drive 9-16, designed for small farms. The F was driven by a floating roller chain between drive gears and tracks. The K-20 shown here was built between 1925 and 1932, and unlike earlier Cletracs, the track was lubricated with a manual plunger. At the same time Cletrac offered the mechanically similar K15-25, which was tested at Nebraska in April/May 1926, in both kerosene and gasoline form. The specifications for this model are given below.

LEFT: *The principle of crawler tracks was simple but effective, spreading the load of the machine over a larger area and so reducing soil compaction and the chances of wheel spin, which also damaged the soil. The company built wheeled tractors briefly, but these were dropped when Oliver took over in 1944. Oliver-Cletrac crawlers continued up until 1965.*

CLETRAC K15-25

Engine: Water-cooled, four-cylinder
Bore x stroke: 4.0 x 5.5 in.
Capacity: 276 cu. in.
Brake Power: 28.4 hp @ 1,375 rpm
Drawbar Power: 4,375 lb.
  (hp not measured)
Transmission: Three-speed
Speeds: Not tested
Fuel Consumption: 9.2 hp/hr
  per gallon
Weight: 4,775 lb.

TWIN CITY 17-28
[1926]

TWIN CITY 17-28

Engine: Water-cooled, four-cylinder

Bore x stroke: 4.25 x 6.0 in.

Capacity: 340 cu. in.

PTO Power: 30.9 hp @ 1,000 rpm

Drawbar Power: 22.5 hp

Transmission: Two-speed

Fuel Consumption: 9.58 hp/hr
per gallon

Weight: 5,895 lb.

BELOW: *The Twin City 17-28's four-cylinder engine was an uprated version of the 12-20. It still came with four valves per cylinder, but now measuring 340 cu. in.*

Four valves per cylinder are now thought of as the height of automotive fashion, but the Twin City 12-20 tractor had them in 1919! It was quite a departure for Minneapolis Steel & Machinery, which sold tractors under the Twin City brand name. Lightweight and strong, with a fully enclosed transmission system and a unit construction (that is, the engine and transmission were stressed members, forming the "chassis" themselves), the 12-20 was certainly advanced for its time. It sold well, too, despite costing twice as much as a Fordson—nearly 3,000 had found homes by the end of its first year. It was so successful that Minneapolis was able to claim fourteen years later that its successor was still selling just as well.

The 17-28 shown here was simply an uprated version of that original, and as ever, the company's marketing team took pains to emphasize its long life and reliability—they claimed that Twin City tractors lasted a good three years longer than the opposition:

"Three extra years is the reputation of all Twin City tractors. The Twin City 17-28 is truly the pioneer of modern tractor design and construction . . . Owners claim the lowest cost per horsepower for more years. The 17-28 has the reputation for keeping lubrication, fuel and upkeep costs down all during its L-O-N-G LIFE. It has that FAMOUS 4-cylinder low speed Twin City engine . . . BURNS kerosene, gasoline or engine distillate without water injection."

MASSEY-HARRIS 20-30

[1926]

Massey-Harris had burned its fingers with the Dent Parrett–designed tractors it sold in the late 1910s and early 1920s. But it did a better job of distributing Wallis tractors, which it began to do in the mid-1920s. The unit construction Wallis was as advanced as the Parrett had been dated. It was so successful that they soon bought the whole Wallis company, and badged the tractors as Massey-Harris machines.

Initially, the range was restricted to the Wallis 15-27, but that was soon uprated into the 20-30, and joined by a smaller 12-20. All were based on the original Wallis Cub of 1913 and shared the same principle of a light, rigid, unit construction frame.

The 20-30 was powered by a 346 cu. in. four-cylinder engine and became Massey-Harris's standard row-crop tractor of the 1930s. It came in various guises, all based around the same engine, chassis, and transmission. An Orchard model offered a low seat, enclosed front wheels, and full mudguards for the rear wheels, while the 20-30 Industrial had the choice of solid rubber or low pressure pneumatic tires, plus higher gearing than the field machines. In 1932 the 20-30 was uprated with more power and renamed the Model 25. Although really intended mainly for belt work, the 25 was often used for plowing as well. By that time, M-H had other, more modern tractors available, but the real significance of the Wallis range was that it established Massey-Harris as a serious player in the business.

MASSEY-HARRIS 20-30 (1931)

Engine: Water-cooled, four-cylinder
Bore x stroke: 4.375 x 5.75 in.
Capacity: 346 cu. in.
PTO Power: 30 hp @ 1,050 rpm
Drawbar Power: 20 hp
Transmission: Two-speed
Speeds: 2.75 & 3.3 mph
Weight: 4,381 lb.

BELOW: *After the failure of their first tractor, Massey-Harris distributed the more successful Wallis Cub. Its trademark U-section unit construction chassis remained a Massey-Harris feature up until the late 1930s.*

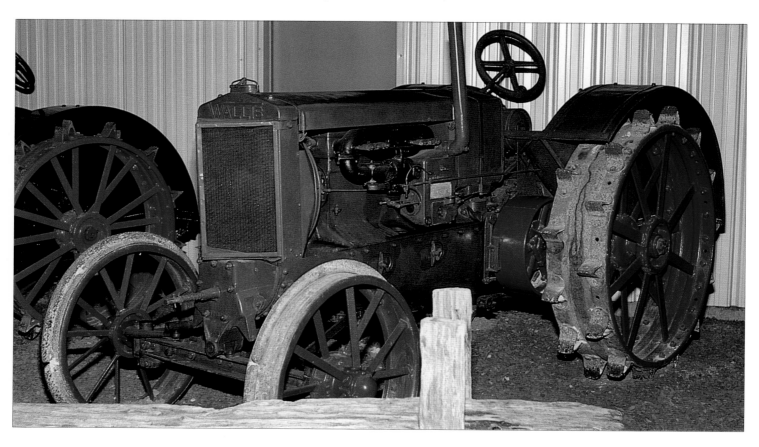

ROCK ISLAND 18-35
[1927]

Heider sounds distinctly Germanic, or maybe even Austrian, but the small manufacturer was in fact based in Cedar Rapids, Iowa, and had been building tractors from as early as 1910.

The company, however, wasn't destined to survive for long as an independent, and after only eight years it was taken over by the Rock Island Plow Company, in 1918. Their tractors continued to be badged as Heiders for several years after the takeover, but in the late 1920s the Rock Island name was gradually adopted across the range. Hence the rather odd acronym of a French tractor of 1919, which was based on the Rock Island Plow design—RIP.

These Heiders—Rock Islands, RIPs, call them what you will—were by no means revolutionary tractors. The gas/kerosene Model D of 1919 was rated at 9 drawbar hp, 16 hp at the PTO. Transmission was by friction discs, giving a speed range of a meager 1–4 mph.

The 18-35 (pictured here) came from the later Rock Island era, and used a Buda four-cylinder engine, Stromberg M3 carburetor, and Dixie-Splitdorf-Aero magneto. Unlike earlier Heiders, it used a sliding gear transmission in place of friction drive.

The G2 model released for the production year of 1929 was really a smaller version of the same thing, rated at 15/25 hp. This particular tractor used a Waukesha four-cylinder engine and weighed 4,200 lb. But Rock Island would not survive the tractor slump of 1930s, and the company was eventually taken over by J. I. Case during 1937. This spelled the end of Rock Island tractor production.

LEFT: *Heider, the name on the hood of this 18-35, came first, but it was independent for only eight years before being taken over by the Rock Island Plow Company. All Rock Island/Heiders were mid-size tractors of conventional design, this 18-35 using a two-speed transmission that gave a top operating speed of 4.5 mph. Power came courtesy of a Buda four-cylinder engine of 382 cu. in., enough for 36.5 hp at the PTO.*

ROCK ISLAND 18-35

Engine: Water-cooled, four-cylinder
Bore x stroke: 4.5 x 6.0 in.
Capacity: 382 cu. in.
PTO Power: 36.5 hp
Drawbar Power: 30.4 hp
Transmission: Two-speed
Speeds: 3 & 4.5 mph
Fuel Consumption: 7.1 hp/hr
 per gallon
Weight: 5,740 lb.

HUBER 40-62
[1927]

Expanding markets always attract speculators, some honest, some not. The early tractor industry was no exception, and some unscrupulous would-be manufacturers made very extravagant claims for tractors that didn't even exist. On the other hand, others were exceptionally modest about their machines. A good example was the Huber 40-62 (pictured here). It had actually started life as a modest 25-50, until it was tested by Nebraska, where it was found to have sixty percent more drawbar power than Huber claimed, and forty percent more at the brake!

In any case, the 40-62 (as it was renamed after Nebraska's revelations) used a Stearns four-cylinder engine of 617 cu. in. It was a valve-in-head unit, rated at 1,100 rpm and consuming fuel at the rate of 6.45 gallons per hour (a rating used before Nebraska came up with its hp/hr per gallon formula).

The smallest Huber, the Light Four 12-25, did not perform as well. During the forty-five hours of running time, it was plagued with minor faults. The carburetor had to be replaced and the magneto adjusted, then readjusted. The fan belt then had to be replaced, as did the water tank, which was leaking. Even the valves had to be reground.

The last Hubers to be tested, an LC and a streamlined B in late 1937, weren't without their problems either. The LC slipped out of gear several times, its fuel tank leaked, and the oil pressure gauge line broke. It was a pity, because the B, one of Huber's last tractors, looked very modern, but there would be a few more tractors bearing the Huber badge after that.

LEFT: *Unusually modest in its power claims, Huber rated this tractor as a 25-50 when it was originally submitted to the University of Nebraska for testing in May 1927. Imagine their surprise when it produced an impressive 40.6 hp at the drawbar and nearly 70 hp at the PTO. In light of this, Huber's big four-cylinder tractor was swiftly rerated as a 40-62, though even this didn't do full justice to the beefiness of its 617 cu. in. Stearns four-cylinder engine.*

HUBER 40-62

Engine: Water-cooled, four-cylinder
Bore x stroke: 5.5 x 6.5 in.
Capacity: 617 cu. in.
PTO Power: 69.8 hp @ 1,100 rpm
Drawbar Power: 40.6 hp
Transmission: Two-speed
Speeds: 2.4 & 3.4 mph
Fuel Consumption: 6.58 hp/hr
  per gallon
Weight: 9,910 lb.

MUNKTELL MODEL 22

[1928]

BOLINDER-MUNKTELL 25 (1934)

Engine: Water-cooled, two-cylinder, two-stroke hot-bulb diesel

Capacity: 325 cu. in.

Power: 32 hp @ 900 rpm

Transmission: Four-speed

Munktell was a long-established engineering concern in Sweden. Founded in 1832, it produced railroad locomotives and portable steam engines before turning to internal combustion engined tractors in 1913. All of these used engines from Bolinder, which had been making internal combustion engines since 1893. The two companies then merged in 1932, to form Bolinder-Munktell.

The first B-M was a huge machine weighing eight tons and with 30 hp, though they later specialized in much smaller machines. Many were powered by Bolinder's hot-bulb engines, an interesting system, derived from a marine engine; it used compressed air to start, after the hot-bulbs had been heated by an integral blowtorch. There were no spark plugs, and the fuel was ignited by a hot spot in the combustion chamber, the hot-bulb.

The company also experimented with wood-fired gas motors, as Sweden imported all of its oil and a practical alternative had great attractions—during the Second World War, when oil was in particularly short supply, over forty percent of the Swedish tractor fleet was converted to run on wood-fired gas. In the early 1920s B-M offered a two-stroke twin-cylinder, with that hot-bulb ignition. This Model 22 was joined by the larger 20-30 in 1930, and a 31 hp machine (still with twin-cylinder hot-bulb motor) in 1939. It wasn't until a takeover by Volvo in 1950 that B-M finally dropped the hot-bulb, unveiling the BM35 and BM55, which both had conventional direct injection diesel engines. The specifications here refer to the later Model 25, after Bolinder and Munktell joined forces, but still using the hot-bulb twin-cylinder engine.

BELOW: *This early Model 25 was powered by a Bolinder hot-bulb engine, not by a conventional ignition system.*

RUSHTON GENERAL
[1928]

George Rushton had an ambition to design and produce an agricultural tractor. Evidently a very persuasive man, he convinced AEC, the long-established bus and truck manufacturer in London, to help him. With one eye on the expanding tractor market (this was 1926, the Wall Street Crash and resulting slump was still a few years away), AEC agreed, and took Mr. Rushton on.

Unfortunately, his experimental Tri Tractor never reached production, but Mr. Rushton had great hopes for his General tractor, which was announced in July 1928. Although it used some existing AEC components, the General (later renamed the Rushton) was basically a copy of the Fordson Model F. It was slightly heavier than the Fordson, a little more powerful, and a lot more expensive.

But as production neared, AEC had a change of heart and decided to pull out. By floating shares, George Rushton found the money to pay off the tractor's development costs and start production at AEC's factory. Despite this difficult birth, the Rushton tractor did get into series production, and the 14-20 pictured here clearly shows its Fordson inspiration. But it didn't last long—the Rushton had no real advantages over the Model F it was based on, and in the 1930 World Agricultural Tractor Trials, the Rushton proved to have a heavier fuel consumption than any other tractor. Rushton was closed in 1932, after only two years in production.

RUSHTON GENERAL

Engine: Water-cooled, four-cylinder
Bore x stroke: 4.125 x 5.0 in.
Capacity: 267 cu. in.
Power: Not known
Transmission: Three-speed
Speeds: 1.3–6.8 mph
Weight: c.2,800 lb.

BELOW: *By the time the Rushton entered production, tractor demand was already beginning to fall into a slump, one of the many consequences of the Wall Street Crash. Costing more than a Fordson, and using more fuel, the Rushton would have found survival difficult even in an economic boom.*

JOHN DEERE GP

[1928]

When the Farmall showed just how useful a general purpose tractor could be, its rivals rushed to follow suit. John Deere had only just unveiled its Model D, so it was another three years before the general purpose C was unveiled. It was rapidly renamed the GP, after only

110 Cs had been built—the story goes that there was confusion between "C" and "D" when dealers put in orders over the phone!

Whatever it was called, the GP was Deere's first successful general purpose machine. There were five versions, all of which used the famous twin-cylinder format. Long after rivals had gone over to four- or even six-cylinder motors, JD stuck with the twin—not as smooth or powerful as younger rivals, but reliable, easy to service, and economical on fuel. "Johnny Popper," as it was affectionately known by generations of farmers, was the mainstay of John Deere for the next forty years.

In the first GP, a side-valve engine of 311 cu. in. was designed to run on kerosene but needed higher octane gasoline to start up. Pre-ignition was a common problem with low grades of fuel, so the GP was fitted with a water valve so the driver could send a squirt of water directly into the combustion chamber, damping down the pre-ignition. At 950 rpm under load, the first GP produced 20 belt hp, 10 drawbar hp, though a more powerful version arrived in 1931. A power takeoff was optional, but the GP's most innovative feature was its mechanical power lift. By means of a foot pedal, attachments could

be raised and lowered using engine power. An option at first, it soon became standard on nearly all general purpose tractors. But as useful as the GP was, it still lacked power and ground clearance compared to International's Farmall.

LEFT: *The General Purpose, or GP, was John Deere's stab at the do-it-all tractor market, exploited so effectively by the International Farmall. The GP lacked some of the Farmall's features but was still reasonably successful.*

BELOW: *There would have been no John Deere GP without this, the Model D, JD's first in-house design.*

JOHN DEERE GP

Engine: Water-cooled twin-cylinder, side-valve
Bore x stroke: 5.75 x 6.0 in.
Capacity: 311 cu. in.
Fuel: Kerosene
PTO Power: 20 hp @ 950 rpm
Drawbar Power: 10 hp @ 950 rpm
Transmission: Three-speed
Speeds: 2.3–4.3 mph
Weight: 3,600 lb.

FORDSON MODEL F
[1929]

By 1928, it looked as if Henry Ford was losing interest in his tractor. It had been a huge success: as early as 1924, the adverts claimed that over seventy-five percent of tractors on U.S. farms were Fordsons, and they were probably right, too. But in over a decade in production,

ABOVE: *Big "orchard fenders" on this Cork-built Fordson helped overcome one of the tractor's major failings: its tendency to rear up on its back wheels when the plow hit an obstruction. All early tractors were prone to this to a certain extent, but the Fordson was particularly vulnerable.*

LEFT: *After twelve years of production, the Fordson Model F had barely changed. Despite its huge success, it was starting to lose its shine by the late 1920s. Ford's single-minded vision had brought it into being, but this turned out to be a double-edged sword as his single-mindedness later became a liability. He refused to change the Model F, which he saw as a successful formula, preferring instead to concentrate on keeping costs down. But technical advances were beginning to overtake the Fordson.*

Henry hadn't made any major improvements to the Model F, preferring to concentrate on churning it out at the lowest possible cost. He had other things on his mind—the Model A car, that long awaited successor to the Model T, was imminent, which meant clearing the production decks throughout the company. With attention focused on the new car, there was no time to spend developing the Fordson, and soon nowhere to make it, either.

Still, after-market manufacturers began to offer a huge range of adaptations from the middle of the decade. There were graders to suit the Fordson, crawler conversions, industrial Fordsons with solid rubber tires, golf course mowers, and pavement sweepers. So in 1928 production was shifted to Cork in Ireland, and a little later on to Ford's giant new plant in Dagenham, in southern England.

The tractor seen here is an Irish Fordson, fitted with the big rear mudguards (sometimes called "orchard fenders") which had the added benefit of preventing the machine tipping over backwards. The short wheelbase Fordson was rather prone to this trouble which, in the days before safety cabs, could be fatal for the driver.

FORDSON MODEL F GASOLINE (1930)

Engine: Water-cooled, four-cylinder
Bore x stroke: 4.13 x 5.0 in.
Capacity: 267 cu. in.
PTO Power: 29.1 hp
Drawbar Power: 15.5 hp
Transmission: Three-speed
Speeds: 2.1–7.8 mph
Fuel Consumption: 9.53 hp/hr per gallon
Weight: 3,820 lb.

FORDSON MODEL N
[1929]

The Fordson Model F had been a huge success, but in the ten years since its first introduction the opposition had moved on. It was still as cheap and as good a value as ever, but by the late 1920s it was looking decidedly old-fashioned and technology had moved on without it.

So during the six months it took to ship all the tooling to Ireland and restart production, there was an ideal opportunity to make some changes. The result was the Model N. Its engine was bigger than that of the F, thanks to a 0.125 in. increase in bore size, and rated speed was boosted from 1,000 to 1,100 rpm, giving 23 hp on kerosene (fifteen percent up on the F), another six on gasoline. The Model T's rather basic ignition system was finally dropped in favor of a conventional high-tension magneto. There were cast front wheels (heavier but stronger than the spoked ones they replaced) and the heavier

LEFT: *Now built in Dagenham, England, the Fordson F became the N, with a bigger engine, more power and stronger front wheels and axle. It was also significantly heavier than the previous model, but it continued to sell well in Britain.*

BELOW: *Pneumatic tires are a later addition to this Dagenham-built Fordson. Sadly, Henry Ford's Irish factory was not a success, being located too far away from the big English market for tractors.*

front axle had a downward bend in the middle. There was also a bigger air cleaner, and the characteristic orchard fenders were a standard feature. And it was just as well the Model N had significantly more power than its predecessor, as it was also nearly half a ton heavier.

But the new Model N didn't last long in its new Irish home. The Cork plant, in the far south of Ireland, was too far from the big tractor market in England, not to mention Ford's London HQ. With all raw materials having to be shipped there, it also made the plant extremely expensive to run. To make

---

FORDSON MODEL N GASOLINE

Engine: Water-cooled, four-cylinder
Bore x stroke: 4.13 x 5.0 in.
Capacity: 267 cu. in.
PTO Power: 29 hp
Transmission: Three-speed
Weight: 3,600 lb.

matters worse, within a couple of years of the plant opening, a worldwide economic slump hit the demand for tractors. Ford's answer to the problem was to cut costs by packing up the machine tools and shifting production again, this time to Ford's new plant in Dagenham, on the outskirts of London. The relocation was complete by early 1933, and the Fordson Model N emerged from its new home sporting a dashing new coat of blue paint and with conventional mudguards. As such, it stayed in production for another twelve years, until 1945. Not bad for a machine that was basically the same as the original 1917 F.

BELOW: *Despite the addition of new options like pneumatic tires, electric lighting and starter, and a rear-mounted PTO, the Fordson was beginning to look seriously outdated by the late 1930s—hardly surprising, as the basic design dated back to 1917.*

ABOVE: *The cast iron front wheels of this slightly later Model N were stronger and heavier than the old spoked ones and the front axle was more heavy-duty.*

BELOW: *Outdated it might be, but thousands of British farmers came to view the Fordson with just as much affection as their U.S. cousins had.*

TWIN CITY 21-32
[1929]

The Twin City 21-32 marked the end of an era, in more ways than one. It was the last design produced by Minneapolis Steel & Machinery as an independent concern—it was introduced for 1929, the year they merged with the Minneapolis Threshing Company and Moline Plow to form Minneapolis-Moline. It was also the final incarnation of the four-valve 12-20, which had been launched back in 1919. The 21-32 followed the same basic format as the 12-20 and its 17-28 big brother, which was sufficiently advanced not to seem out of date ten years later. In fact, the 21-32 was to stay in production with only minor changes for another fifteen years.

The four-cylinder 16-valve engine was only slightly larger than that of the 17-28, but according to Nebraska, it had significantly more power. Rated 21 hp at the drawbar, it delivered 31! At first, it had only a two-speed transmission, though a three-speed was added later. A catalog of the time emphasized the 21-32's lubrication system, including a gear-driven pump for the engine, an oil pressure gauge, and a large reservoir of oil for the gearbox (which also enclosed the steering gear). Also known as the FT, the 21-32 was renamed FTA in 1935, which signified a slightly bigger engine with a bore of 4.675 in.

LEFT: *With a slightly bigger 382 cu. in. engine than the 17-28, the 21-32 enjoyed a power boost to 36 hp at the PTO. It had another power boost in 1935.*

BELOW: *Clean lines and a neat appearance for the last four-valve Twin City, though back in 1929, no tractor would have stayed this clean for very long!*

ABOVE: *"The NEW 21-32," wasn't quite that new, being an update of the four-valve-per-cylinder 12-20.*

TWIN CITY 21-32 (1929)

Engine: Water-cooled, four-cylinder
Bore x stroke: 4.5 x 6.0 in.
Capacity: 382 cu. in.
PTO Power: 35.9 hp @ 1,000 rpm
Drawbar Power: 31.1 hp
Transmission: Two-speed
Speeds: 2.2 & 2.9 mph
Fuel Consumption: 9.64 hp/hr per gallon
Weight: 6,819 lb.

JOHN DEERE GP WT

[1929]

John Deere's GP, the tractor the company hoped would take sales away from the all-conquering International Farmall, was not a great success. By comparison, it lacked ground clearance and power, while the standard tread rear axle could not straddle two rows, an essential feature for row-crop work. In the Southern United States in particular, cotton growers preferred the Farmall.

John Deere partially answered these inadequacies with the introduction of its GP WT (Wide Tread), which combined a two-row rear axle with a two-wheel tricycle front end, just like the Farmall. It still wasn't quite as powerful, though it had slightly lower gearing than the standard GP, which helped a little. In any case, in 1931 a larger version of the John Deere twin-cylinder motor, now 339 cu. in., helped address the power problem as well. Another big change was the addition of an overhead steering linkage in 1932. The original side-mounted system, with the linkage running down the offside of the machine, was subject to front-wheel whip.

The GP WT did retain the GP's three-speed transmission and chain drive, but it was over 26 in. wider, with an 8-inch longer wheelbase, and the rear tread width was now 76 in. Plus it also had a narrower hood and radiator to improve the driver's visibility. To compliment and enhance the WT, John Deere introduced a new series of two- and four-row implements. The GP400 for example, was a four-row cotton and corn planter, which, they claimed, allowed one farmer to plant, "from 35 to 45 acres per day."

Despite all the effort the company put into their new tractor, the John Deere GP WT still failed to topple the Farmall from its wide-tread pedestal, but it did go some way to regaining ground lost with the first GP.

LEFT: *To counter the criticisms of the basic GP, the John Deere WT featured, as the name suggested, a wider rear track, to make it suitable for row-crop work, though it didn't have power to match the Farmall until 1931. John Deere offered two- and four-row implements to match the tractor.*

JOHN DEERE GP WT

Engine: Water-cooled twin-cylinder, side-valve
Bore x stroke: 6.0 x 6.0 in.
Capacity: 339 cu. in.
Fuel: Kerosene
PTO Power: 26 hp @ 950 rpm
Drawbar Power: 29 hp @ 950 rpm
Transmission: Three-speed

CASE MODEL L
[1929]

By the late 1920s, the Crossmotor concept was sadly out of date. New boss Leon Clausen set about turning the company around, and he gave the go ahead for a brand-new range of machines to replace the Crossmotors. When it finally arrived in 1929, the Model L couldn't have been more conventional. The four-cylinder engine sat along (not across) the frame, driving through a three-speed gearbox and (less usual) chain drive between the differential and rear axle. Being of unit construction (using the engine as part of the chassis frame) made it lighter, so while the L was the same size and weight as the 18-32 Crossmotor, it had the capabilities of the bigger 25-45.

The simple four-cylinder motor was of 403 cu. in., and rated at 1,100 rpm. There was also a rear power takeoff for easy use of the new generation of shaft-powered binders and combines. The L came along at just the right time for Case, and over 30,000 were sold before production ended in 1940. It was a very different beast to the John Deere D, its closest rival, with its higher-revving four-cylinder engine against the Deere's two-cylinder slogger. But it was more powerful and only used a little more fuel.

Rubber tires were offered from 1934 and the industrial Model LI came with dual turning brakes. The basic layout of the L was a great survivor. As the LA, it was built until 1953, and as the re-engined 5/600 it went on into the 1960s.

LEFT: *The Model L signified a new era for Case, leaving behind the old Crossmotors in favor of a new line of conventional tractors with in-line mounted engines. Lighter and smaller than the equivalent Crossmotor, the L was also very long lived, and the basic design was built right through to the 1960s.*

BELOW: *The Case Model L was unit construction— that is, the engine and transmission themselves formed part of the chassis, which made for a stronger, lighter structure than a traditional separate chassis frame layout. It also confirmed Case's commitment to the four-cylinder engine.*

CASE MODEL L

Engine: Water-cooled, four-cylinder
Bore x stroke: 4.625 x 6.00 in.
Capacity: 403 cu. in.
PTO Power: 45.0 hp @ 1,100 rpm
Drawbar Power: 36.8 hp @ 1,100 rpm
Transmission: Three-speed
Speeds: 3.5–5.6 mph
Fuel Consumption: 10.05 hp/hr
    per gallon
Weight: 8,025 lb. (on rubber tires)

CASE MODEL C
[1929]

A few months after the Model L was launched came this, the C. It was really a baby version of the L, with another three-bearing four-cylinder engine that had removable cylinder liners, though this one was of smaller capacity, at 324 cu. in. While the Model L was aimed fairly and squarely at the John Deere D, the C's natural rival was the all-conquering Fordson. Naturally, it couldn't compete with Henry's tractor on price, one reason why Ford was still selling 2,000 Fordson Fs a month in the late 1920s, while Case moved around 300 Model Cs. But in other respects it was competitive. It was about thirty percent heavier at 4,000 lb. but far less likely to tip over backward (a serious Fordson failing). The Case C had slightly less power than a Fordson (29.8 belt hp and nearly 20 at the drawbar, according to Nebraska), but it was a lot more economical (11 hp/hrs per gallon against 5.9).

That Model C tested at Nebraska was kerosene-fueled, despite which it was relatively fuel-efficient, as it recorded 11.36 hp/hr per gallon at maximum load of 29.8 brake horsepower. The three gear ratios allowed speeds of 2.3, 3.3, and 4.5 mph, and in the lowest of these it was capable of pulling 3,289 lb., or seventy-nine percent of its own weight, which translated as a respectable 19.6 drawbar hp. During thirty-five hours of running time, it needed no attention apart from some clutch adjustment and cleaning of the fuel line.

After a year, it was joined by the CC, a general purpose version of the same machine. Case had little choice but to do this, as every major manufacturer had produced a machine to rival the Farmall. The CC was useful enough, but it cost more than any of its rivals.

LEFT: *Case quickly followed up the Model L with the C, a smaller machine aimed at the Fordson market. It was never built in Fordson quantities, but it was clear that more specialist tractors could survive the Ford onslaught.*

BELOW: *The Case Model C with period steel wheels. These, rather than the pneumatic tires seen on the tractor on the left, would have been the correct factory fitment. Pneumatic rubber tires were not generally available until the late 1930s.*

CASE MODEL C

Engine: Water-cooled, four-cylinder
Bore x stroke: 3.875 x 5.50 in.
Capacity: 259 cu. in.
PTO Power: 29.8 hp @ 1,100 rpm
Drawbar Power: 19.6 hp @1,100 rpm
Transmission: Three-speed
Speeds: 2.3–4.5 mph
Fuel Consumption: 11.36 hp/hr
  per gallon
Weight: 4,155 lb.

The 1930s:
GREAT LEAPS FORWARD

If anyone in the tractor business had thought the 1920s were tough, worse was to come. The decade had ended on a high in the United States, with 229,000 tractors produced in 1929. The following year saw a modest fall, to 202,000. But by 1932, actual tractor sales in the U.S. slumped to just 19,000. Even allowing for exports, it was a disaster. In just three years sales had plummeted to less than one-tenth of the previous production figure. Even Fordson wasn't exempt—the Cork plant had been producing fifty machines a day in late 1930, but according to R. B. Gray *(The Agricultural Tractor)*, in May 1931, "production was practically discontinued owing to a lack of new orders."

Just as in earlier hard times, many smaller tractor companies went out of business. In 1921, there were an estimated 186 manufacturers; fifteen years later, only twenty were left. And of those twenty, just nine controlled ninety percent of U.S. tractor production. The big nine didn't include Fordson, now mass producing tractors in Britain, but only exporting in very small numbers to the U.S.

So who were the big nine? First and foremost, there was International Harvester, still riding high on the success of the Farmall, and with three factories busy building tractors in Chicago, Milwaukee, and Rock Island. John Deere was doing well, too, making a virtue of the simplicity of its two-cylinder Johnny Poppers. J. I. Case was third, thanks to the up-to-date Model L and Model C launched in 1929 to replace the aging Crossmotors. Fourth biggest was the token Canadian company, Massey-Harris,

doing well out of the U-framed Challenger. Then came Oliver—recently merged with the stronger Hart-Parr, it would make its mark during the 1930s with the six-cylinder 70. Minneapolis-Moline was another child of merger, three small companies joined to form one that could survive. Then came Allis-Chalmers, held back by its limited dealer network, which was solved by taking over Advance-Rumely and its dealers. Finally in the big nine, there were two crawler manufacturers: Cleveland, which had been building Cletrac crawlers since 1916, and, of course, Caterpillar.

Between them, these nine U.S. manufacturers were to produce a whole raft of new innovations: diesel engines (Caterpillar); high octane six-cylinder gasoline engines (Oliver); the mechanical implement lift (Case); pneumatic rubber tires (Allis-Chalmers); and enclosed cab (Minneapolis-Moline). However, the most significant advance of the decade would have nothing to do with any of them.

Pneumatic rubber tires were a long time in coming to tractors. Bare steel rims with stick-out spade lugs, which most early tractors used, were strong and relatively cheap. But the lugs caused field damage, and on the road steel rims limited speed to little more than that of a horse. The most common solution was to fit steel bands over the lugs, which allowed slightly higher speeds, but were cumbersome and time

RIGHT: *What's the most significant item on this Persian Orange Allis-Chalmers Model U? Answer: pneumatic rubber tires, which made it faster, more efficient, and more comfortable.*

consuming to fit. Solid rubber tires were commonly fitted to industrial tractors, which spent all their time on hard surfaces, but these gave zero traction in the field. In the late 1920s, however, Allis-Chalmers came up with the perfect solution—massive, low pressure pneumatics. After early experiments with 70 psi aircraft tires, the real breakthrough came when the pressure was reduced to 12 psi. They transformed the Allis-Chalmers Model U, the first machine with an air tire option. It was more efficient in the field, needing half the power of a steel-rimmed tractor, and could run up to 15 mph on the road. As icing on the cake, it was more comfortable for the driver, not to mention easier to steer. Despite costing a substantial $150 extra, the U's rubber tires made a huge impact and within a few years, every major manufacturer was offering them. At first, U.S. farmers balked at the high option price, and in 1935 only fourteen percent of new wheeled tractors were air-equipped.

But the economies were so great that rubber tires paid for themselves, and by 1940 only five percent of new tractors ran on steel.

Diesel power, now almost universal in tractors, took longer to gain wide acceptance, again because of the high initial cost. The real pioneers were in Europe. Benz of Germany was producing a diesel-engined tractor as early as 1921; five years later in Italy, Francesco Cassani (later to build SAME tractors) built a twin-cylinder diesel machine; and in 1928, the British company of Marshall began the development of its big single-cylinder tractor, which would remain in production until 1957.

These were wheeled tractors, but in the U.S., the first diesels were all crawler machines, used in construction work as well as farming. Caterpillar was the first

BELOW: *This TracTractor is gasoline-powered, but crawlers pioneered diesel power in 1930s America—their greater efficiency made them hard to ignore.*

BELOW: *The U.S. soon became the world's leading manufacturer of crawler tractors, some of which were used in agriculture, though they were primarily built for the construction industry.*

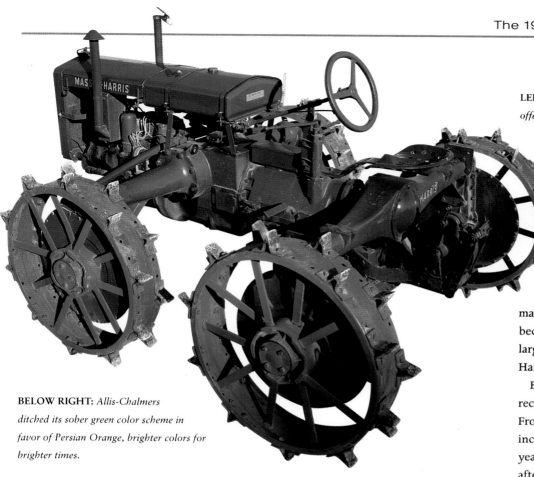

LEFT: *Massey-Harris GP was not a big seller, but offered unrivaled traction for a wheeled tractor, thanks to four-wheel drive.*

1,500 rpm unit produced a respectable 30 hp at the PTO, and, of course, being a small six, it was much smoother than two- and four-cylinder rivals. Not that Oliver had pioneered the use of six cylinders—Eagle and Advance-Rumely both unveiled six-cylinder machines in 1930. Later in the decade, sixes became far more popular, especially in larger sizes; Graham-Bradley and Massey-Harris 101 are suitable examples.

By this time, U.S. tractor sales had recovered well from the early 1930s slump. From that low of 1932, production increased by eighty percent the following year, and another forty percent the year after, to 50,000. It was a sign of just how bad things had been that this figure was little more than one-fifth of the 1929 high. But in 1935 production shot back up to over 160,000 tractors, and the following year it almost matched the 1929 figure. There were now well over a million tractors

BELOW RIGHT: *Allis-Chalmers ditched its sober green color scheme in favor of Persian Orange, brighter colors for brighter times.*

U.S. manufacturer in the field, after first experimenting with converted gasoline engines. It started big, with the 77 hp Diesel Sixty of 1930. The new Sixty was a great success, setting a new fuel economy record of 13.87 hp/hr per gallon, when tested at Nebraska. It was so successful, that the following year a whole range of smaller diesel Cats were unveiled—the Thirty-Five, Fifty, and Seventy-Five. Within a few years, most Caterpillars had a diesel option, and the other crawler manufacturers had all followed suit. If they insisted, customers could opt for a kerosene or gasoline version of the little R2 crawler, but more Nebraskan tests showed that the diesel was at least fifty percent more efficient. However, the high initial cost and the Second World War were to delay the widespread use of diesel in American-made tractors for another fifteen years.

Meanwhile, farmers wanted more power. Higher octane gasoline, of 68-70 rating compared to the previous 50-65, was now commonplace, and Oliver was the first tractor manufacturer to take advantage of it. The Oliver 70 of 1935 was specifically designed for high-octane gas, with a high-

compression six-cylinder engine of 202 cu. in. Not all farmers wanted to pay out for expensive high-octane fuel though, and the 70 was also available in a low-compression kerosene form. Although relatively small, the Oliver's high-revving

LEFT: *International didn't just make Farmalls—they also sold standard-tread equivalents in the 1930s, wearing the McCormick-Deering badge.*

rounded housing. Even the wheels were redesigned to give an impression of both lightness and strength. John Deere followed suit in 1939, calling in designer Henry Dreyfuss to transform the sheet metal on its machines. The style here was more a softening of the old square-rigged lines, rather than full-on Art Deco streamlining. Whatever, it suited the no-nonsense John Deere image very well.

Perhaps the most dramatically restyled tractor was the Minneapolis-Moline UDLX, or Comfortractor. Based on the standard Minneapolis-Moline U series, it looked more like a 1930s automobile than a tractor, with its weatherproof all-steel cab and voluminous mudguards. The prtective cab came equipped with all mod cons, including a heater and radio, but there was also a rare open top version, which looked for all the world like a boulevard-cruising Chevrolet. Unfortunately, the UDLX was too far ahead of its time, and few were sold—it would be many years before farmers were prepared to pay extra for comfort.

in use on American farms, twice as many as in 1925. In short, the slump was over!

Almost in celebration of this, U.S. tractor manufacturers appeared to discover the delights of styling and color schemes. Just like automobiles and motorcycles, not to mention more static items like refrigerators and toasters, tractors entered the elegant new streamlined age with a vengeance.

Some companies did the work themselves. Oliver's six-cylinder 70 already looked pretty sleek, but was improved further with rounded off styling in 1937. Other manufacturers brought in outside help. International went to Raymond Loewy, whose famous design studio had been at the forefront of transforming quite mundane items into stylish pieces of Art Deco. Loewy set to work, and enclosed the International tractor's fuel tank, steering rod, and radiator in a single

A simpler way to make tractors look more attractive was to give them bold new color

ABOVE: *By the mid-1930s, Caterpillar was the largest manufacturer of diesel engines in the world.*

RIGHT: *Sleek and slim, the Oliver 70 made use of high octane gasoline to power its high-compression, high-revving six-cylinder engine. It got a more streamlined look in 1937.*

schemes with romantic names—hence Allis-Chalmers's Persian Orange, Case's Flambeau Red, and Minneapolis-Moline's bright yellow, Prairie Gold.

But things were changing under the skin as well. Tractors were becoming ever more adaptable, a trend kickstarted by the International Farmall of 1927, with its high clearance and maneuverability for row-crop work and enough power to be useful for hauling and belt work as well. Times had moved on since the Fordson Model F, which was simple and cheap but essentially a compromise for many jobs on the farm. Ford itself realized this, and belatedly offered the Fordson All-Around in 1935. Although more useful than the basic Model N, it was still outdated in many ways, and sales were disappointing.

The way to success for a modern row-crop tractor was to combine all those original Farmall selling points, with a high level of adjustability to suit different crops. John Deere's smaller A and B models, for example, offered the choice of tricycle, fixed front, or adjustable front axles, plus a fully adjustable rear axle. The rear axle on the latest Farmall, the F14, could be varied between 44 and 78 inches. Making such adjustments was still quite laborious, depending on muscle power and large hammers, but they did bring a new adaptability to tractors. Later, power adjustment would make life easier still.

One particularly back-breaking job was attaching and removing implements such as plows and cultivators, whether to the rear or to mid-mountings. You could either use muscle power alone or resort to a jack, but either way the result was a lot of hard work and very time consuming. The market was ripe for a new means of implement control, and the single-most important leap forward in tractor design was the result—the Ferguson three-point hydraulic hitch.

There had been power hitches before, of course. The British-made Ideal tractor offered a power-operated implement lift in 1912, and U.S. manufacturer Hackney began producing its Auto Plow, complete with mechanical lift, a year earlier. John Deere developed a mechanical lift in 1927 on the Model C, following that with a hydraulic version in 1932—to lift the implement, you just stepped on a pedal or pushed a lever. J. I. Case, too, offered its customers the "Motor Lift," in 1935. It was

ABOVE: *What a transformation! This is the Model D before it was restyled, showing what a difference some sheet metal changes could make to a tractor.*

driven by engine power via an enclosed worm gear, and a whole range of implements was designed to suit it.

But none of these had the sophistication of the Ferguson system. They were purely designed to lift implements and set them down again. Harry Ferguson's three-point system took into account the relationship between tractor and implement, their stability and their traction. Harry Ferguson was an Irishman, a highly gifted engineer with a natural flair for business. He sold U.S. Waterloo Boy tractors in Ireland during the First World War, and became interested in the way implements were attached. He soon designed a plow specifically for the Fordson Model F, with two struts which reduced the risk of the tractor tipping over backward and helped to maintain a more even working depth.

The three-point hitch, which Ferguson began developing in the late 1920s, was a more advanced version of the same thing. There were three attachment points instead of two, and hydraulic lift operation. Tests showed it was more stable in operation than a conventional system, it prevented tipping up, and had automatic draft sensing. And, of course, the hydraulic system made attaching implements far easier than

before. Ferguson even designed a tractor to suit, the low-slung Type A, which was produced for him by the David Brown company of England in 1936. The Type A

BELOW: *Minneapolis-Moline UDLX was the first tractor with an all-steel glazed cab, complete with heater and radio.*

BELOW: *Adjustability was the name of the game in the late 1930s. This John Deere BWH, a hybrid of parts taken from the B, BN, and BW, has adjustable tread both front and rear.*

RIGHT: *Demonstration of the Ferguson three-point hitch—this was the single biggest advance in tractor design of all time.*

proved itself so efficient that it could outpace far more powerful tractors.

But the partnership of Ferguson/David Brown was hardly a marriage made in heaven. The Type A sold poorly, thanks to a high price, and the partners disagreed on how to improve it. In the end, they split up—David Brown went its own way, and became a major tractor manufacturer in its own right, while Harry Ferguson set up a meeting with Henry Ford at Dearborn. It was a landmark in tractor history. Ford was keen to get back into the tractor market—the Fordson Model N was now a British responsibility, and U.S. sales had dwindled. Ferguson, for his part, wanted to see his three-point system on a mass-production tractor. Ford was so impressed by the Irishman's field demonstration that he struck a deal there and then. He would develop a brand-new tractor to suit the Ferguson system, and would build it in huge quantities—Harry Ferguson would market and sell it.

Only eight months after that famous handshake agreement (nothing was ever put in writing) the new Ford 9N went into production—that alone was a remarkable achievement. The 9N proved to have much the same impact as the original Fordson. Smaller and lighter than many of its rivals, it had the huge advantage of the Ferguson hitch system. It was thoroughly up-to-date, too, with pneumatic rubber tires and an electric starter.

The 9N's attractions were obvious, and 10,000 were built in those first six months of production. All in all, it had been quite a decade—from disastrous slump to rapid recovery via some highly significant technological leaps. The 1940s would not be quite so eventful.

BELOW: *The Ferguson-Brown was designed to suit the new three-point hitch, and was remarkably advanced, but a high price put buyers off.*

RUMELY 6A
[1930]

Advance-Rumely, like many of the tractor pioneers, started out making monster-sized rivals for the steam traction engines. The famous Oil Pulls, with their huge slow-revving kerosene engines, even looked just like the old traction engines. In their day, they had their advantages, but by the late 1920s they were looking seriously outdated next to the new breed of lighter, handier, and cheaper gasoline tractors. Advance-Rumely had to do something to catch up, and tried with the Toro Motor Cultivator line—the little four-cylinder DoAll weighed a reasonable 3,000 lb. and used a conventional Waukesha engine. But it was not a success, and the remaining stocks were sold off to the dealers at a bargain $543—not much more than half the original list price.

There was one final stab at a modern tractor, before Rumely was driven into the arms of Allis-Chalmers. The 6A of 1930 was as far from the old Oil Pulls as it was possible to get: modern Waukesha six-cylinder engine, and a six-speed transmission where the opposition offered three. It could pull 4,273 lb. at 9.96% wheel slippage. Could this be the tractor to save Advance-Rumely? Sadly, sales didn't match up to the specification, and 700 unsold 6As were still held at the factory when Allis-Chalmers took over in 1931. A classic case of too little, too late.

LEFT: *The 6A, a belated attempt to produce a modern six-cylinder tractor, but many were still unsold when Allis-Chalmers took over. It was tested by Nebraska in April 1931. It should have been October 1930, but the first 6A to be tested was withdrawn after just two hours. They tried again later in the month, but that test was abandoned after three weeks, due to cold weather. Finally, in the following spring, it was completed, though even that last bout of testing wasn't without incident—the 6A's valves needed regrinding, and the fan hub broke up, destroying both fan and radiator. The Waukesha engine, which on the test tractor was equipped with an American Bosch magneto and Zenith carburetor, produced 43 hp at maximum load, at a fuel efficiency of 8.79 hp/hr per gallon.*

RUMELY 6A

Engine: Water-cooled, six-cylinder
Bore x stroke: 4.25 x 4.75 in.
Capacity: 504 cu. in.
PTO Power: 43 hp @ 1,365 rpm
Drawbar Power: 33.6 hp
Transmission: Three-speed
Speeds: 2.8–4.7 mph
Fuel Consumption: 8.79 hp/hr per gallon
Weight: 6,370 lb.

EAGLE 6A
[1930]

By the late 1920s, Eagle found itself in a similar position to Advance-Rumely. Well, not quite the same. The company had produced a whole range of two- and four-cylinder tractors through the 1920s, and its first four actually appeared in 1911. But it was an increasingly outdated lineup, especially compared to the Fordson. Next to Henry's mass-produced baby, the Eagles were heavy, expensive, and old-fashioned.

Like Rumely, it tried using a Waukesha six-cylinder engine to tempt the buyers back. The Eagle 6A was even introduced in the same year as Rumely's, 1930. It was a quite different machine though, using a much smaller 226 cu. in. Waukesha instead of the Rumely's 504 cu. in. unit. According to the Nebraska tests, it wasn't far behind on power though, with 28/40 hp against the Rumely's 34/43.

There were three variations on the theme. The 6A pictured here was designed for three- or four-plow use, the 6B was a row-crop machine, and the 6C a utility. These might have been a big step for Eagle, but they weren't enough for the company to resume production after the Second World War. The company stopped making tractors in the early 1940s.

LEFT: *The Eagle 6A was tested at Nebraska just before the Rumely 6A test was abandoned, and although it looked similar (both were powered by Waukesha six-cylinder engines) was actually a very different machine. Eagle did not give the 6A a power rating, but according to the ASAE (American Society of Agricultural Engineers) it was a 22-37. The Nebraskan tests found it could manage slightly more than that, and not far short of the Rumely outputs, which was quite an achievement, given the Eagle's smaller engine. It was also a lighter tractor than the Rumely (5,670 lb. as tested, against 6,370 lb.) so its work rate wouldn't have been that far off. It was slightly more fuel-efficient too, with 9.2 hp/hr per gallon at maximum load of 40.4 brake horsepower. The maximum drawbar pull, in low gear, was 4,650 lb., so it could pull its own weight. The 6A helped Eagle persevere through the 1930s, but the company didn't survive the war.*

EAGLE 6A GASOLINE

Engine: Water-cooled, six-cylinder
Bore x stroke: 4.0 x 4.5 in.
Capacity: 226 cu. in.
PTO Power: 40.4 hp @ 1,416 rpm
Drawbar Power: 27.9 hp @ 1,416 rpm
Transmission: Three-speed
Speeds: 2.5–4.5 mph
Fuel Consumption: 9.2 hp/hr
  per gallon
Weight: 5,670 lb.

MASSEY-HARRIS
GENERAL PURPOSE [1930]

By 1930, Massey-Harris had been in the tractor business for fifteen years, but had yet to build its own machine, preferring to market other makes. The General Purpose changed all that. The GP was the first tractor to be designed and built by Massey-Harris itself in Canada.

But despite the name, which attempted to imply a ubiquitous do-it-all tractor like the Farmall, the General Purpose was anything but.

In some ways, it was far ahead of its time. It had permanent four-wheel drive and an articulated chassis, features which are now almost compulsory among high-horsepower supertractors, but they were almost unheard of then. Unfortunately, the design also had some serious drawbacks that made it far from a genuine do-it-all. Four-wheel drive restricted the turning circle, so this GP wasn't as nimble as a Farmall or John Deere GP. It also meant the track width was not adjustable, an essential feature for an all-around tractor.

But if Massey's first in-house tractor failed to be a genuine all-arounder, it did have some unique attributes of its own. The

LEFT: *Lateral thinking from Massey-Harris produced the four-wheel drive, articulated chassis General Purpose—great traction, but expensive.*

BELOW: *Until 1936, all GPs were powered by a 25 hp (rated at 22 hp) Hercules four-cylinder engine of 226 cu. in.—later models used an in-house Massey-Harris unit.*

four-wheel drive from equal-sized wheels gave it unrivaled traction amongst other wheeled machines; the articulated chassis allowed the rear axle to follow rough ground independently; and weight distribution was carefully thought out, for optimum placing on all four driven wheels.

These advantages did help to secure Massey-Harris a niche in forestry and specialty crops, but priced at $1,000 it was too expensive for most farmers. There was little attempt to change the GP over its production run, though there were plans for a six-cylinder version, but it remained ahead of its time.

MASSEY-HARRIS GENERAL PURPOSE

Engine: Water-cooled, four-cylinder
Bore x stroke: 4.0 x 4.5 in.
Capacity: 226 cu. in.
PTO Power: 24.8 hp @ 1,200 rpm
Drawbar Power: 19 hp
Transmission: Three-speed
Speeds: 2.2–4.0 mph
Weight: 3,861 lb.

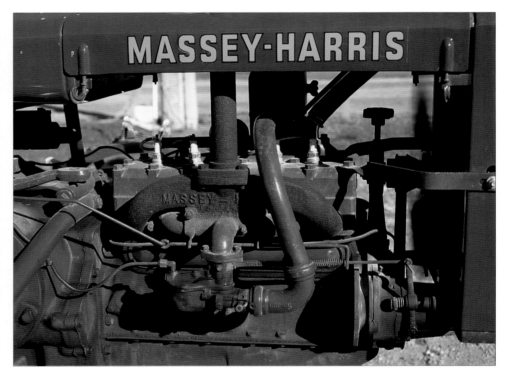

BELOW: *The GP's wide track and high ground clearance is obvious in this shot, showing the similarity with a crawler machine. GPs were sometimes used as substitutes for crawlers.*

ABOVE: *Although the GP's track width was unadjustable (which really ruled it out for row-crop work) a number of different widths could be built in at the factory. Note the optional power lift just behind the driver's seat.*

LEFT: *This is an early General Purpose, according to the serial number—not many were sold.*

RIGHT: *The GP's forward-mounted engine was intended to counter-balance the weight of an implement at the rear, thus producing roughly equal weight distribution over the four driven wheels. It was a clever design.*

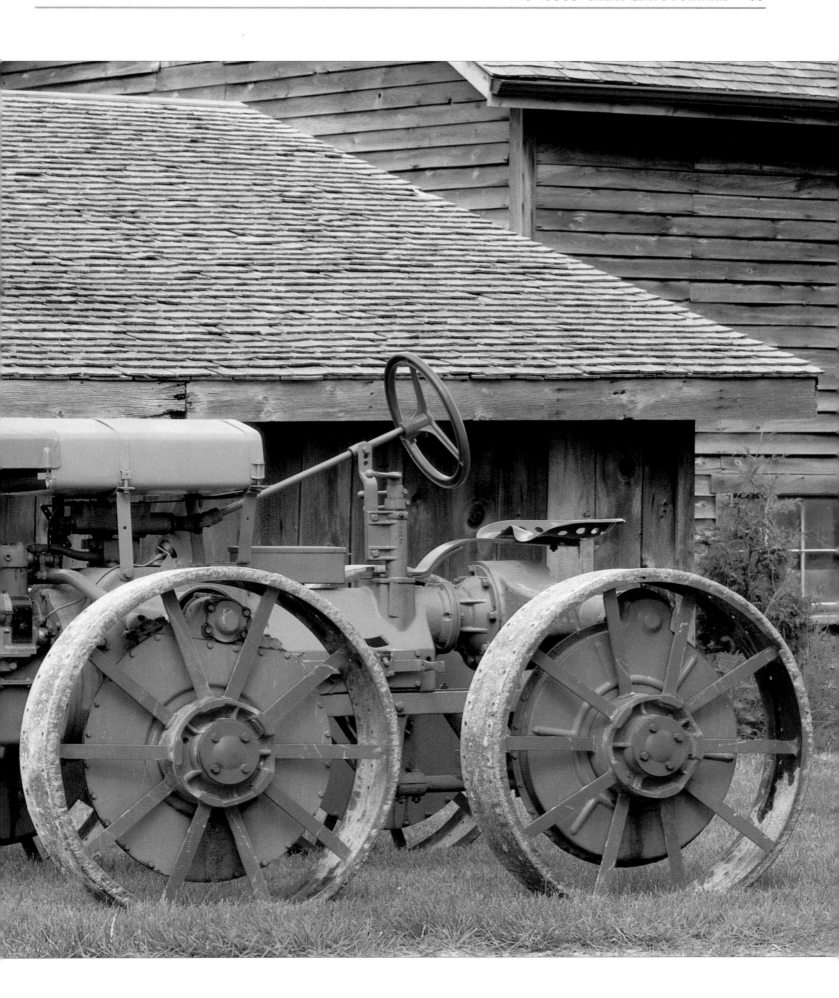

OLIVER MODEL A/28-44
[1931]

The year 1929 was a good year for mergers. Three companies joined to create Minneapolis-Moline, brought together by the hardships of the 1920s. That same year, the U.S. seeding Machine Company (seeders and planters), Nichols and Shepherd (threshers), Hart-Parr (tractors), and the Oliver Chilled Plow Works (plows) all joined forces. It was a good marriage—Oliver had a new tractor on the drawing board, while Hart-Parr had the expertise to build it.

At first, Oliver tractors were built by Hart-Parr and both names appeared, though the H-P name was dropped after a few years. The first fruit of this merger was the Oliver-Hart-Parr Row Crop of 1930. Rated at 18/27 hp, it was fitted with a single front wheel—the rear pair were adjustable by sliding them in and out on a splined

axle. The uprated 22/44 hp Model A soon followed, with standard treads, along with a Model B 18/28 standard tread. Both became known by their power ratings only—the Row Crop became 18-27 and the same year was updated with dual front wheels and improved steering and brakes. Later, it was renamed the 80 Row Crop.

LEFT: *Designed by Oliver, built by Hart-Parr, this 28-44 was an early result of the merger between four smaller companies that became known as Oliver.*

BELOW: *The big 28-44 was later updated as the Oliver 90, although it was still powered by the same hefty 443 cu. in. four-cylinder engine.*

OLIVER A/28-44

Engine: Water-cooled, four-cylinder
Bore x stroke: 4.75 x 6.25 in.
Capacity: 443 cu. in.
PTO Power: 49 hp @ 1,125 rpm
Drawbar Power: 28 hp
Transmission: Three-speed
Speeds: 2.7–4.3 mph
Weight: 6,415 lb.

FARMALL F30
[1931]

No one could accuse International Harvester of rushing things. It had taken seven years for them to bring the revolutionary Farmall to production. It took another seven before a more-powerful version appeared, despite the threat from John Deere, Case, and Allis-Chalmers, all of whom had come up with their own Farmall rivals some time before.

The new F30 Farmall, with 30 hp and thirty percent bigger than the original, was really little different to the first one. The engine was substantially bigger, with an extra half-inch on the bore to give a capacity of 284 cu. in.—these dimensions were the same as the older 10-20, which was still selling steadily. Despite a slightly lower rated speed of 1,150 rpm, the result was 20 hp at the drawbar, and a genuine 30 hp at the belt. Perhaps with one eye on the perceived clash between its standard tread tractors and the Farmall, IHC had already uprated the 15-30 into a 22-36, to distance it from the new F30. The first Farmall incidentally was now named the Regular, to differentiate it from big brother, and was given slightly more power and better steering as the F20 in 1932.

In standard form, the F30 was well equipped, with regular or narrow tread, a belt-pulley, solid-rim wheels (rubber tires later became an option), and adjustable radiator shutter. But despite the extra power and features, it failed to emulate the success of the original, 40,000 of which had been sold in 1930 alone. There were plenty of farmers seeking an alternative to the first Farmall, but they wanted a smaller, cheaper version, not thirty percent more power.

LEFT: *Encouraged by the success of the original Farmall, International developed a whole range, with standard-tread spin-offs based on the same mechanical parts. The F30 was the first variation, offering more power. It was otherwise very similar to the first Farmall, which was renamed the Farmall Regular. Although heavier at 5,300 lb., it was still nimble compared to 30 hp rivals, and had the same high-clearance, crop-straddling capabilities as the tractor it was derived from. It was never as successful as the smaller Farmalls.*

FARMALL F30

Engine: Water-cooled, four-cylinder
Bore x stroke: 4.25 x 5.0 in.
Capacity: 284 cu. in.
Drawbar Power: 20 hp @ 1,150 rpm
PTO Power: 30 hp
Transmission: Four-speed
Speeds: 2.0–3.75 mph
Weight: 5,300 lb.

FARMALL F12
[1932]

International may have taken a while to come up with the original Farmall and the powered-up F30, but the little F12 followed far more quickly. The United States was still the land of small farmers, (those with only a hundred acres). They loved the idea of the Farmall, but couldn't justify, or plain couldn't afford, the full-size 20 hp version.

In 1932, they got what the wanted. Just as the 30 hp F30 was simply a bigger brother of the original Farmall, so the F12 was no more, or less, than a scaled-down version of the pioneering original. It was actually much smaller than the machine it was derived from—the F30 was thirty percent bigger, but F12 had a little 113 cu. in. engine, less than half the size of the first Farmall's. With everything on a smaller scale, it came in at a featherweight 2,700 lb., which gave its modest 10 hp more of a fighting chance. In any case, it was enough for a one-bottom plow, and just like the bigger Farmalls, this one could fit between rows, and was able to cultivate two rows at a time. One new feature shared with the larger Farmalls was the adjustable width rear axle, altered by sliding the rear wheels along splines.

For the first five months of production, the F12 used Waukesha engines, but in May 1933 IHC's own power unit replaced it. Whatever its power unit, the little F12 was a great success, and it was five years before IHC felt the need to uprate it, and the F12 became the 15 hp F14 in 1938.

LEFT: *This was more like it. Although a huge country, the United States in the 1930s was still overwhelmingly a land of small farmers who didn't want or couldn't afford a 20 hp Farmall, let alone the new 30 hp F30. The F12 was designed just for them; much smaller and lighter than the original Farmall, it was scaled down in every way. It actually weighed twenty-five percent less, so was able to use a tiny 113 cu. in. four-cylinder engine without seeming underpowered. The Waukesha unit (International later introduced its own) was beefy enough to pull a one-bottom plow or cultivate two rows at one pass. The smallest Farmall sold well and soon became an established part of the range.*

FARMALL F12

Engine: Water-cooled, four-cylinder
Bore x stroke: 3.0 x 4.0 in.
Capacity: 113 cu. in.
Drawbar Power: 10 hp @ 1,400 rpm
PTO Power: 15 hp
Transmission: Three-speed
Speeds: 2.25–3.75 mph
Weight: 2,700 lb.

ALLIS-CHALMERS MODEL U
[1932]

This is a true landmark tractor, but not because of its engine, transmission, or price—in fact, the Allis-Chalmers Model U had a very ordinary specification, except for one thing: pneumatic tires.

Until then, all agricultural tractors ran on steel rims. They were tough, but limited speed on the road to a good walking pace, while the spade lugs could do a lot of damage during field work. At first, A-C experimented with Firestone aircraft tires, but the results were disappointing when run at the standard 70 psi. Then someone had the idea of reducing the pressure to 12 psi. The effect was dramatic, and new purpose-designed tires halved the Model U's power requirements, which allowed a high-speed fourth gear to be added to the transmission. A-C claimed 5 mph while plowing, 15 mph on the blacktop, though the Model U tested at Nebraska in 1935 (see specifications) was geared for 10 mph. Extra speed meant less working time, lower costs, and higher profits.

There were other benefits too—the new tires made the tractor quieter, easier to steer, and more comfortable to ride on. Traction was not compromised either, and fuel economy was much improved. Still, the company wisely started off by making the new-fangled pneumatics a $150 option, rather than bumping up the price of the whole tractor. Take up was slow at first, until A-C geared-up a few Us and held high-speed tractor races at county fairs, with well-known racing drivers at the wheel. It worked, and the take-up on pneumatics soon increased dramatically. Given the huge benefits, A-C's rivals had no choice but to follow suit, and by 1937 nearly half of the new tractors in the U.S. had pneumatic tires.

LEFT: *Pneumatic tires, as pioneered on the Allis-Chalmers Model U, were one of the great leaps in tractor technology during the 1930s. They reduced power requirements, were more comfortable, and allowed a higher road speed for hauling, or when traveling between fields. Rubber-equipped tractors used less fuel than those on steel rims, and traction was unaffected.*

ALLIS-CHALMERS MODEL U

Engine: Water-cooled, four-cylinder
Capacity: 301 cu. in.
PTO Power: 31 hp
Drawbar Power: 22.7 hp
Fuel Consumption: 9.94 hp/hr
  per gallon
Speeds: 2.3–10 mph
Weight: 5,140 lb.

ALLIS-CHALMERS WC
[1933]

With their rubber-tired Model U, Allis-Chalmers had scored a technical triumph, but it still hadn't cracked the mass tractor market. However, the WC, which would be one of the most successful tractors Allis-Chalmers ever made, did just that.

Launched in 1933, there was little new about the WC, but it did come along at just the right time, enabling it to take advantage of the boom in two-plow tractor demand. It also had the option of rubber tires. They were not cheap at $150, but the tractor trade was swiftly overcoming its initial resistance to pneumatics. Better still, no rival was offering them yet.

As with the U, rubber tires made the WC a far more efficient tractor. Nebraska tests showed that the WC gave 5.62 hp/hours per gallon of fuel running on steel rims, but achieved 10.17 when running on rubber. Not only that, but rubber was much quieter, it allowed higher speeds and easier steering, and it certainly didn't hurt off-road traction either.

All of these obvious advantages were then backed up with a lightweight high-tensile steel chassis, which helped to make the best of the 201 cu. in. engine's 21 hp at the drawbar. The four-cylinder motor, incidentally, was the first in a tractor to feature the same bore and stroke dimensions—four inches all around. A drive-in attachment for implements was another very useful feature on the WC, which combined with the optional power lift arm to give a simpler antecedent to the Ferguson system.

ABOVE: *The WC's light weight gave its small 201 cu. in. motor an easier time, enabling it to haul relatively heavy loads.*

LEFT: *Two innovations on the WC—the "square" dimensioned bore and stroke, and the high-tensile steel chassis—made it light and relatively powerful.*

It was little wonder that the WC sold so well. In total 178,000 were built, and it remained part of the A-C lineup for fifteen years. Above all, it was a useful, adaptable machine. With its individual rear brakes, the WC could make 180-degree turns; with rubber tires, it could top 9 mph on the road; and there were lots of options.

ALLIS-CHALMERS WC (1934)

Engine: Water-cooled, four-cylinder
Bore x stroke: 4.0 x 4.0 in.
Capacity: 201 cu. in.
PTO Power: 21.5 hp
Drawbar Power: n/a
Fuel Consumption: 10.17 hp/hr
  per gallon
Transmission: Four-speed
Speeds (pneumatic): 2.5–9.25 mph
Weight: 3,792 lb.

CLETRAC 60-80

[1933]

In the United States, diesel tractors didn't really begin to feature until the mid-1950s, and it would be another decade before they became the dominant power unit. But crawlers took to diesel power much earlier. Heavier and more expensive than wheeled tractors, for crawlers the extra weight and cost of a diesel power unit was less of an issue, but its superior fuel consumption was a great attraction. A big crawler could guzzle 100 gallons of gasoline a day, but only 50 gallons of diesel.

This 60-80 of 1933 was Cletrac's first diesel. It was really playing catch-up with Caterpillar, the U.S.'s leading crawler maker. By this time, Caterpillar was building more diesels than the rest of the U.S. tractor industry put together. The 60-80, Cletrac's biggest machine to date, used a six-cylinder Hercules diesel, with electric start (as were all the Cletrac diesels). Steering was by controlled differential, which used band brakes, allowing both tracks to be driven whilst turning, improving traction on tough terrain.

But Cletrac couldn't survive on its own, and was taken over by Oliver in 1945. Production continued, and apart from acquiring Oliver badges, the Cletrac crawlers were little changed. The tractors themselves were also much the same, albeit with the Oliver badge. In 1960, Oliver itself was bought by White. So history had come full circle, as Rollin White had been one of the Cleveland Tractor Company's chief shareholders back in the early days. The new association didn't last long though and Cletrac production ceased in 1965.

LEFT: *Most early Cletracs were small crawlers, but in the 1930s the company made a determined attempt to catch up to Caterpillar, who dominated the U.S. market. Diesel engines and bigger machines such as this 60-80, were its chief tools. With 90 hp from a 617 cu. in. Hercules diesel and over 80 hp available at the drawbar, the 60-80 had all the right ingredients to be a true Caterpillar rival. The Cleveland Motor Company was founded in 1916 by Rollin H. and Clarence G. White, with the intention of building crawlers for the agricultural sector.*

CLETRAC 60-80

Engine: Water-cooled, six-cylinder
Bore x stroke: 5.5 x 6.5 in.
Capacity: 617 cu. in.
Brake Power: 90 hp @ 1,050 rpm
Drawbar Power: 83.5 hp @ 1,050 rpm
Transmission: Three-speed
Speeds: 1.8–3.6 mph
Fuel Consumption: 12.1 hp/hr per gallon
Weight: 22,840 lb.

FORDSON N ROADLESS
[1933]

FORDSON N ROADLESS

Engine: Water-cooled, four-cylinder

Bore x stroke: 4.13 x 5.0 in.

Capacity: 267 cu. in.

PTO Power: 29 hp

Transmission: Three-speed

Weight: 3,600 lb. plus track bogies

BELOW: *Roadless half-track conversions provided a genuine halfway house between a conventional wheeled tractor and a crawler. They were cheaper than the real thing, and enabled owners to make use of their existing conventional tractors.*

Long before four-wheel drive became commonplace, the search was on for more traction. In Britain, specialist companies sprang up like County, Northrop, and Muir-Hill, all of whom converted mainstream tractors to four-wheel drive. Roadless was different, as they specialized in half-track conversions, which were the answer in extremely soft conditions where even four driven wheels weren't enough.

The company was created by Henry Johnson, an engineer. During the Boer War, while working for the British Army, he had the chance to study the use of big heavy vehicles off-road. A spell in India soon afterward saw Johnson working for steam engine manufacturer Fowler, once again pondering the problem of off-road traction.

Back at home during the First World War, he began working on tank development, and when peace broke out, set up as Roadless Traction Ltd., replacing the rear wheels on Foden and Sentinel steam trucks with tanklike treads and bogies.

Motor trucks followed, and in the late 1920s Johnson turned his attention to tractors. His thorough conversion of the Fordson N (which was officially approved by Fordson), was very popular in Britain. Roadless would move on to four-wheel-drive conversions after the Second World War ended.

FARMALL W12
[1934]

The Farmall had been a new type of tractor, combining a decent pulling power with the agility of a small row-crop. It filled a repressed demand, and was a huge success. But through the 1930s, there was still a demand among U.S. farmers for a more traditional standard-tread tractor.

International's response was to update the old 15-30 with the Farmall F30's engine, renaming it the W30. Predictably, a standard-tread version of the little F12, the W12, soon followed, though rather oddly there was never a W20 version of the original Farmall.

Mechanically, the W12 was very similar to the small Farmall, albeit with rated engine speed increased to 1,700 rpm, and 16 hp at the belt, rather than 15. There was a pneumatic rubber tire option, and there were several versions, including the McCormick-Deering badged W12, the International I12, the Orchard O12, and the Fairway 12, which was introduced in 1934, and was adaptable to orchard and golf course work, as well as the field. "What the W12 Will Do," announced a brochure of the day: "1) Will more than pay its way on any diversified farm . . . 2) Will plough from 4 to 7 acres a day, double-disk from 16 to 30 acres a day . . . 3) With pneumatic tires will do most of the hauling, field and roadway . . . 4) On many farms will advantageously supplement the work of larger tractors."

But the market for standard-treads was limited now by the success of the Farmall, and only 3,622 W12s were built between 1934 and 1938.

FARMALL W12

Engine: Water-cooled, four-cylinder
Bore x stroke: 3.0 x 4.0 in.
Capacity: 113 cu. in.
Drawbar Power: 10 hp @ 1,700 rpm
PTO Power: 16 hp
Transmission: Three-speed
Speeds: 2.14–3.6 mph
Weight: 2,900 lb.

BELOW: *Alongside the hugely successful Farmall, International offered an equivalent range of standard-tread tractors, closer in type to the postwar utility-type tractor. This little W12 was cousin to the smallest Farmall F12, and used the same 113 cu. in. four-cylinder engine.*

JOHN DEERE MODEL A
[1934]

John Deere had produced its own rival for the all-conquering Farmall in 1928. But the GP had never really fulfilled its promise, so six years later, Deere unveiled its second attempt at a modern row-crop tractor, the Model A. This was more like it. In place of the GP's twin front wheels, this had the tricycle front end that was rapidly becoming the standard for row-crop machines. It had excellent visibility and plenty of ground clearance, plus an adjustable rear tread and comfortable driver's platform—all the essentials for a successful row-crop. As well as all the basics, the Model A included some innovative features as well. It had the first fully hydraulic lift system, where most rivals offered cruder mechanical lifts—it wasn't a Ferguson three-point hitch, but it was a step in the right direction. There was a center-line hitch as well, and a PTO.

But the masterstroke was that alongside all this innovation the Model A was as simple to build, maintain, and drive as any other John Deere. The famous twin-cylinder engine was updated with overhead valves, but still very simple, with thermo-syphon cooling instead of a water pump. Rated at 16 drawbar hp, 24 hp at the belt, it was uprated to 20-26 hp in 1939 and 26-33 after the war, while a six-speed trans-mission replaced the four-speed. It was finally replaced in 1953 after over 200,000 had been sold.

LEFT: *John Deere lost money in the early 1930s tractor slump, but invested in new models, and thrived as a result.*

JOHN DEERE MODEL A

Engine Type: Water-cooled
 twin-cylinder, ohv
Bore x stroke: 5.5 x 6.5 in.
Capacity: 206 cu. in.
Fuel: Gasoline or kerosene
PTO Power: 24 hp @ 975 rpm
Drawbar Power: 16 hp @ 975 rpm
Transmission: Four-speed (later six-speed)

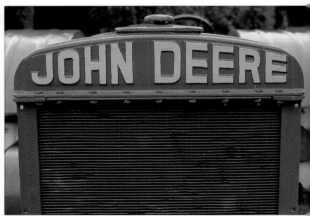

ALLIS-CHALMERS MODEL M
[1935]

Although specialists like Caterpillar and Cletrac led the crawler market, some of the tractor makers produced their own crawlers. The Allis-Chalmers Model U was available with crawler tracks early on. The Trackson Co. of Milwaukee did the conversion, naming the result GU or LU.

The LU had a four-speed transmission and could reach 9.5 mph, which was respectable speed for a crawler.

These must be presumed successful in the market, for A-C later produced its own crawler version of the Model U, the M. "M" stood for "Monarch," as A-C had bought the Monarch crawler company. Mechanically, it was very similar to the U, with the same 301 cu. in. four-cylinder unit, rated at 22.8 drawbar hp and 31.6 at the belt. However, the gearing was very much lower than that of the agricultural tractor, a fact underlined when the M was tested at Nebraska in August 1935. In low gear it pulled just over 5,000 lb., or seventy-three percent of its own weight—that was at a speed of 2.05 mph while developing 27.4 hp. In second gear, the pull was reduced to 2,700 lb., albeit at 3.13 mph. No repairs or adjustments were needed after fifty hours of Nebraskan testing, a testament to the strength of A-C's basic design. But the market for crawlers was limited compared to that for farm tractors, and would remain so until the late 1990s.

LEFT: *In the 1930s, a few tractor manufacturers moved into the crawler market. Allis-Chalmers acquired the necessary expertise by buying up Monarch, and produced this crawler version of the Model U.*

ALLIS-CHALMERS MODEL M

Engine: Water-cooled, four-cylinder
Capacity: 301 cu. in.
PTO Power: 31.6 hp
Drawbar Power: 22.8 hp
Fuel Consumption: 9.79 hp/hr per gallon
Speeds: 1.8–4.2 mph
Weight: 6,855 lb.

BELOW: *Cabs were still a rarity on 1930s tractors, but there were various aftermarket conversions for those who wanted them.*

BOTTOM: *Not many crawlers were sold to farmers, but they still had a niche, and companies like Allis-Chalmers were well placed to exploit it.*

CASE MODEL RC

[1935]

CASE MODEL RC (1936)

Engine: Water-cooled, four-cylinder
Capacity: 133 cu. in.
PTO Power: 17.6 hp @ 1,425 rpm
Drawbar Power: 11.6 hp @ 1,425 rpm
Fuel Consumption: 9.87 hp/hr per gallon
Speeds: 2.3–4.5 mph
Weight: 3,350 lb.

There's no doubt that the lightweight Case RC, aimed at the general purpose market, would have seen production much sooner were it not for Leon Clausen. Case's president resisted the pleas of dealers and salesmen to come up with a sub-20 hp Case, insisting that such a tractor would steal sales from their existing Model C. He finally relented, but insisted there should be no launch fanfare, and even vetoed the addition of fourth gear to the transmission, which would have cost a mere seventy-two cents! Clausen seemed vindicated when the RC was not a great seller, but maybe launched three years earlier with full publicity, things might have been different.

Case didn't make an engine small enough to suit the RC, so it bought in a 133 cu. in. four-cylinder unit from Waukesha. It was gasoline only, rated at 1,425 rpm, and had no water pump, as the thermo-syphon effect was considered sufficient to keep the coolant circulating. The RC also had an adjustable rear track of 44 to 80 inches, achieved by a combination of sliding the wheels on splines and reversing them. An adjustable front track was among the options, as were rubber tires. A standard tread version was launched in 1938, which was otherwise identical. Both used Case's trademark chicken roost steering rack, but this looked untidy in the new era of stylish tractors, and the RC was launched with overhead steering. Both R and RC got that seventy-two-cent fourth gear in 1939, as well as the new "sunburst" radiator grille and Flambeau Red color. But later that year, both were replaced by the Model V.

BELOW: *A belated competitor for the smaller Farmalls, the Case Model RC was only introduced after much internal corporate wrangling.*

HSCS K40 "STEEL HORSE"

[1935]

Hofherr-Schrantz-Clayton-Shuttleworth (or HSCS) was a joint venture between Hungarian business interests and the British company Clayton & Shuttleworth, which did good business in central Europe with its steam plows. Founded in Budapest

BELOW: *"Steel Horse" was an apt name for the simple, basic HSCS, a straightforward workhorse if ever there was one. It owed something to the Lanz Bulldog layout, with a single horizontally mounted cylinder working on the semi-diesel principle. This was a popular layout in Europe, built in Britain, France, and Italy, as well as Germany and Hungary. Renamed Red Star tractors in 1951, HSCS went on to adopt the name "Dutra," which was allegedly derived from the words Dumper and Tractor, its two major products.*

in 1900, HSCS became a wholly Hungarian concern in 1912.

It started building gasoline engines in 1919 and its first tractor appeared four years later. This was powered by a single-cylinder gasoline motor, but it wasn't long before the company turned to semi-diesels. The semi-diesel is mechanically simple and will run on almost any type of fuel, including waste oil, though it is rather crude compared to multicylinder four-stroke diesels.

Although it only found limited favor in Britain and the U.S., the semi-diesel was very popular with many makes throughout Europe, particularly Lanz of Germany, Landini in Italy, and SFV in France. HSCS's motor was rated at 14 hp, and was

intended for plowing and as a stationary power source, and derivatives continued to power a range of wheeled and tracked tractors through the next few decades. To suit the new Communist regime, HSCS was renamed (appropriately enough) Red Star tractors in 1951. It used the Dutra brand name after 1960, specializing in big four-wheel-drive tractors.

HSCS K40 "STEEL HORSE"

Engine: Single-cylinder, semi-diesel
Power: Not known
Transmission: Not known
Weight: 7,500 lb.

JOHN DEERE MODEL B
[1935]

Just as International built a smaller version of the Farmall to meet demand from small farmers, so did John Deere. The Model B was about "two-thirds the size in power and weight," of the full size Model A, according to the publicity. In the United States in 1930, small farms of less than one

ABOVE: *Right through the 1920s and 1930s, all John Deeres used the same horizontal twin-cylinder layout that would serve the company well for a very long time. They now also came in a range of sizes.*

LEFT: *A nicely restored Model B, with later Henry Dreyfuss styling, in a sylvan setting. This example belongs to tractor historian Bob Pripps.*

hundred acres still made up more than half the total farming area, so there was certainly plenty of demand for a single-plow general purpose machine.

Despite its small size, the Model B was a genuine miniature of the bigger Deeres, with a little 149 cu. in. version of the classic twin-cylinder water-cooled engine, though unlike the A, it retained the side-valve format of older JDs. It ran slightly faster than its bigger brothers, at 1,150 rpm, and produced 14 hp at the belt, 9.4 hp at the drawbar, according to Nebraska.

There were many variations on the theme: the basic B used a two-wheel tricycle front end; BN denoted a single front wheel; BW, wide-front model; BR, standard front; BO, orchard version; BNH, high-crop version of the BN; BWH, high-crop version of the BW; BO Lindemann, a crawler model converted by Lindeman Power & Equipment; and finally, BI, the industrial tractor. All benefited from larger engines: 175 cu. in. in 1939 and 190 cu. in. in 1947—the latter was offered in both all-fuel and high-compression gasoline versions. Less successful was the Model H, smaller and less powerful than the B, but only $100 cheaper. However, the B was a genuine miniature of the mid-size Model A—later, it even received a six-speed transmission along with its bigger brother.

JOHN DEERE MODEL B

Engine Type: Water-cooled twin-cylinder, side-valve
Bore x stroke: 4.25 x 5.25 in.
Capacity: 149 cu. in.
Fuel: Gasoline or kerosene
PTO Power: 14 hp @ 1,150 rpm
Drawbar Power: 9.4 hp @ 1,150 rpm
Transmission: Four-speed (later six-speed)
Speeds: 2.3–5.0 mph
Weight: 2,731 lb.

MINNEAPOLIS-MOLINE MTA
[1935]

Mergers usually mean rationalization, and so it was with the new Minneapolis-Moline company, a 1929 joint venture between three companies in the agricultural machinery business.

They faced a considerable overlap in tractor production and M-M lost no time in dropping the Minneapolis Threshing's 27-44, as the Minneapolis Steel 27-42 was a superior model. Another casualty was Minneapolis Steel's Twin City brand name. For a few years, the new MM logo was combined with the old one, but soon Twin City was dropped altogether.

On a more positive note, there was a new four-wheel row-crop tractor, the 15-23 hp KT, though this had been under development by Minneapolis Steel before the merger. The next few years saw a general renewal of the tractor range: the 17-28 and 27-42 were phased out in 1935, while the KT, FT, and MT were all updated the same year, as the KTA, FTA, and MTA.

The MTA pictured here, basically a tricycle row-crop version of the KTA, shows the layout that had now become the norm for most U.S. row-crop tractors. Tricycle wheel format; big four-cylinder engine; transmission forming the chassis; fuel tank mounted on top and driver sitting between the rear wheels. It was also uprated to 19-30 hp (the specifications below are for the earlier MT). By this time, it had been joined by the smaller JT, another row-crop intended to compete with the Farmall F20.

LEFT: *The new Minneapolis-Moline era brought in new innovations like five-speed transmissions and enclosed cabs. The MTA (pictured here) was the tricycle row-crop version of M-M's mid-size tractor. The pre-update KT, FT, and MT all used M-M's own four-cylinder I-head engine, whose 4.25 in. pistons ran up and down a five-inch stroke, pushing the crank at a rated 1,000 rpm. Tested by Nebraska in October 1931, the MT ran for fifty-nine hours without a single repair or adjustment needed, not something that all tractors tested there could boast.*

MINNEAPOLIS-MOLINE MODEL MT (1931)

Engine: Water-cooled, four-cylinder
Bore x stroke: 4.25 x 5.0 in.
Capacity: 284 cu. in.
PTO Power: 26.7 hp @ 1,000 rpm
Drawbar Power: 18.2 hp
Transmission: Three-speed
Speeds: 2.1–4.2 mph
Fuel Consumption: 5.64 hp/hr
  per gallon
Weight: 5,235 lb.

OLIVER 70 ROW CROP

[1935]

"Power when you want it," trumpeted an early ad, "power when you need it— power when field conditions are right and time and help are limited. That's the power you'll find in an Oliver Row Crop 70." Oliver's 70 was sold on its speed, and with good reason. Although smaller than the existing Oliver 80 and 90, it was powered by a higher revving six-cylinder engine. At the time, most tractors used low compression, low-revving gasoline or distillate engines, usually of two or four cylinders. So the 70, with its high compression six, really stood out. It was small for a six-cylinder motor, at 202 cu. in. but that made it particularly smooth compared to the less-sophisticated opposition, and more powerful. The only downside was that the 70 needed expensive high octane fuel—but for farmers who couldn't bring themselves to pay out for such a rich diet, the 70 was also available in low-compression distillate form.

Not only that, but the streamlined, carlike Fleetline styling in 1937 set the 70 apart from its boxy rivals.

ABOVE: *Oliver emphasized the 70's looks and speed—"It has everything, it does everything, it's a beauty." Some farmers were sufficiently impressed to buy one.*

LEFT: *With streamlined Fleetline styling and wrap-around grille, an Oliver 70 was surely the best-looking U.S. tractor available in the 1930s.*

BELOW: *As launched, the 70 came with flat grille, and a long hood to accommodate that six-cylinder engine. This example has Oliver's "tip-toe" steel wheels, though rubber tires were an option.*

OLIVER 70 ROW CROP
(1940)

Engine: Water-cooled, six-cylinder
Bore x stroke: 3.13 x 4.38 in.
Capacity: 202 cu. in.
PTO Power: 30.4 hp @ 1,500rpm
Drawbar Power: 22.7 hp
Transmission: Six-speed
Speeds: 2.6–13.4 mph
Fuel Consumption: 9.81 hp/hr per gallon
Weight: 4,370 lb.

LANDINI 65F
[1935]

Giovanni Landini never lived to see the tractor that bore his name. An Italian blacksmith's apprentice, he went into business in 1884, opening a machine shop. By 1911 he was building steam engines, and six years later had developed portable internal combustion engines, though Landini didn't begin developing tractors until the early 1920s. Sadly, he died in 1924, but his sons then took over the business and announced a 30 hp semi-diesel machine in the following year.

Its power unit was based on one of Landini's earlier stationary engines. Instead of a radiator and closed cooling system, there was a simple hopper system, while the engine itself was of the *testa calda,* or hot-bulb, type. Neither a true diesel nor a spark-ignition engine, the fuel was ignited by a hot spot in the cylinder head, which had to be heated up each morning before the engine would start. The layout was based around a large single cylinder, mounted horizontally in the chassis, with the hot-bulb poking out between the front wheels, for easy access. A very popular type in much of Europe through the 1930s, 1940s, and early 1950s, it was heavy and slow, but simple to maintain. Semi-diesels or hot-bulb engines were smoky, rough, and inefficient, but they were also cheap, simple, and reliable.

Landini made its name with semi-diesel tractors. By the late 1930s they were well built and reliable, producing a solid 40 hp. Engines were bigger and more powerful than ever, with the Super L powered by a 749 cu. in. version of the venerable hot-bulb single. Nine hundred Landini tractors were built in 1934, when two hundred and fifty workers assembled four every day. By U.S. standards, the Landini was a long way from mass production, but it was successful in its own right. Production resumed after the Second World War, with similar models, and a full diesel version was added in 1958. By this time, however, the single-cylinder Landinis were looking decidedly old-fashioned against the multicylinder opposition. But Dr. Flavio Fadda took over Landini in the nick of time, and immediately began a licensing deal with Perkins, whereby the new range of tractors would use Perkins multicylinder engines.

LEFT: *Landini made its name with heavy single-cylinder semi-diesel tractors, but had to drop them in favor of more modern designs in the late 1950s.*

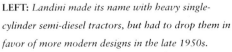

LANDINI 65F

Specifications: Unavailable

INTERNATIONAL WK40
[1935]

International Harvester made its name, reputation, and fortune with small tractors: the 8-16 Mogul, McCormick-Deering 10-20, and of course the Farmall. But this meant they were missing out on a growing part of the tractor market, especially in the wheatland prairies of the Midwest U.S., where farmers needed something rather bigger than even the most powerful Farmall.

International's response was certainly different. The WD40 was the U.S. tractor industry's first mass-produced diesel. With 53 hp at the belt and 38 at the drawbar, the WD40 took IHC up to a new power class. It was also unique in that the diesel engine had to be started on gasoline before it would run on pure diesel. So as well as the usual diesel injectors and pump, it was equipped with a carburetor and spark plugs! This was a big tractor for its time: the engine measured 355 cu. in., the cooling system held 14 gallons and the fuel tank over 30. Ready to ship, the complete tractor weighed 7,550 lb. and came with steel wheels or pneumatic rubber tires.

But International wisely didn't put all its eggs in the diesel basket, and the WK40 shown here was the distillate version, with very similar power to the WD40 but a completely different, six-cylinder engine. It came out of a truck, and was already built in-house by International. There was a gasoline version, too, in which case the tractor was a WA40.

LEFT: *The WD40 also came as the distillate-powered WK40 (shown here) or as a gasoline WA40. These machines took International into a new market for heavyweight tractors. All of them could break the 50 hp barrier at the PTO, which was quite an achievement for the industry at the time. This was maximum power, and International's recommended rating was about seventy-five percent of that. The gasoline WA, distillate WK, and hybrid diesel WD all gave nearly identical power figures: 38 rated hp at the drawbar for the WA and WK (WD, 27.99) and 53 rated at the PTO (WD, 44.04). The WA/WK matched the WD's power with a smaller 298 cu. in. engine, underlining how diesel power was still in its infancy for tractor use.*

INTERNATIONAL WK40

Engine: Water-cooled, six-cylinder
Bore x stroke: 3.75 x 4.5 in.
Capacity: 298 cu. in.
Drawbar Power: 38 hp @ 1,750 rpm
PTO Power: 53 hp
Transmission: Four-speed
Speeds (pneumatic): 2.4–12.0 mph
Weight (WD40): 7,550 lb.

MINNEAPOLIS-MOLINE MODEL Z [1936]

Minneapolis-Moline was never famed for its small tractors, but the Universal J of 1934 was a well-equipped machine that weighed only 3,450 lb. It boasted a power lift, as well as power takeoff, and a five-speed transmission. The latter was a first for tractors, and soon became an M-M trademark. With four field-speed gears plus a higher ratio for the road, it enabled the rubber-equipped J to reach 18 mph on tarmac. A two-plow machine, the J also had adjustable rear treads (54–76 in.) and a three-fuel four-cylinder engine, "built to stand the gaff," as an advert of the time put it. A fine tractor, but it was very slightly under powered at 14-22 hp.

A couple of years later it was replaced by the Z, which used a slightly smaller all-new 185 cu. in. four-cylinder motor, albeit with more power. Like the J, the Z had a five-speed transmission and was also designed with easy home maintenance in mind. For example, the valves were mounted horizontally, opened by long vertical rocker arms, which eased the work of valve adjustment. Another feature was the Visionlined styling. This wasn't just to look good, the hood tapered back toward the driver, to optimize his view of front-mounted implements. And the gray color scheme was replaced by Prairie Gold yellow with red wheels. A standard tread version, ZTS, soon followed. In updated form, the Z carried on into the 1950s—specifications for the 1950 model are given below.

Incidentally, M-M's three-letter model names are quite easy to decipher: the first letter (K, J, Z) refers to the model, "T" stands for tractor, and the final letter refers to chassis type.

LEFT: *A five-speed transmission, with one very ultra-high ratio for the road, enabled the little Z to reach up to 13.1 mph on tarmac. Five speeds was a first and became an M-M trademark at the time.*

BELOW: *Another Minneapolis trademark was Prairie Gold, the bright and bold color in which all its tractors were finished, set off by bright red wheels. Many manufacturers were using bolder colors now, reflecting the more cheerful economic climate.*

MINNEAPOLIS-MOLINE MODEL Z (1950)

Engine: Water-cooled, four-cylinder
Capacity: 185 cu. in.
PTO Power: 34.8 hp @ 1,500 rpm
Drawbar Power: 25.1 hp
Transmission: Five-speed
Speeds: 2.4–13.1 mph
Fuel Consumption: 8.55 hp/hr
  per gallon
Weight: 4,290 lb.

MASSEY-HARRIS CHALLENGER

[1936]

MASSEY-HARRIS CHALLENGER

Engine: Water-cooled, four-cylinder

Bore x stroke: 3.88 x 5.25 in.

Capacity: 248 cu. in.

PTO Power: 27.2 hp @ 1,200 rpm

Drawbar Power: 16.3 hp

Transmission: Four-speed

Speeds: 2.4–8.5 mph

Fuel Consumption: 6.65 hp/hr per gallon

Weight: 4,200 lb.

"CHALLENGER. Here's a trim looking tractor as you've ever seen. Note the clean, flowing lines, nothing there to obstruct your vision of the field ahead . . . You'll like this tractor's husky 2-3 plow power—the eagerness with which it responds to the toughest jobs. Learn the advantages of more power for every job at low cost."

After the failure of the innovative four-wheel-drive GP, Massey-Harris had another go at designing an all-purpose row-crop tractor to rival the Farmall. The Challenger of 1936 was simply an adapted version of the old 12-20, with the same 248 cu. in. engine (now in overhead valve form) and a unit frame. The 12-20, of course, was originally a Wallis Cub since Massey-Harris had bought the Wallis company in 1928.

Instead of the 12-20's standard-tread, the Challenger had narrow front wheels and large rear wheels, whose track could be altered by moving them in or out on splined axles. This was fast becoming the standard arrangement on American row-crop machines. It was simple and it worked, and no serious row-crop could afford to be without it. With the engine uprated to 16-27 hp and a reasonable all-up weight of 4,200 lb., the new Challenger was far more successful than the clever but flawed GP.

BELOW: *"Challenger" was an effective name for the Massey-Harris row-crop, as it was an true competitor for the Farmall. It still used the U-frame chassis, which Massey had inherited from the Wallis Cub. Buyers had the choice of single or twin-wheel tricycle front end, and four-wheel, or four-wheel high-clearance versions.*

RANSOMES MG2

[1936]

In 1930s England, there was a demand for crawler tractors, but they had to be quite different from the U.S. variety. Market gardeners, or small-scale vegetable growers, formed the main market, and what they needed was a miniature crawler. Ransomes, based in England, had never built a tractor like this before, but entered into an agreement with Roadless Traction (makers of half-track tractor conversions). The result, unveiled in 1936, was the Ransomes MG2—MG stood for Market Garden. It was powered by a 37 cu. in. side-valve Sturmey-Archer. It was so successful that Ransomes would be making small crawlers for the next thirty years.

The MG2 used a directly mounted rear frame for implements, single-bottom plows and so on, which was arguably a cruder,

simpler version of Harry Ferguson's three-point hitch. So popular was the Ransome— 15,000 were made over three decades—that a whole range of implements to suit it were soon on the market, an example being the Demon Spray Pump made by A&G Cooper. The little engines were built to last too. On one MG2, left derelict for years, the power unit needed only a good service and valve job before being ready for work.

The MG2 itself developed into variants such as the MG6. When production ended in 1966, the MG40 was diesel powered and equipped with a hydraulic lift for implements. The company was bought out in 1997 by Textron, the American makers of Jacobsen mowers. The specfications here refer to the Ransomes MG5, a later update of the same basic concept.

RANSOMES MG5 (1953)

Engine: Water-cooled
Power: 5 hp
Transmission: Single-speed
   forward/reverse
Weight: 1,800 lb.

BELOW: *The little Ransomes machine was an ideal size for market gardeners in Britain. Power was derived from a small side-valve single-cylinder built by the Sturmey-Archer company, better known for its cycle components. Five horsepower wasn't a lot, but it was certainly sufficient for the MG2, which was strong enough to pull a small single-bottom plow. Pictured here is the MG6 variant of the original MG2 machine.*

INTERNATIONAL TD40
[1936]

International, like many rivals, built its own range of crawlers, based on tractor components. Bearing the ingenious name TracTractors, they were based on the 20, 30, and 40 hp machines, though the most popular was the smallest T20. Introduced in 1931, this was small enough to be profitable for farming as well as construction work and came in low-seat form for orchards.

The TD40 (shown here) was the most powerful crawler offered by International, with that unique diesel engine which also saw service in the WD40 tractor. Today, we are used to diesels which start instantly, hot or cold, thanks to electronic injection and quick-heat glow plugs. But tractors and crawlers of the 1930s brought different solutions. One was the so-called "hot-bulb" semi-diesel, used by manufacturers such as Lanz and Landini. First job of the morning was to heat up the cylinder head with a blow torch, after which the big single-cylinder would (hopefully) thump into life. Once running, the engine's own heat would keep it going. International's four-cylinder four-stroke, by contrast, started on gasoline using its own carburetor, spark plugs, and magneto. Once running, the driver would switch over to diesel. A complicated solution, but one worthwhile for farmers needing the extra economy of diesel for long days in the fields.

LEFT: *When is a diesel not a diesel? International's engine which powered both this TD40 and the WD40 wheeled tractor was a hybrid, which started on gasoline and ran on diesel once warmed up. The advantage was gasoline-style quick starting from cold (which could be tricky with early diesels), but diesel economy and efficiency once warmed up. With a 14-gallon cooling system, this was a big engine, and if you weren't convinced by the economic argument, the most powerful TracTractor was available with a conventional gasoline/kerosene six-cylinder engine as well. But for crawlers, the diesel era was just beginning, and would soon be the dominant power source—wheeled tractors would take a little longer to catch on.*

INTERNATIONAL TD40

Engine: Water-cooled, four-cylinder hybrid diesel
Bore x stroke: 4.75 x 6.5 in.
Capacity: 355 cu. in.
Compression Ratio: 17:1
Drawbar Power: 37 hp
PTO Power: 52 hp
Injection/Ignition: Precision fuel injection pump, model R carburetor, F-4 magneto

ALLIS-CHALMERS MODEL A
[1936]

The 1930s looked like a good time for Allis-Chalmers. They'd taken the market by storm with pneumatic tires; the WC was a roaring success; and the little Model B had opened up a new market for mini-tractors. But the big Model A was the exception. It was intended as a direct replacement for the heavyweight 18-30/20-35 series, and in fact there were some useful updates. The old two-speed transmission was replaced by a new four-speeder (really just a beefed-up version of the smaller U's transmission), and there was a pneumatic tire option, of course. In fact, the engine was the only major component that remained unchanged. Using gasoline, it had a 4.75 in. bore and produced 33 hp at the drawbar, 44 hp at the belt.

This all looked very promising, except that by 1936, times had changed. With its large powerful engine, the A was designed more for powering threshers than towing implements. But in the late 1930s, the first combines began to trickle onto the market—self-powered, these didn't need tractors to tow them. Even A-C itself ceased production of Advance-Rumely threshers the same year that it announced a tractor to suit them!

With this *raison d'être* removed, the Model A seemed like a dinosaur compared to the new breed of lightweight machines. It weighed a cumbersome 3.75 tons, and was thirsty—some said that the smaller U could do nearly as much work on half the amount of fuel. Sales reflected that fact, and even in its best year, less than 600 Model As found homes. When it was dropped after five years, a mere 1,200 had left the works. Fortunately, Allis-Chalmers had plenty of good-selling tractors as well.

LEFT: *The Allis-Chalmers Model A was a heavyweight tractor of the old school, intended primarily for belt work, but that role would soon be obsolete, thanks to powered combine harvesters. It was a direct descendent of Allis-Chalmers's 18-30/ 20-35, the company's first successful tractor, but fifteen years later the world had changed, and most farmers wanted lighter, more adaptable tractors like the Farmall or A-C's own Model U, with its pneumatic rubber tires.*

ALLIS-CHALMERS MODEL A

Engine: Water-cooled, four-cylinder
Capacity: 461 cu. in.
PTO Power: 44 hp
Drawbar Power: 33 hp
Fuel Consumption: n/a
Speeds: n/a
Weight: 7,425 lb.

ALLIS-CHALMERS MODEL B
[1937]

After the huge success of the Fordson Model F (three-quarters of a million were sold), you could be forgiven for thinking that every U.S. farmer who wanted a tractor now had one. Not a bit of it. By the late 1930s, the Model F had been out of production for some ten years, and its Model N replacement (now imported from Britain) looked very old fashioned. What small farmers wanted was a tractor that was small, cheap, and modern. The A-C Model B was all three.

It cost a mere $495 brand new, partly thanks to its simple, light construction.

Allis returned to unit construction with the Model B, using the engine, transmission, and torque tube as stressed members which absorbed loads and helped support each other and the rest of the tractor. They also allowed a clean, wasp-waisted look, courtesy of the famous industrial designer Brooks Stevens, with good visibility as icing on the cake.

The engine was a little 116 cu. in. unit produced by A-C itself, though the first batch of Model Bs were actually Waukesha powered. The Allis produced 10.3 hp at the bar, 14 at the belt, according to Nebraska tests. It wasn't much, but A-C did increase the capacity to 125 cu. in. in 1943, which gave a useful power boost.

Although it came in fairly basic form, the Model B could easily be upgraded: a PTO shaft and belt pulley, for example, cost an extra $35, an adjustable-width front axle, just $20 (allowing ten different spacings from 38 to 60). And recognizing that small farmers' needs were just as varied as big ones, A-C offered a whole range of Model Bs, including a high-clearance Asparagus Special and narrow-track Potato Special. Rubber tires were standard on all of these, except in the depths of wartime, when a rubber shortage forced A-C temporarily back to solid-steel wheels. The Model B stayed in production right up to 1957, by which time over 100,000 had been sold.

LEFT: *Cheap, modern, and simple, the Allis-Chalmers Model B filled the same role that the Fordson Model F had twenty years earlier. It cost less than $500, brand new and ready to work.*

ALLIS-CHALMERS MODEL B

Engine: Water-cooled, four-cylinder
Capacity: 116 cu. in.
PTO Power: 14.0 hp
Drawbar Power: 10.3 hp
Fuel Consumption: 11.14 hp/hr per gallon
Speeds: 2.5–7.75 mph
Weight: 2,260 lb.

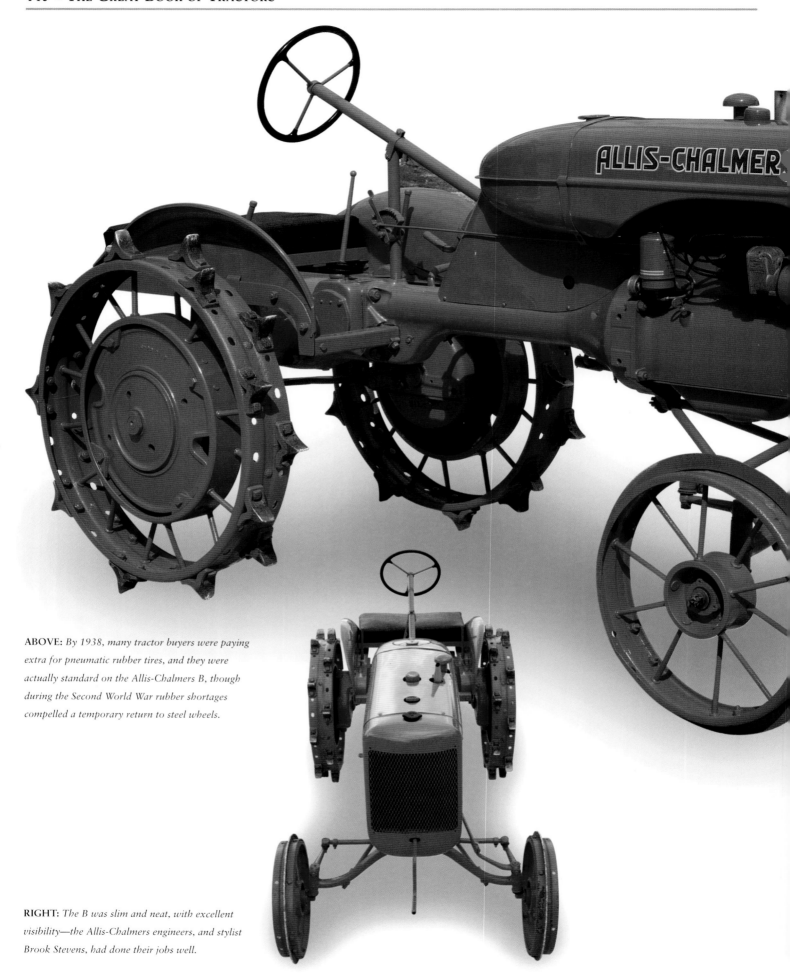

ABOVE: *By 1938, many tractor buyers were paying extra for pneumatic rubber tires, and they were actually standard on the Allis-Chalmers B, though during the Second World War rubber shortages compelled a temporary return to steel wheels.*

RIGHT: *The B was slim and neat, with excellent visibility—the Allis-Chalmers engineers, and stylist Brook Stevens, had done their jobs well.*

TOP RIGHT: *Everything on the B was finished in Persian Orange, even these control lever serrations, still pristine on this newly restored example.*

RIGHT: *Oil filter and pressure gauge on the Allis-Chalmers B—that was often the sole instrument on tractors of the time, as with a top speed of just under 8 mph, a speedometer was a bit superfluous.*

OLIVER 80

[1937]

OLIVER 80 STANDARD HC (1940)

Engine: Water-cooled, four-cylinder
Bore x stroke: 4.25 x 5.25 in.
Capacity: 298 cu. in.
PTO Power: 38 hp @ 1,200 rpm
Drawbar Power: 28 hp
Transmission: Four-speed
Speeds: 2.8–6.4 mph
Fuel Consumption: 9.5 hp/hr per gallon
Weight: 8,145 lb.

Oliver had made a bold step forward with the six-cylinder 70, a very modern, streamlined machine that set new standards for smoothness. However it was shrewd enough not to put all its eggs in the six-cylinder basket. The bigger four-cylinder tractors may have stemmed from an earlier era, but they were still proven and reliable machines, and Oliver continued to stick with them.

So the Oliver 80 of 1937 was based heavily on the old Hart-Parr 18-27 and 18-28, with the Oliver-Hart-Parr 80 industrial tractor providing the link between them. On sale for the 1938 model year, there was little new about the 80. It was still powered by a simple four-cylinder motor in high-compression gasoline or low-compression kerosene versions. Power outputs for the two machines were virtually the same, though the kerosene was slightly bigger to counteract its lower efficiency—bore was 4.50 in. against 4.25 in. A diesel option was added to the lineup for the 1940 model year, using a Buda-Lanova engine, and this was available on both standard and row-crop 80s.

Oliver certainly didn't flinch from updating its oldest tractor. The year before, it had added an ASAE standard PTO and hitches, plus a four-speed transmission. It was ten years before the 80 was finally replaced by the six-cylinder 88.

LEFT: *Alongside the modern mid-size 70, the bigger Olivers were updates of the four-cylinder Hart-Parrs. In fact, the big four-cylinder Olivers were excellent examples of how older designs could be kept competitive through judicious upgrades. These were needed because the Oliver 80 and 90 had been designed by Hart-Parr in the late 1920s and although there was nothing essentially wrong with them, they were becoming decidedly outmoded. As the Hart-Parr name was phased out, the Hart-Parr 18-27 became the Oliver 80 in 1937. The following year, the old three-speed transmission was replaced by a four-speed, and ASAE standard PTO and hitches were also added. In 1940, the 80 gained a diesel option, though this was only fitted to around seventy-five row-crop 80s during that production year and just a few of the standard-treads. Oliver didn't make its own diesel, so a suitable Buda unit had to be bought in. The only update that wasn't possible on the Model 80 was electric starting, a discrepancy the company would eventually resolve in 1947.*

OLIVER 90

[1937]

Like the Oliver 80, the 90 was no more than a rebadged, updated version of the original Hart-Parrs. It was based on the biggest Hart-Parr, the 28-44 or Model A, which by 1937, when the 90 was first announced, had already been in production for six years. But in its latest form it did get a much more thorough update than the 80 had done.

Oliver used the same big 443 cu. in. four-cylinder engine, rated at 1,125 rpm and with 4.75 x 6.25 in. dimensions. But now it had high-pressure lubrication, an electric start, and centrifugal governor. There were both gasoline and kerosene versions, but no high-compression option—that came rather later with the 99. Transmission was four-speed as standard, but a PTO cost extra. The 90 was, of course, Oliver's flagship tractor, the heaviest and most powerful in the line. But year by year, the biggest tractors on the market were getting more powerful. It would take too long to design an all-new six-cylinder 90, so Oliver's quick response was simply to raise the compression ratio and call the result the 99. Available from the late 1930s, the Oliver 99 proved substantially more powerful than the original Hart-Parr 28-44. That produced 44 belt hp, in line with its rating, while the new 99 managed 54.5 rated hp at the belt, and 59 hp at the belt at maximum load. It was an impressive amount of power from the same in-house 443 cu. in. four-cylinder unit, and enough to keep up with the big Minneapolis-Moline GTA.

OLIVER 90

Engine: Water-cooled, four-cylinder
Bore x stroke: 4.75 x 6.25 in.
Capacity: 443 cu. in.
PTO Power: 49 hp @ 1,125 rpm
Drawbar Power; 28 hp
Transmission: Three-speed
Speeds: 2.7–4.3 mph
Weight: 6,415 lb.

BELOW: *In its last year, production of the old-style Model 90 was moved from Charles City to the Oliver plant in South Bend. When production was eventually ceased, Oliver's last link with the old Hart-Parr tractors was severed.*

JOHN DEERE MODEL G

[1937]

They must have had a saying at John Deere: If you've found a winning formula, stick with it. Other manufacturers tinkered with four cylinders or six. John Deere stuck with two, regardless of the size of tractor or its intended use. So the original Model D led to the row-crop GP and Model A, then the downsized Model B and even smaller Model H. The Model G (seen here) went the other way, the biggest, most powerful row-crop JD to date.

All of them used the same basic layout of a low-revving twin-cylinder engine, which was mounted horizontally. The Model G

certainly had plenty of power to tackle big acreages, notching up 31 hp at the PTO on its first Nebraska test and 21 drawbar hp. John Deere's biggest-yet motor measured 410 cu. in., was lower revving than the equivalent four-cylinder motors, rated at 975 rpm, but wasn't lacking in power or torque, being the first over-30 hp general purpose machine. JD had yet to follow the new fashion for streamlining, and the Model G remained unstyled until 1942, but that didn't make it outdated. Also in 1942, a six-speed transmission arrived and rubber tires were standard.

As befitted a row-crop tractor, the rear wheel tread was adjustable between 60 and 84 inches with up to 112 inches possible with optional axles. A power takeoff was standard, and hydraulics optional. There were some overheating problems early in the G's life, but a larger capacity radiator solved that, after about 3,000 Model Gs had left the line. And it became another JD success story, with over 60,000 built by the time production ceased in 1953.

LEFT: *In the 1950s and 1960s, the U.S. tractor market saw a power/transmission race in which manufacturers sought desperately to outdo each other, with more horsepower and ever more sophisticated transmissions. Back in the late 1930s, things were simpler. The easiest way to increase power was to make a bigger engine, so that's what John Deere did with the Model G. At 410 cu. in. and 31 hp it was their biggest row-crop yet.*

JOHN DEERE MODEL G

Engine Type: Water cooled
  twin-cylinder, ohv
Bore x stroke: 6.125 x 7.0 in.
Capacity: 410 cu. in.
PTO Power: 31 hp @ 975 rpm
Drawbar Power: 21 hp @ 975 rpm
Transmission: Four-speed (six-speed
  from 1942)
Speeds (4spd): 2.3–6 mph
Weight: 4,400 lb.

MINNEAPOLIS-MOLINE UDLX

[1938]

A spacious, weatherproof cab, a nice comfortable seat, a radio, heater, and windshield wipers—the very height of luxury. Today we take it for granted that most modern tractors will have all these things as standard, but in 1938 none of them did, that is until Minneapolis-Moline

unveiled their new "Comfortractor" to an astonished farming industry.

Better equipped than even many cars of the time, the UDLX Comfortractor had an integral steel cab, with real glass in the windows, and came with every conceivable extra. You didn't have to clamber up to the

UDLX's cab, you stepped into it via convenient rear doors. As well as that heater and radio, the package also included safety glass, a defroster, and foot accelerator, even a passenger seat. Nor was it simply about comfort. Minneapolis-Moline's trademark high top gear gave a road speed of 40 mph, a full half a century before the JCB Fastrac appeared.

It looked very elegant, too, clean and streamlined in a way that some cars of 1938 failed to emulate. This was a new sort of tractor. There was even a sleek-looking open top variant, without the cab. In theory, you could plow in comfort all day (whatever the weather), then drive out to town for the evening—all in the comfort of your own tractor.

In practice the enclosed cab provided poor visibility, especially in the wet (take another look at those windshield wipers!) though the tractor was good enough for field work.

Ahead of its time? Yes, and maybe too far ahead for the average 1938 tractor buyer. Despite using standard Model U components under its shapely bodywork, the Comfortractor cost a whopping $2,155. Its huge price tag put the tractor firmly out of the reach of most farmers, and consequently the company only managed to sell one hundred and fifty machines.

LEFT: *The brightly colored Comfortractor was elegant, comfortable, and well-equipped—this Minneapolis-Moline machine was years ahead of its time, and way out of most farmers' price range.*

MINNEAPOLIS-MOLINE
UDLX

Engine: Water-cooled, four-cylinder
Bore x stroke: 4.25 x 5.0 in.
Capacity: 283 cu. in.
PTO Power: 38 hp @ 1,275 rpm
Drawbar Power: 31 hp
Transmission: Five-speed
Weight: 6,000 lb.

ABOVE AND RIGHT: *Who could resist it? Well, the majority of farmers, as it turned out—the ones who couldn't afford the $2,000-plus asking price.*

BELOW: *Beneath the skin, a UDLX Comfortractor used standard U-series components, including the 283 cu. in. four-cylinder engine, though the five-speed transmission had an extra-tall top ratio to allow 40 mph on the road.*

RIGHT: *Minneapolis-Moline, with a chunky new "MM" logo, described themselves as "The Modern Tractor Pioneers." With the UDLX, they were.*

FAR RIGHT: *No more undignified climbing over the fender, one stepped through the rear door into the Comfortractor.*

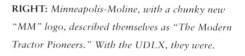

ABOVE: *Was this the best-looking tractor of the 1930s? This sleek open-top version of the UDLX forsook the major selling point of the whole machine—its cab. Few were sold, but it did look nice.*

MASSEY-HARRIS 101 JUNIOR
[1939]

By 1938, Massey-Harris was a well-established make, and it was busy updating its entire range. The 101, launched that year, slotted in between the Challenger and the now aging Model 25. Its engine was more sophisticated than either, a smooth Chrysler straight six of 201 cu. in.

The success of tractors like the Oliver 70 had proved that some farmers liked the extra smoothness of six cylinders. The unit frame, which could trace its roots back to the 1913 Wallis Cub, was discarded for the 101, although it is debatable whether the heavy cast-iron frame that replaced it was actually much of an improvement. There were more genuine enhancements with a four-speed gearbox and modern, streamlined styling.

A year later, it was joined by the 101 Junior (pictured here.) This was much smaller, a whole 2,000 lb. lighter, and powered by a little 124 cu. in. four-cylinder engine in gasoline form only. With 16–24

LEFT: *Massey-Harris took the six-cylinder route with the 101, complete with streamlined styling to match—could the days of the lumbering four-cylinder monsters be drawing to a close?*

BELOW: *By the late 1930s, Massey-Harris was a respected, well-established manufacturer that built its own tractors.*

hp, it was a two-plow tractor that filled a gap at the bottom of the Massey-Harris range.

The 101 Junior Twin Power had a slightly larger 140 cu. in. version of the Junior's Continental engine, but what really marked it out was the Twin Power feature. This was a Massey-Harris first, a two-speed governor first seen in the Challenger. All the 101s were replaced shortly after the Second World War.

MASSEY-HARRIS 101 JUNIOR

Engine: Water-cooled, four-cylinder
Bore x stroke: 3.0 x 4.39 in.
Capacity: 124 cu. in.
PTO Power: 25.4 hp @ 1,800 rpm
Drawbar Power: 16.4 hp
Transmission: Four-speed
Speeds: 2.6–17.4 mph
Fuel Consumption: 9.75 hp/hr per gallon

FORD 9N
[1939]

To build one revolutionary tractor is quite something. To build two, well, that's something else. But that's exactly what Henry Ford did. The 1917 Fordson Model F was the first truly mass-produced tractor, bringing one within reach of many small farms. Twenty-one years later, the Ford 9N had a similar impact, though this had more to do with its new technical features than its price.

Henry did have some help the second time around. Irishman Harry Ferguson had much in common with Ford: he was another farmer's son, a self-made man who could be difficult and irascible, but also came close to genius. He had designed a revolutionary new means of attaching tractors to implements. Ferguson's patented three-point hydraulic hitch enabled quick and easy coupling and decoupling; its clever geometry allowed some of the implement's drag to be applied as downforce to the tractor's rear wheels, improving traction; it had draft control; and it was far safer than a conventional hitch, as it prevented the tractor rearing up and flipping over.

In 1938, he crossed the Atlantic to demonstrate the system to Henry Ford, who was so impressed that he immediately agreed to build an all-new tractor to incorporate the three-point system. No contracts, no lawyers, just a handshake, which was later to prove a headache to both sides. The 9N of 1939 was the result. Like the Model F, it was small, light, and possessed an excellent power-to-weight ratio—it could do the work of a tractor of twice the price and weight. It was certainly a case of history repeating itself.

LEFT: *The 9N proved to be something of a poisoned chalice for Ford. It was a huge leap forward in tractor technology, in its way just as revolutionary as the original Fordson, thanks largely to the Ferguson three-point hitch that came as standard. But the gentleman's agreement with Harry Ferguson didn't work out, and Ford failed to make a cent of profit on any of the early 9Ns. Not until the contract was finally terminated by Henry Ford II in 1947, and Ford gained full control of tractor distribution, did the chalice turn into a horn of plenty.*

FORD 9N

Engine: Water-cooled, four-cylinder
Capacity: 199 cu. in.
PTO Power: 20 hp
Drawbar Power: 12.7 hp
Transmission: Three-speed
Weight: 2,340 lb.
Speeds: 2.0–6.3 mph
Weight: 4,088 lb.

JOHN DEERE D (STYLED)
[1939]

John Deere tractors were sold on solid, sensible virtues—strength, simplicity, and reliability. But even they couldn't afford to look even slightly old-fashioned in an increasingly fashion-conscious world. Many tractor manufacturers rushed to restyle their machines in the late 1930s, and

John Deere was not to be left behind. They enrolled the help of well-known industrial designer Henry Dreyfuss. The story goes that one of John Deere's engineers turned up at Dreyfuss's smart New York office in a fur coat and straw hat. Apparently the leading designer was so struck by this fashion-free ensemble that he agree to take on the job right away!

He certainly did a good job on the D, not to mention all other John Deeres, which were restyled along the same lines. Trim, neat, and sleek, they carried John Deere well into the 1950s. It was hard to believe that the restyled D had been conceived in the early 1920s. But it wasn't just cosmetic, and there were plenty of other changes during its thirty-year production run. Many small engine improvements saw power rise from 27 hp at first to 42 bhp by 1953. A third transmission speed was added in 1935, and the Henry Dreyfuss styling came in four years later.

John Deere played a canny game with the Model D—tried and tested running gear, suitably updated from time to time, with Dreyfuss styling to make it seem very contemporary. It repaid the compliment by fighting off tough competition from Fordson, Case, and Farmall, and establishing JD as a serious tractor manufacturer.

ABOVE: *The original design—practical and reliable it may have been but stylish it was not. This comparative shot of the Model D enables you to compare the two machines before it received the Henry Dreyfuss restyle. Rubber pads on the wheels were supposed to improve comfort for the driver on tarmac roads.*

LEFT: *A well-preserved example of Henry Dreyfuss's restyled Model D—the boxy lines suited the tractor's no-nonsense reliability. The Model D established John Deere as a mainstream mass maker of tractors, and helped them to survive tough times and even tougher competition from rival manufacturers such as Fordson, J. I. Case, and Farmall—a truly landmark tractor.*

JOHN DEERE D (STYLED)

Engine Type: Water cooled
twin-cylinder
Bore x stroke: 6.8 x 7.0 in.
Capacity: 508 cu. in.
PTO Power: 40 hp @ 900 rpm
Drawbar Power: 34.5 hp @ 900 rpm
Transmission: Three-speed
Speeds: 3.0–5.3 mph
Fuel Consumption: 10.1 hp/hr
per gallon
Weight: 8,125 lb.

MINNEAPOLIS-MOLINE R
[1939]

Despite the sales flop of the Comfortractor, M-M persevered with an all-steel cab, offering it as an option on some other models. However, it was very different to the luxury specification of the Comfortractor, being purely a means of keeping the weather off. The little R, for instance, could be bought with a cab. It was a new two-plow tractor designed to fit into the range beneath the 2–3-plow Z. The R was really a smaller version of the Z, powered by a 16-25 hp 165 cu. in. engine with all the same easy-maintenance features, like those horizontal valves, which meant very easy clearance checking. Crankshaft and con-rods could be examined without even draining the sump, and the engine could be overhauled without having to dismantle the entire machine.

"For the economy-minded farmer," went M-M's publicity, "a Minneapolis-Moline R is RIGHT. He knows that it is better to have a little extra power than not quite enough. The R offers four kinds of power for immediate use, with economy of cost: drawbar, Uni-Matic Power, power take-off and belt pulley." Most were available through to 1955, and specfications for a 1951 Model R are shown here.

RIGHT: *Note the rear power takeoff on this Model R, but there's still no three-point linkage. Otherwise, the R was quite an advanced small tractor.*

LEFT: *M-M learned from the costly Comfortractor, and thereafter offered simple steel cabs without the luxury features, but still weatherproof.*

BELOW: *The R's 165 cu. in. engine was designed with easy maintenance in mind. Its thoughtful design meant the crankshaft could be checked without even draining the sump.*

MINNEAPOLIS-MOLINE MODEL R (1951)

Engine: Water-cooled, four-cylinder
Bore x stroke: 3.63 x 4.0 in.
Capacity: 165 cu. in.
PTO Power: 25.9 hp @ 1,500 rpm
Drawbar Power: 18.3 hp
Transmission: Four-speed
Speeds: 2.6–13.2 mph
Fuel Consumption: 7.95 hp/hr
  per gallon
Weight: 3,414 lb.

FARMALL A
[1939]

FARMALL A

Engine: Water-cooled, four-cylinder

Bore x stroke: 3.0 x 4.0 in.

Capacity: 113 cu. in.

Drawbar Power: 17.4 hp @ 1,400 rpm

PTO Power: 19.1 hp

Transmission: Four-speed

Speeds: 2.3–9.6 mph

Weight: 1,870 lb.

BELOW: *The smallest Farmall F12 was later upgraded as the F14 and later still as this, the A— still lightweight, nimble, and adaptable, but now with more power and the "Cultivision" chassis.*

Miniature single-plow tractors were a popular feature of the Farmall range from the first 1932 F12 onwards. That was later upgraded into the F14 and in 1939 updated again as this, the Farmall A. Like the F14, the A was a small single-plow machine, though the 113 cu. in. overhead valve engine was uprated to give 17.4 drawbar hp, 19.1 at the belt.

The smallest Farmalls were invariably bought for crop cultivation, so the A was redesigned with this in mind. Named the "Cultivision," the chassis was offset to the left, giving the driver a clear view ahead, and the front tread was adjustable as well as the rear. Until then, most row-crop tractors had rear tread adjustment only.

At just 1,870 lb., the A was a remarkably light tractor, and one interesting option (available on other Internationals) was high-altitude pistons. These altered the compression ratio to cope with running in higher country, and came in 5,000-feet or 9,000-feet versions.

Produced right through the Second World War, the A's best year was actually 1941, when nearly 23,000 were built. However, at the war's height only 105 Farmall As left the line, reflecting a factory busy on war work. In 1947, the smallest Farmall was given hydraulics, as the Super A. That in turn was replaced by the more powerful 100 in 1954, later upgraded as a 130 and 140.

FARMALL AV

[1939]

As with most tractor ranges, there were lots of variations on the Farmall A theme. In International Harvester terms in 1939, "V" signaled high-crop, so the AV was simply a high-crop version of the standard A. There were high-crop versions of the bigger H and M Farmalls as well.

Under the skin, the AV was virtually identical to the standard A, but it did share new styling. In fact, the A and AV were part of a new generation, with special attention paid to styling and ergonomics. In the mid 1930s, several tractor makers brought in designers from outside the industry to give their machines a fresh, up-to-the-minute look, and International went to Raymond Loewy for inspiration.

The Farmalls had been quite neat-looking tractors before this makeover, but Loewy improved on that, encasing the fuel tank, steering bolster, and radiator in a single streamlined housing. He also styled the wheels to give an impression of both strength and lightness, and even hired an orthopedic surgeon to shape the seat.

It was a quirk of history that IHC agricultural tractors were still badged "McCormick-Deering" and the crawlers "TracTractors." To add to the confusion, "Farmall" was so well known it had virtually become a marque in its own right. The Deering name was finally dropped in the late 1940s, and McCormick was scraped soon after.

FARMALL AV

Engine: Water-cooled, four-cylinder
Bore x stroke: 3.0 x 4.0 in.
Capacity: 113 cu. in.
Drawbar Power: 17 hp @ 1,400 rpm
PTO Power: 19 hp
Transmission: Four-speed
Speeds: 2.9–12.8 mph
Weight: 2,280 lb.

BELOW: *The AV was the high-clearance version of the Farmall A, and it enjoyed the same advances of styling and ergonomics, designed by renowned industrial designer Raymond Loewy.*

The 1940s:
WAR & PEACE

At first, the Second World War had little effect on the U.S. tractor industry. The tractor manufacturers were on a roll, enjoying the fruits of relatively high farm incomes and over a decade of technological innovation. Production continued to climb, to nearly 250,000 in 1940 (up thirty percent from the previous year), and over 300,000 in 1941, a new record. Ford was struggling to meet demand for its new 9N, and International launched eleven new models in 1940.

But when the U.S. entered the war late in 1941, things soon began to change. The tractor industry represented a huge engineering resource, and it was soon being directed into the war effort, to make tanks, munitions, and every kind of military material. Even where tractor production continued, skilled manpower proved an increasing problem, as men were called into the armed services, and material shortages made themselves felt as well.

The first cutbacks were in new model research and development, one of the reasons why there were very few technical advances during the 1940s. Tractors in production had their specifications down-graded to cope with shortages. The Ford 9N, for example, became the simpler, cheaper 2N, with steel rim wheels replacing the standard rubber tires and magneto ignition in place of the battery system—that meant the electric starter was ditched as well. In fact, most tractors produced during the war came with plain steel wheels, and there were other economies under the sheet metal. Steel back bearings were used to replace solid bronze, and

certain steel and iron alloys were changed to use less rare metals.

Reflecting the lack of new models, the University of Nebraska suspended tractor testing in 1942, for the duration of the war. It was the only break in testing at Nebraska from Test No.1 in 1920, to the present day. Meanwhile, production of new tractors fell sharply, to just over 172,000 in 1942 and 105,000 in 1943. But that was the low point, and production more than doubled the following year. By the end of the decade, another record would be broken, with over half a million wheeled tractors built in 1949.

In fact, the late 1940s were a boom time for tractor producers. There was a huge backlog of orders in the United States, while a Europe devastated by war needed a whole new generation of farm machinery to get agriculture moving again. This burgeoning demand, the ending of material shortages, and the return of the skilled engineers, home from the war, led to an explosion of tractor production.

It also tempted many new entrants into the tractor market. Perhaps the most interesting was the Universal Jeep, built by Willys-Overland. In 1945, with one eye on the imminent end of the war (and less demand for its famous military Jeep), Willys adapted the Jeep for farm work. It actually differed little from the military spec machine, but had a lower rear axle ratio and first gear, a larger radiator, and

RIGHT: *Shown here is the Farmall BMD, a wider tread version of the Farmall A. It was a relatively low-volume tractor—only 75,000 were sold in eight years.*

ABOVE: *Oliver, the pioneer of high-compression six-cylinder tractor power, faced the postwar world with a new commitment to diesel.*

RIGHT: *Gasoline power still dominated in the 1940s, but the following decade would see a gradual shift towards diesel.*

lower towing hitch. Like the standard Jeep, it could be switched between two- or four-wheel drive. The Willys Farm Jeep would be produced into the 1950s, and was tested by Nebraska in 1953.

Not all the new arrivals came with such impeccable credentials. According to R. B. Gray *(The Agricultural Tractor)* some of them were "fly-by-night manufacturers," producing machines "of inferior design and quality." All the established U.S. manufacturers were obliged to export part of their production to aid Europe's recovery, which left plenty of unfulfilled demand on the home market—a fly-by-nighters dream?

But not all the new tractor producers were like that. The Empire Tractor Co. of Philadelphia launched its Model 88 in 1946, powered by a 40 hp Willys-Overland engine, though this company only lasted a couple of years. Or there was the Earthmaster Model C of the same year, a little 1/2-plow machine with "Duomatic" hydraulic control. Other examples were the four-wheel-drive Cimco PH31, Continental-powered with a four-speed transmission and two power takeoffs. Jumbo Steel Products built the three-plow Simpson Jumbo, said to be designed for the western U.S.'s rugged climate, and the oddly named Haas "Atomic" tractor used a single-

cylinder 12.5 hp aero engine with six forward speeds. None of these tractors were particularly innovative, but in 1947 one

ABOVE: *A very smart Ford 9N, with polished hood and rubber tires—it would never have left the factory like this in wartime.*

genuine step forward did take place. The Canadian Cockshutt company announced a continuously running power takeoff, which would carry on spinning when the clutch was released. Until then, PTO-driven machinery like sprayers and combines would stop when the clutch was released, so continuous operation was very useful. Cockshutt called it a "live" PTO, and within a few years many U.S. manufacturers had followed suit. Another new feature that year, though a less dramatic one, was John Deere's "Roll-O-Matic." This was designed for the two front wheel tricycle model, and amounted to independent suspension for each of the wheels, allowing one wheel to roll over obstructions while the other stuck to level ground.

Meanwhile, in Europe, the tractor industry was slowly getting its act together. This was most noticeable in eastern Europe and Soviet Russia. A new factory at Minsk in Belarus was opened in 1946 to build crawler tractors, though wheeled models soon followed. Belarus, as the tractors were badged, served the massive U.S.S.R. market, and was to become the largest manufacturer in the world—by 1995 it had produced three million machines. Tractor production

restarted in Poland as well, where the Ursus concern began making a version of the German-designed Lanz Bulldog machine under license. In Hungary, the prewar HSCS resumed production (though it was soon renamed "Red Star Tractors" in keeping with the new regime), and Zetor, probably

ABOVE: *Oliver went on producing its 1930s star, the six-cylinder 70, right through the 1940s, albeit on steel rims during the war.*

BELOW: *David Brown, after falling out with Harry Ferguson, went on to become a tractor manufacturer in its own right. This is a postwar Cropmaster.*

the most successful of the East European manufacturers, began production in 1946.

In Britain, Fordson still dominated the tractor industry, with David Brown the only large-scale domestically owned manufacturer in early postwar years. In fact, at first it looked as if the rest of Britain's tractor industry would be U.S.-owned or operated. In 1947 Allis-Chalmers opened a factory in Southampton, on the south coast of England, and later in Lincolnshire, in the northeast. The British arm of Allis-Chalmers produced variations on U.S. A-C machines for over twenty years. At first the little Model B was

ALLIS-CHALMERS

ABOVE: *Allis-Chalmers established a factory in Britain in the late 1940s, and they continued to build tractors in the country for twenty years.*

assembled from parts imported from the U.S., but later machines, such as the Perkins diesel-powered D272 and ED40, had more English input.

A-C's British production closed in 1968, but International Harvester's was longer-lived. It built a new factory in Doncaster,

ABOVE: *Bristol of England built small and mid-size crawlers—at this time, there wasn't really a big market in Britain for the largest crawlers.*

BELOW: *Ford 9N in original gray finish. The '40s would see Ford wrest control of its tractor back from Harry Ferguson.*

northern England, in 1949, and like A-C, the early tractors made there were U.S. models, but British designs followed. The Doncaster factory is still producing tractors today, now as the McCormick brand. In fact, Britain seemed to be a favorite European production base for U.S. companies—Massey-Harris had a factory in Scotland, while Minneapolis-Moline sent over tractors without engines, to be fitted with British diesels.

But Britain's homegrown tractor industry was expanding as well. Harry Ferguson's handshake agreement with Ford was in tatters, so he needed someone else to build his machines. He found a suitable partner in the Standard Motor Co., which had spare capacity in their factory in central England. The first Ferguson TE20 rolled off the line in 1946, the start of a highly successful factory that would produce Fergies and Massey-Fergusons for nearly sixty years.

The TE20 was superficially similar to the Ford 9N, and of course featured the famous three-point hitch. Meanwhile, Ford of Britain was following its own path, quite separately from U.S. Ford tractors. Still using the Fordson name, which was highly respected in Britain, it gradually updated the venerable E27N (which was based on the much older Fordson Model N) with a Perkins diesel engine in 1948 and later a hydraulic linkage. Morris, the British car maker, also moved into the tractor market in 1948, and its Nuffield Universal proved a great success, and was soon being exported in large numbers.

So Europe was getting back on its feet, but what of the United States? Its domestic production continued to boom: from 258,000 wheeled tractors in 1946, to 433,000 the following year, then 529,000 in 1948, and 555,000 in 1949. But technical innovations were few and far between as manufacturers struggled simply to keep up with demand. Until 1949, when John Deere gave a pointer to how things would develop in the 1950s.

It was the John Deere Model R, the biggest, most powerful machine JD had

ever made, its first five-plow machine and its first diesel. The company had actually been working on diesel development since 1935, though the war had evidently slowed things down. The 51 hp Model R retained the classic John Deere twin-cylinder layout, measuring a meaty 416 cu. in. A small donkey gasoline engine was provided to start the big diesel. Despite its complexity (by John Deere standards), the Model R was very popular, simply because it was the most fuel-efficient big tractor you could buy.

ABOVE: *The herald of a new era. The Model R was John Deere's biggest, most powerful tractor ever, and its first diesel.*

BELOW: *The 1947 Fleetline look was Oliver's new face for the postwar world. This 77 replaced the 70 that year.*

This was a clear message to the other American manufacturers—diesel was clearly the way to go, especially for big machines. Anyone who ignored that particular message would not survive.

OLIVER 70 ORCHARD
[1940]

Orchard tractors have a following all of their own, and you can see why. The faired-in bodywork looks terrific, giving the tractor a sleek, streamlined appearance. Of course, it's there for a practical reason—to prevent tree branches catching on the tractor and getting damaged. Modern orchard tractors usually get around that by being rather smaller and narrower—more effective, but less aesthetic!

Oliver's six-cylinder 70 was already a good-looking tractor in standard form, and a real stunner when set up for orchard work. Over 60,000 70s were sold, and they allowed Oliver to hit the big time. Not all of those were standard row-crop machines, and as well as the orchard version featured here, there was the appropriately named Airport 25, designed for towing aircraft. The green color was said to have been the result of extensive market research, 1930s style. Several 70s were painted in a variety of colors (red, green, orange, silver, and gold) and displayed at country fairs to gauge public reaction. Green got the most favorable reviews, so that's how Olivers were finished from then on.

There were many options on the 70—an electric starter, rubber tires, a wide front axle—which could push the price up over $1,000, but some were willing to pay the price for a handsome tractor.

LEFT: *"Ready for take off." This winged Oliver 70 Orchard looks as if it really could fly, but the giant, graceful fenders were there for a purpose, to prevent tree branches from snagging on the passing tractor and getting damaged. Under the shapely skin, the orchard model was the same as any other Oliver 70, with gasoline and kerosene options. The same was true of most orchard models, mechanically identical with their row-crop or standard-tread farming counterparts, but with that extra bodywork, often a lower seating position (to keep the driver away from overhanging branches) and rerouted exhaust. The University of Nebraska tested a row-crop specification Oliver 70 in 1940, with Oliver's own high-compression six-cylinder engine. As ever, it ran at a relatively high 1,500 rpm, maybe part of the reason why Oliver provided a six-speed transmission to go with it—this allowed speeds of between 2.6 and 13.4 mph. In forty-nine hours of testing, no adjustments or repairs were needed. The test machine came with pneumatic rubber tires, but materials shortages would soon make steel rims the only available option.*

BELOW: *The Oliver 70 looked more like a car than a tractor with its sleek, long hood, especially after the streamlined "Fleetline" styling it received in its 1937 model year. This 1940s orchard model just enhanced its smooth lines even further. The only thing letting this Oliver 70 down are its steel rims, introduced due to shortages caused by the war.*

OLIVER 70 ORCHARD

Engine: Water-cooled, six-cylinder
Bore x stroke: 3.13 x 4.38 in.
Capacity: 202 cu. in.
PTO Power: 30.4 hp @ 1,500 rpm
Drawbar Power: 22.7 hp
Transmission: Six-speed
Speeds: 2.6–13.4 mph
Fuel Consumption: 9.81 hp/hr
   per gallon
Weight: 4,370 lb.

CASE MODEL S
[1940]

In the history of Case tractors, at least some of it fits into neat categories. The Crossmotor era stretched from 1916 to 1928; then the general purpose Models L and C took over until 1939. The third era was that of Flambeau Red. Not just a new color in 1939, but the beginnings of a new

LEFT: *The Case Model S was part of a general renewal of the Case range in 1939, easily recognized by this new Flambeau Red color.*

ABOVE: *The S was a thoroughly modern two-plow machine, with four-speed transmission and high-speed four-cylinder power unit.*

range of tractors. Over the next couple of years, the whole range was affected. A new D replaced the C model; LA replaced the L; the V was a new single-plow machine; and the S was a two-plow general purpose tractor replacing the R and RC.

Not all these tractors were new, but the S was, with a four-speed transmission and a whole range of different versions. You could have it in standard tread as the S; SC denoted the general purpose tractor; SO for orchard work; and SI was the industrial model. There was also an SC-4 with a fixed-tread wide front axle. All were powered by a relatively short-stroke, high-revving four-cylinder engine of 154 cu. in. with a rated speed of 1,550 rpm. There were few major changes to the S, but it did acquire

hydraulics and a foot clutch. While in its final year of 1953, the engine was upped in size to 165 cu. in.

CASE MODEL S GASOLINE (1953)

Engine: Water-cooled, four-cylinder
Bore x stroke: 3.625 x 4 in.
Capacity: 165 cu. in.
PTO Power: 32 hp @ 1,600 rpm
Drawbar Power: 28 hp @ 1,600 rpm
Transmission: Four-speed
Speeds: 2.5–10.3 mph
Fuel Consumption: 10.28 hp/hr per gallon
Weight: 5,007 lb.

CASE MODEL D
[1940]

The Case Model D was a good example of how to keep an aging tractor up to date. When launched in 1939, it was little more than a restyled Model C—which itself dated back ten years. However, constant updates over the next decade kept the Model D reasonably up to date.

A four-speed transmission replaced the three-speed in 1940, along with a foot clutch to replace the old hand clutch. Case had already introduced a mechanical Motor Lift, to help attach implements, and this was updated with hydraulics. Later, disc brakes replaced the band type, and for the first time, Case offered an LPG (Liquid Petroleum Gas) conversion; soon a water pump did away with having to rely on the thermo-syphon effect, and a live PTO became standard.

Rubber pneumatic tires were still optional, but the final big change came in 1952. The Eagle Hitch was Case's answer to the Ferguson-Ford three-point hydraulic hitch. This had already revolutionized the use of implements: with in-built draft control, it made plowing far easier and safer than before, while attaching and removing implements was simplicity itself.

Farmers, dealers, and sales force all began pressuring for a comparable system, though Case president Leon Clausen had dismissed Harry Ferguson's invention as "a cheatin' system." They couldn't ignore it though, and the Eagle Hitch did allow rapid snap-on fitting of implements. What it didn't have was draft control—a genuine three-point hitch was the only answer.

LEFT: *The Case Model D looked new, but was really a cleverly updated Model C. Restyled, and with a four-speed transmission and foot clutch, it was a genuine advance, and Case gave it regular updates through the 1940s and early 1950s, to keep it competitive: a mechanical (later hydraulic) implement lift, disc brakes, the option of an LPG engine, a live PTO, and a water pump cooling system. Plus, of course, the significant Eagle Hitch was a partial answer to the revolutionary Ferguson three-point hitch, which was making the Ford 9N such a roaring success.*

CASE MODEL D

Engine: Water-cooled four-cylinder
Bore x stroke: 3.875 x 5.5 in.
Capacity: 259 cu. in.
PTO Power: 35.5 hp @ 1,100 rpm
Drawbar Power: 24.4 hp @ 1,100 rpm
Transmission: Three-speed
Speeds: 2.5–5.0 mph
Fuel Consumption: 12.1 hp/hr per gallon
Weight: 7,010 lb.

INTERNATIONAL W4

[1940]

INTERNATIONAL W4

Engine: Water-cooled, four-cylinder

Bore x stroke: 3.31 x 4.25 in.

Capacity: 152 cu. in.

Drawbar Power: 22.5 hp @ 1,650 rpm

PTO Power: 25 hp

Transmission: Five-speed

Speeds: 2.3–14.0 mph

Weight: 3,890 lb.

By the end of the 1930s, row-crop tractors dominated the U.S. market, with just a trickle of demand for the less-adaptable standard-tread machines. Take the Farmall H and its standard-tread equivalent, the W4 pictured here. During thirteen years on the market, just over 24,000 W4s were sold. In the same period (plus one year) International shifted over 300,000 Farmall H's!

It's a good comparison, because the W4 and Farmall H were almost identical under the skin. Both used exactly the same 152 cu. in. four-cylinder engine, in the same state of tune. The only substantial differences were the standard-tread front axle, though the W4 was also slightly lower geared than the Farmall, on which it was based, and also a little heavier. Top speed on the standard rubber tires was 14 mph.

The other reason for persevering with a standard-tread tractor was that it formed the basis of specialist tractors for orchard or industrial work—the O4 and OS4 were for orchards, and the industrial I4 came in standard and heavy-duty forms. There was also a much larger W9 (or WD9 diesel), with a 335 cu. in. four-cylinder engine producing 35 hp at the drawbar, and 45 hp on the belt.

BELOW: *This standard-tread W4 was badged as a McCormick-Deering in its various forms, but the industrial I4 was an International. The equivalent row-crop tractor of course, was still a Farmall. Regular equipment on the W4 included a 152 cu. in. gasoline engine, adjustable-tread front axle, swinging drawbar, hydraulic deluxe foam rubber seat, disc brakes, hydraulic Touch Control, belt pulley and PTO, muffler, heat indicator, exhaust valve rotators, starter, lights, and battery ignition.*

INTERNATIONAL W6

[1940]

"Farmall M has easy operation, comfort, and all those other refinements that go to make up a tractor that is a delight to use . . . It will pull three 14- or 16-inch bottom ploughs under harder than average soil conditions at good plowing speed . . . In a word, Farmall M has what it takes to deliver satisfactory and economical power under any field conditions."

International Harvester was right to be so proud of the Farmall. It owed a great deal, maybe even its independent survival up to the 1980s, to the whole Farmall concept. So, just as the ultra-successful Farmall H replaced the mid-range Farmall F20, so the bigger Farmall M did the same job for the

F30. Both sold by the truckload in the 1940s and early 1950s (the M wasn't quite as a big a seller as the H, but it was still hugely popular); over 270,000 of them had been produced by the time production finally ended in 1952. And of course, just as the W4 was the standard-tread version of the Farmall H, the W6 pictured here was an M, but with fixed axles.

Both combined the new Loewy styling, with that rounded radiator grille and ergonomic design, with a 248 cu. in. four-cylinder engine in gasoline or distillate form. This was a 33 hp three-plow tractor and, until the arrival of the 45 hp W9, it was the biggest offered by International.

INTERNATIONAL W6	
Engine: Water-cooled, four-cylinder	
Bore x stroke: 3.86 x 5.25 in.	
Capacity: 248 cu. in.	
Drawbar Power: 33 hp @ 1,450 rpm	
PTO Power: 37 hp	
Transmission: Five-speed	
Speeds: 2.3–14.5 mph	
Weight: 4,830 lb.	

BELOW: *The Farmall W6 was more nimble and easier to operate than the little F12, yet it could do four times the amount of work.*

INTERNATIONAL WD6

[1940]

An outsider to the tractor industry might wonder why diesel power took so long to catch on. After all, the principle had been around since 1910, and the very strengths of diesel (long life, efficiency, and high torque) were ideal for tractors. The trouble was, diesels were more expensive to build and buy, and since every farmer was his own businessman, that was an important factor in holding back sales, especially while gasoline fuel was relatively cheap. But in the 1930s, Caterpillar demonstrated the advantages of diesel in its crawlers, and International wasn't far behind—it built its first diesel crawler in 1932 and a diesel tractor, the WD40, only three years later. It used a hybrid diesel/gasoline motor, equipped with both injectors and a carburetor—it could run on either fuel.

The WD6 was rather more conventional, using a straight diesel conversion of International's existing 248 cu. in. four. It produced almost identical power figures, 31/36 hp against 33/37 hp, and was rated at the same 1,450 rpm. The diesel engine added 420 lb. to the weight of the tractor, though gearing was unchanged. It was cheaper to run, of course, but it would take most farmers several years to see the savings. In 1951, the WD6 cost $3,124, over thirty percent more than the gasoline W6.

LEFT: *International was the first mainstream U.S. manufacturer to offer a diesel-engined tractor in 1935. But the WD40 was more of a hybrid than a true diesel. The WD6 launched five years later was a genuine diesel, using International's own conversion of its 248 cu. in. four-cylinder engine which powered the W6. With a compression ratio of 14.2:1 (the standard gasoline unit ran on 5.9:1) the new diesel was rated at 1,450 rpm, the same speed, and produced very similar power figures. It drove through a five-speed transmission, which provided ground speeds of 2.3–14.5 mph. The WD6 was much heavier than the W6 and cost nearly $800 extra. The point was that it was far more fuel efficient—over time, it could pay for itself. Shown here is a BWD6— the "B" denotes the front axle/wheel arrangement.*

INTERNATIONAL WD6

Engine: Water-cooled, four-cylinder
Bore x stroke: 3.86 x 5.25 in.
Capacity: 248 cu. in.
Drawbar Power: 31 hp @ 1,450 rpm
PTO Power: 36 hp
Fuel Consumption: 14.85 hp/hr
  per gallon
Transmission: Five-speed
Speeds: 2.3–14.5 mph
Weight: 5,250 lb.

ALLIS-CHALMERS MODEL WF
[1940]

The WC was Allis-Chalmers's Farmall, a mass-production row-crop tractor that sold in huge numbers. But, just like International, they couldn't ignore the continuing demand for a simple standard-tread machine. So the WF, announced in 1940, was no less than a standard-tread version of the WC. Both used A-C's own W-type engine with its four-inch bore and stroke, the first tractor engine to have these "square" dimensions. Rated at 1,300 rpm, it produced a reliable 21 hp at the drawbar, and was quite economical, giving 5.62 hp/hr per gallon on rubber tires.

But the WF hadn't been in production long before the Second World War affected it. In 1941, only a year into production, the electric starter and lights had to be dropped. Like many tractors of the 1940s, the WF was affected by material shortages. In fact, production was stopped altogether in 1943, though it resumed the following year. By 1948, all the peacetime goodies were back, and a WF with electric start and lights cost $971 on steel wheels, or $1,210 on pneumatics, which were now the industry standard.

The WF could also blame war restrictions for the fact that it was never tested at Nebraska—unusual for a U.S.-made tractor. Nebraska testing was suspended in November 1941, and didn't resume again until 1946. Still, figures for the almost-identical WC can be used as a guide.

LEFT: *Just as International offered standard-tread equivalents to the Farmall, this was A-C's standard-tread version of its own row-crop WC. Like those Internationals, the WF was little more than a modified version of its row-crop cousin. It used the same 202 cu. in. four-cylinder power unit, with "square" bore and stroke. This was a first for a tractor engine, and it proved lighter than long-stroke units, but reliable and economical as well. Something else that kept the overall weight down was the high-tensile steel chassis, though it was not unit construction. There was no hydraulic three-point hitch, but A-C already offered a drive-in attachment for implements, with an optional power lift.*

ALLIS-CHALMERS WC (1934) PNEUMATIC TIRES

Engine: Water-cooled, four-cylinder

Bore x stroke: 4.0 x 4.0 in.

Capacity: 202 cu. in.

PTO Power: 21.5 hp

Drawbar Power: n/a

Fuel Consumption: 10.17 hp/hr
per gallon

Speeds: 2.5–9.3 mph

Weight: 3,792 lb.

JOHN DEERE BWH

[1940]

As the jobs they had to do became more specialized, so did the tractors. Even the most adaptable general purpose model couldn't handle all crops, so specialized versions evolved. Hence the Model B, the smaller of John Deere's do-it-all machines. This came in BN and BW forms, narrow and wide front axle respectively. The BW was offered all the way from early 1935 to the summer of 1952, and its front end could be adjusted between 56 and 80 inches, in four-inch steps. It was a useful feature, as setting the front axle to the same width as the rear reduced soil packing. Then there were also the BNH and BWH, high-clearance versions of both.

The BWH high-cropper shown here didn't arrive until 1940, and together with the BNH was a hybrid of parts taken from the B, BN, and BW, with some all-new components as well. Forty-inch drive wheels in place of the standard 36-inch brought an extra two inches of clearance under the rear axle, and there was an extra three inches of clearance at the front, thanks to lengthened front axle knuckles. The wider front tread was adjustable between 42.625 inches and 54.625 inches and if that wasn't enough, both 7- and 13-inch extension assemblies were available as well. A farmer who couldn't find something to suit him had very strange needs indeed!

LEFT: *One of the most striking things about John Deere's twin-cylinder layout was its adaptability. The company was able to offer a wide range of machines, all based on this format. Some were bigger than the original Waterloo Boy, such as the Model G row-crop, the long-running Model D, and the diesel-powered Model R. But they also had to compete with Farmalls and Fordsons, so they offered the smaller two-plow Model A from 1934 and this, the scaled-down Model B, soon afterward. It offered 16 hp against the A's 24 hp, and weighed only 2,763 lb. But for some, even the B was too much, and for 1937 JD unveiled the L, a 9 hp 1,570 lb. tractor with a vertical twin-cylinder engine. It was the first JD to abandon the horizontal cylinder layout, but it wasn't a great success. They followed it up with the Model H, a genuinely scaled-down B.*

JOHN DEERE BWH

Engine Type: Water-cooled twin-cylinder, side-valve
Bore x stroke: 4.25 x 5.25 in.
Capacity: 149 cu. in.
Fuel: Gasoline or kerosene
PTO Power: 14 hp @ 1,150 rpm
Drawbar Power: 9.4 hp @ 1,150 rpm
Transmission: Four-speed (later six-speed)
Speeds: 2.3–5.0 mph

FORD 2N
[1941]

All of the U.S. tractor makers were affected by the war in some way. Many were kept busy with government contracts. Massey-Harris, for example, built tanks; John Deere produced all sorts of things, including mobile laundry units. That not only put tractor development on hold, but as we've seen, serious shortages of raw materials hit production as well. Pneumatic tires were an early casualty, thanks to the shortage of imported rubber, and for the duration of the war most new tractors reverted to steel wheels. Some manufacturers suspended their tractor production altogether, but Ford persevered. After all, the new 9N had only been in production a couple of years when the U.S. officially entered the war. In that short time, it had gained a fine reputation: it was lightweight, a good value, and easy to use, plus, of course, it was the first mass-production tractor equipped with a Ferguson three-point hitch.

So rather than drop its new arrival, Ford downgraded it to the wartime specification 2N. Out went the rubber tires (a standard fitment on the 9N, despite its budget price), as did the battery and generator electrics in favor of a magneto.

Even with these economic measures in place, production had to be cut back, from over 40,000 tractors in 1941 to less than 16,500 the following year. In 1942 Ford actually stopped its tractor line for several months. But as soon as the war was over, the 9N, complete with rubber tires and electric starter, was back in production. In fact, 1946 was its best ever year, with 74,004 tractors built.

LEFT: *During the Second World War, the specification of many American-built tractors had to be downgraded to take account of material shortages; rubber tires and non-essential electrical equipment were the first to go. The changes were significant enough for Ford to rename the successful 9N (which had had all these things as standard) as the 2N, its wartime austerity version. Of course, many 2Ns were upgraded back to the original 9N specification after the war, as was this restored example, but the stripped-down tractor enabled Ford to carry on building tractors right through the war, apart from a gap of just a few months.*

FORD 2N

Engine: Water-cooled, four-cylinder
Capacity: 199 cu. in.
PTO Power: 20 hp
Drawbar Power: 12.7 hp
Transmission: Three-speed
Weight: 2,340 lb.

CASE MODEL DEX

[1941]

CASE MODEL DEX (1942)

Engine: Water-cooled four-cylinder

Bore x stroke: 3.875 x 5.5 in.

Capacity: 259 cu. in.

PTO Power: 35.5 hp @ 1,100 rpm

Drawbar Power: 24.4 hp @ 1,100 rpm

Transmission: Three-speed

Speeds: 2.5–5.0 mph

Fuel Consumption: 12.1 hp/hr per gallon

Weight: 7,010 lb.

BELOW: *This three-plow tractor produced 35.5 hp at maximum load, with a fuel efficiency of 12.13 hp/hr per gallon. The maximum drawbar pull was 24.4 hp, which equated to 4,128 lb.*

There were lots of variations on the Case Model D theme, all of them finished in the smart new Flambeau Red sheet metal that heralded the 1939 model year. The name Flambeau, incidentally, came from the French for flame, or flaming torch. Either that or the Flambeau River region of North Wisconsin, the original home of Old Abe the eagle, Case's trademark since the days of Jerome Increase Case himself.

As for the Model D, it wasn't enough to produce this three-plow tractor in one basic version, Fordson style, with the aim of driving down the price. Farmers now wanted different tractors for different jobs: row-crop work, industrial, specialist crops such as sugarcane or vines—the list was endless. So D denoted standard-tread: DC3,

DC4, and DH were all-purpose tractors, and the DC4 came as a Rice Special as well; DO was the orchard machine; DV for vineyards; there were two industrial tractors, the DI Standard and DI Narrow Tread; DCS sugarcane special; export versions of the D and DO were different again; and finally, there were military versions of the DI during the Second World War.

As if this weren't enough, there were various wheel options, such as pneumatic tires or steel, and single or twin front wheels. The best selling D models were the standard tread D and general purpose DC, with the more specialized models reflecting more limited markets. But the best of the rest was the DEX (pictured here). Over 7,000 were built between 1940 and 1952.

MASSEY-HARRIS SUPER 101

[1941]

Massey-Harris had taken time to find its feet as a mainstream tractor manufacturer. The unit frame Challenger and Pacemaker proved a great success in 1936, and from then on the company concentrated both on regular updates and on new models.

The 1938 101, with its smooth six-cylinder Chrysler engine, brought a new sophistication, and after only three years it was updated as the Super 101, shown here. The Chrysler engine was boosted to 218 cu. in., though the original 201 cu. in. unit was still available, and a 101 Senior was added to the range, powered by a 244 cu. in. Continental six. These were quite highly tuned, high-compression machines that required 70 octane gasoline. They were rated at 1,500 rpm for the first three gears,

and 1,800 rpm in top or for the belt. In top gear on tarmac with pneumatic tires, that equated to a heady 16.1 mph. Both the new 101s also came with Twin Power, the two-speed governor that allowed different engine speeds for top gear and the belt, and that was still unique to Massey-Harris.

Also in 1940, the aging Model 25 (which could trace its roots back to the Wallis Cub of the 1920s) was replaced by the 201, a larger four-plow tractor based on the 101 layout. This came with standard-tread only (the 101 was standard or row-crop) with a 242 cu. in. 57 hp Chrysler gasoline engine; the similar 202 offered a little more power (60 hp Continental) and there was a 64 hp 203 as well. None of these should be confused with the 101 Junior, which was a smaller four-cylinder tractor.

MASSEY-HARRIS SUPER 101

Engine: Water-cooled, six-cylinder
Bore x stroke: 3.25 x 4.375 in.
Capacity: 218 cu. in.
PTO Power: 36 hp @ 1,800 rpm
Drawbar Power: 24 hp
Transmission: Four-speed
Speeds: 2.4–16.1 mph
Fuel Consumption: 7.46 hp/hr per gallon
Weight (steel wheels): 3,805 lb.

BELOW: *With its long, handsomely louvered hood, the Super 101 put one in mind of a 1940s aircraft or a long, low sports car. At least, it would if you squinted a bit and used your imagination.*

OLIVER 60
[1941]

Oliver had done well with the 70, a sleek six-cylinder tractor that made some rivals look crude. Meanwhile, the bigger, less sophisticated four-cylinder Olivers were still well respected. What they didn't have was a smaller tractor to compete with the Allis-Chalmers B, John Deere H,

ABOVE: *As an alternative to the adjustable two-wheel front end, the row-crop 60 could be had with a twin-wheel tricycle front, the classic row-crop format. This allowed the front wheels to run between rows, without the need for adjustment.*

LEFT: *There was a wide range of both front and rear tread adjustment on this Oliver 60. Power adjustment still hadn't arrived, so it was a case of loosening off the clamp bolts, jacking up the relevant wheel, and laboriously knocking it in or out by hand. Labor-intensive perhaps, but it did make one tractor adaptable to a wide variety of crop row spacings. Power adjustment (for the rear wheels) did arrive in the 1950s.*

Farmall A, and now the Ford 9N as well. Given the success of the 70, you would have expected the 60 to be a smaller four-cylinder version of the same thing. And that's exactly what it was. The 60's 108 cu. in. power unit was really just a four-cylinder version of the famous six, running to the relatively high speed of 1,500 rpm, and like the 70, there was a four-speed transmission. Eighteen hp at the PTO wasn't much, but it was enough to compete with the new Ford.

Pneumatic tires were standard, though during the Second World War the Oliver 60, like many other tractors, had to temporarily revert to steel wheels due to material shortages. But the modern engine, rubber tires, and four speeds underlined the fact that this was by no means a cut-price special. An electrical system cost extra though, and the ignition varied between Wico magnetos and car-type distributor systems. The 60 established Oliver in the smaller tractor market, and was in production until 1948.

OLIVER 60

Engine: Water-cooled, four-cylinder
Bore x stroke: 3.13 x 3.5 in.
Capacity: 108 cu. in.
PTO Power: 18.3 hp @ 1,500 rpm
Drawbar Power: 13.6 hp
Transmission: Four-speed
Speeds: 2.6–6.1 mph
Fuel Consumption: 10.13 hp/hr
  per gallon
Weight: 2,450 lb.

MASSEY-HARRIS 81

[1941]

Massey-Harris was kept very busy in the late 1930s and early 1940s, simply by expanding its range. It also kept customers guessing. Just when it seemed as though a nice, neat, logical numbering system was in place—101, 102, 201, 202, 203—along came the 81.

It was really a lighter, cheaper alternative to the 101 Junior, using the same 124 cu. in. Continental gasoline engine. There was a similar distillate-powered 82 as well, which used a slightly larger bore of 3.188 in. to give 140 cu. in. This was a common option at the time, to make up for the lower efficiency of distillate, and a lower 5:1 compression ratio—the 81 used a 6.75:1 compression.

These were M-H's smallest, cheapest two-plow tractors, available in standard-tread or row-crop form. Despite being at the budget end of the market, both had the Twin Power governor, though it wasn't called that any more. Soon after the war, the 81 and 82 were updated as the Model 20, and it was still a particularly lightweight machine, weighing in at 2,700 lb.

LEFT: *The latest addition to the Massey-Harris range for 1941 was the 81, essentially a cheaper version of the existing 101 Junior. Like the 101, it was fitted as standard with a Continental gasoline engine of 124 cu. in., though this was enlarged to 140 cu. in. if the optional distillate setup was specified. Just like the bigger M-H's, the 81 came with the now-familiar two-speed governor, allowing 1,500 rpm in the first three gears, and 1,800 in top or for belt work—this gave speeds of 2.4, 3.5, 4.7, or a comparatively quick 15.8 mph. There were individual rear disc brakes, but you had to pay extra for lighting equipment, a PTO extension, and (on early models) fenders and a belt pulley.*

BELOW: *Both 81s shown here are the standard-tread versions, but the tractor was also available as a row-crop version, with twin-wheel tricycle front end and adjustable rear tread.*

MASSEY-HARRIS 81

Engine: Water-cooled, four-cylinder
Bore x stroke: 3.0 x 4.375 in.
Capacity: 124 cu. in.
PTO Power: 26 hp @ 1,800 rpm
Drawbar Power: 16.4 hp
Transmission: Four-speed
Speeds: 2.4–15.8 mph
Fuel Consumption: 10.91 hp/hr
  per gallon
Weight: 2,895 lb.

MINNEAPOLIS-MOLINE GTA
[1942]

The 1930s had really been the decade of the lightweight, handy tractor, with modest power. But toward the end of the decade there was a glimpse of what was to happen once the war was over—a power race. Farms were getting bigger and more competitive. Bigger, more powerful tractors could do the work more quickly, fast enough to recoup their extra cost.

Minneapolis-Moline could see this coming, and had obliged with the big four-cylinder GT in 1938. There wasn't much radically new about the GT, and in fact it used the same engine that had originally seen light of day in the 21-32 of 1926. Still, in 403 cu. in. form it produced 36 hp at the drawbar, and 49 at the belt, which made it strong enough to draw a five-bottom plow.

Old it may have been, but the GT's beefy four-cylinder motor had plenty of potential. In 1942, the uprated GTA boasted 56 PTO horsepower and 39 for towing duties. The GTA incidentally, can be discerned from the GT by its Prairie Yellow grille, to match the rest of the machine—the GT had a red grille. A GTB followed in 1947, while the LPG-fueled GTC was available between 1951 and 1953. Finally, a diesel GTB-D was available from 1953, using a big 425 cu. in. engine. Two years later, it was updated as the GBD, giving similar power to the gasoline version. Either way, M-M's flagship was one of the last big four-cylinder tractors.

LEFT: *An unlikely looking candidate in a horsepower race, but that's what the GT and GTA amounted to. Big five-plow machines, they were the first mainstream tractors of the time to offer over 50 hp to farmers who thought they could make good use of it. But to do this, M-M didn't buy in a super-smooth six-cylinder engine, as Oliver and Massey-Harris were doing, but instead adapted their own big four-cylinder. It was interesting how the top horsepower tractors of the late 1930s to late 1940s had two or four cylinders rather than six. The agricultural market was fairly conservative, and six-cylinder motors were still something of a novelty for field work.*

MINNEAPOLIS-MOLINE MODEL GTA (1950)

Engine: Water-cooled, four-cylinder
Bore x stroke: 4.63 x 6.0 in.
Capacity: 403 cu. in.
PTO Power: 55.9 hp @ 1,100rpm
Drawbar Power: 39.2 hp
Transmission: Five-speed
Speeds: 2.5–13.8 mph
Fuel Consumption: 9.72 hp/hr per gallon
Weight: 7,230 lb.

CASE MODEL SC
[1942]

An ad in a 1941 issue of *Successful Farming* promised the happy buyer, "22 New Conveniences . . . synchronized steering with castor action stays free from play . . . deep-cushioned backrest seat . . . simplified 4-speed gearshift . . . electric starting . . . 2-rate generator . . . self-sealed cooling pump, lubricated for life . . . built-in implement mounts . . . adjustable drawbar . . . No-one can tell you in words the feel of . . . the thrill of driving this new SC Case."

The object of all this hype was the general purpose version of the Case Model S, which had been launched in November 1940.

Mechanically, it was identical to the basic standard tread S, with the same relatively high speed, short-stroke gasoline engine. We hadn't entered the diesel era yet, especially for tractors of this size. This was the two-plow class, which no manufacturer could ignore and where competition was ultra-fierce.

A few years before, eyebrows were raised at the Oliver 70, whose engine was rated at a relatively high 1,500 rpm. By 1941, engine speeds like that were common, especially on the smaller tractors, and this Case Model SC was rated at 1,550 rpm. The company's relatively short-stroke (3.5 x 4.0 in.) motor played its part in these higher speeds, and running on distillate produced 21.6 hp at maximum load, with an efficiency of 10.55 hp/hr per gallon. The Nebraska test, conducted in April/May 1941, usually gave alternative drawbar power figures, depending on the gear ratio used. For the SC, first gear gave a pull of 3,168 lb. (19.33 hp) at 2.29 mph, and second gear 1,794 lb. at 3.38 mph. It was neat illustration of elementary physics: lower gear ratios produced more torque, and thus more pulling power, albeit at a lower speed. Like the S, the SC was offered through to the early 1950s.

LEFT: *This SC model was the general purpose version of the two-plow Case S, which itself was replaced in 1956 by the 400. Note the "chicken roost" steering linkage, just visible on the far side.*

CASE MODEL SC

Engine: Water-cooled, four-cylinder
Bore x stroke: 3.5 x 4.0 in.
Capacity: 154 cu. in.
PTO Power: 21.6 hp @ 1,550 rpm
Drawbar Power: 16.8 hp @ 1,550 rpm
Transmission: Four-speed
Speeds: 2.5–9.7 mph
Fuel Consumption: 10.55 hp/hr
  per gallon
Weight: 4,200 lb.

MINNEAPOLIS-MOLINE ZTX

[1943]

1943 ZTX

Minneapolis-Moline was working on the conversion of tractors to military use as early as 1938, and the ZTX shown here was one of these. It used the engine and chassis of the ZTS, with the cab from the smaller R series. It wasn't designed for off-road use, but for the short haulage of heavy loads, such as aircraft—many agricultural tractors were converted as aircraft tugs during the Second World War.

The five-speed transmission gave a top speed of 15.3 mph, and the heavy protective front grille was a feature unique to this model, though oddly the ZTX was painted M-M's standard Prairie Yellow. Only twenty-five ZTXs were built. In the early 1950s, a military version of the RTI industrial tractor was produced, for use in the Korean war. It was equipped with lifting lugs for loading by crane.

The Z series dated back to 1936, and remained in production right through the Second World War: the ZTU (the original row-crop) and ZTN ran from 1940 to 1948, alongside the standard-tread ZTS. The ZA series (ZAU, S, E, and N) took over in 1949. But as with the other tractor lines, there were few updates in wartime, as Minneapolis-Moline was heavily committed to producing military vehicles. One example was a prototype Jeep for the U.S. Navy in 1944. This was based on M-M tractor components, and betrayed its origins with a hood that extended backward between driver and passenger.

LEFT: *Agricultural tractors were popular conversions as military tugs. A field tractor's low-revving, torquey engine and very low gearing in a relatively compact package made it ideal for this sort of work. For the military, all-weather capabilities were vital, so the 25 Minneapolis-Moline ZTXs were all fitted with the steel cab from the Z model. Although the Comfortractor of 1938 had not been a huge success, Minneapolis-Moline used the experience to offer simpler steel cabs on some of its other tractors. It was years ahead of its rivals, though it would be another twenty years before factory-fitted cabs became a common option.*

MINNEAPOLIS-MOLINE
ZTX

(Note: Mechanically similar to ZT)
Engine: Water-cooled, four-cylinder
Bore x stroke: 3.625 x 4.5 in.
Capacity: 186 cu. in.
PTO Power: 25.2 hp
Drawbar Power: 19.8 hp
Transmission: Five-speed
Speeds: 2.2–15.3 mph
Weight: 4,280 lb.

CO-OP E3
[1945]

In 1938, the Cooperative Manufacturing Co. of Battle Creek, Michigan, had offered three tractors, the four-cylinder No.1 and six-cylinder No.2 and No.3. The No.2 was said to be capable of 28 mph on the road! All had been sold by Duplex the previous year, so it seems likely that they were built by Duplex as well. Certainly after 1945, Co-op tractors were just Canadian Cockshutt machines, repainted and rebadged to suit. There was nothing new in this badge engineering. The Allis-Chalmers U was originally built at the request of a Chicago-based farmers' co-op.

In fact, the Cockshutt 30, the Canadian company's first in-house tractor, was marketed by both Canada's farm cooperative as the CCIL 30 and by the American Farmers Union Co-op as the Co-op E3, the one pictured here. The latter was treated to a repaint in Pumpkin Orange. Mechanically, it was identical to the Cockshutt.

Unlike the short-lived Allis-Chalmers arrangement, this one evidently worked, as the E3 was followed by the Co-op E4, based on the Cockshutt 40 but again with the corporate orange livery. Cockshutt's little 20 hp 20 was sold as the Co-op E2 and the big six-cylinder 50 as the E5. Cockshutt was later taken over by White.

LEFT: *Over the years, many different tractors have worn the Co-op badge. Co-op No.2 and No.3 (shown here) for example, were both offered in the mid-1930s. Both were originally built by Duplex Machinery Co. of Battle Creek, Michigan, but after a year the company changed its name to the Co-operative Machinery Company. By 1940, a new manufacturer was listed as making the Co-ops, the Arthurdale Farm Equipment company. Another source states that the Co-ops were later produced by the Farmers Union Central Exchange of St. Paul, Minnesota, and sold under the Co-op brand. Both Co-op tractors were notable for offering a high-speed five-speed transmission, allowing road speeds of up to 20 mph on the No.3 and an alleged 28 mph on the No.2. Production ceased during the Second World War and was never restarted, so the Cockshutt-based Co-op tractors of the late 1940s and 1950s bear no relation to these Duplex-derived machines.*

CO-OP E4

Engine: Water-cooled, six-cylinder
Bore x stroke: 3.4 x 4.1 in.
Capacity: 230 cu. in.
PTO Power: 38.7 hp @ 1,650 rpm
Drawbar Power: 30.3 hp
Transmission: Six-speed
Speeds: 1.6–12.0 mph
Fuel Consumption: 9.7 hp/hr per gallon
Weight: 5,305 lb.

CASE MODEL VA
[1945]

There's one problem with building your tractor out of bought-in parts—it usually costs more than making them yourself. On the other hand, it saves time, manpower, and effort, so that's exactly what Case did in 1940. It urgently needed a small single-plow tractor to compete with machines like the John Deere L and Allis-Chalmers B. As ever, president Leon Clausen was suspicious of the whole idea of making a smaller tractor, convinced it would steal sales from its bigger siblings.

In the end, he relented, but to save time the new Model V was unveiled with a Continental 124 cu. in. motor and gear final drive from the Clark Equipment Company. Even the sheet metal was bought in. And in typical Case fashion, the Model V was both heavier and more powerful than its rivals, but its price was held down to stop it encroaching on Model S territory.

The V was soon replaced by the much longer-lived VA, which was part of the Case lineup for the next decade or so. Much was new, such as the 124 cu. in. ohv engine, now built by Case itself at the Rock Island plant. It was also the first machine to use the Case Eagle Hitch. There were lots of variations on the VA theme: VAC was the general purpose version; VAC-14 had a low seat with the driver straddling the transmission, like the Ford-Ferguson; 15,000 VAI industrial tractors were built; VAS was a high-clearance row-crop machine, of which only 1,600 were made; and the VAH pictured here had adjustable front wheel spacing. In all, nearly 60,000 VA tractors were built over a thirteen-year production run. Maybe now Mr. Clausen was finally convinced.

LEFT: The little VA proved to be quite a success for Case, despite Leon Clausen's fears that it might take sales away from existing Case models. Initially, many parts were bought in.

BELOW: Eventually, 60,000 Case VA tractors were sold—this is the VAH, with adjustable front tread, but there were many other variations on the theme.

CASE MODEL VAC

Engine: Water-cooled, four-cylinder
Bore x stroke: 3.25 x 3.75 in.
Capacity: 124 cu. in.
PTO Power: 17.0 hp @ 1,425 rpm
Drawbar Power: 12.5 hp @ 1,425 rpm
Transmission: Four-speed
Speeds: 2.3–8.4 mph
Fuel Consumption: 10.8 hp/hr per gallon
Weight: 3,199 lb.

FORDSON E27N
[1945]

In Britain, the venerable Fordson Model N would get a second chance. For the farmers in the United States, the N (which was only a mildly updated version of the original 1917 Model F, don't forget) was looking sadly outdated by the late 1930s. But things were different in Britain.

Farms were smaller and the tractor competition was less intense. Also, the Fordson had developed a very good reputation, not due just to service in the fields, but thanks to the part it played in the war effort. One-hundred and fifty thousand Fordson Ns had been built in

Ford's British factory during the Second World War. Finally, in the difficult economic conditions of 1945, there just wasn't the time and materials available to come up with something new, or to build the Ford 9N—it would have to be an update on the faithful old Fordson N.

In fact, there were some changes made. There was more power from an engine rated at 1,200 rpm. A water pump was also added, but the four-cylinder motor still used splash lubrication. It was powerful enough to make the updated E27N a three-plow machine, thanks to a new bevel-drive rear axle, updated from the old worm-drive which couldn't take the extra load. The whole thing weighed 4,000 lb. (a far cry from Henry Ford's lightweight original), though it did at least have the option of a hydraulic implement lift. The "E," incidentally, stood for "English," "27" was to identify the horsepower, and the inclusion of the "N" was to make the lineage of the tractor clear.

Thus updated, and soon with the option of a Perkins diesel engine, as well, the final incarnation of Henry Ford's Model F sold respectably well and managed to hang on right up until 1952, at which point Ford of Dagenham introduced its own new tractor, the New Major.

LEFT: *The E27N was a British update on the original Fordson Model F, now stronger, heavier, and with more power. For years, Henry Ford was unable to use his own name on tractors, as a rival American manufacturer (the Ford Tractor Co. of Minneapolis) was already producing machines under that name. Hence the name Fordson.*

FORDSON E27N GASOLINE

Engine: Water-cooled, four-cylinder
Bore x stroke: 4.13 x 5.00 in.
Capacity: 267 cu. in.
Power: 27 hp @ 1,200 rpm
Transmission: Three-speed
Weight: 4,000 lb.

MASSEY-HARRIS 102 JUNIOR
[1946]

The Massey-Harris range of tractors was looking increasingly complex by now. The 102 Junior (pictured here) was a slightly more powerful version of the 101 Junior, using a 162 cu. in. Continental power unit in place of the 101's 124 cu. in.—it was announced in 1946.

But there was a bewildering array of variants as well. The 102G and GS Junior were the standard-tread versions, the G only listed with steel wheels, the GS with pneumatic rubber tires—though the GS was also described as a 2–3 plow tractor and the G as 2-plow. There were row-crop versions of both of these, the 102 Junior Rowcrop G and GRC. And there was also an Orchard model, of course.

Without the "Junior" tag, the 102 turned into a completely different machine. As the 102G Twin Power, it replaced the four-cylinder Continental engine with one of 226 cu. in. As the name suggested, it also had M-H's well-proven twin-speed governor to allow 1,800 rpm at the belt. For 1944–45 there were G and GS versions, with either the 226 cu. in. or a 244 cu. in. Continental, depending on who you ask.

Relief was at hand. In 1947 the lineup was simplified by the new 44, which replaced all the various 102s. It turned out to be M-H's most successful machine.

LEFT: *Despite its rapidly growing range (in both size and complexity), Massey-Harris still chose to buy in engines rather than build its own. Continental was the most common choice, this being used on the entire 102 range, which was basically a powered-up version of the 101 Junior, slotting in between that tractor and the six-cylinder Super 101 and 101 Senior. There were nearly a dozen variations on the 102 theme, tagged "Junior" or "Senior," according to engine size and number of cylinders—all Juniors were four-cylinders while the Seniors were sixes. All were built in the U.S., though the confusing lineage of Massey-Harris led to tractors being built in Canada, France, and Britain all bearing the Massey-Harris badge. And all came with the company's well-proven Twin Power system, which allowed a higher-rated engine speed for belt work, and for a few more miles per hour on the road—1,500 and 1,800 rpm were the two settings.*

MASSEY-HARRIS 102 JUNIOR

Engine: Water-cooled, four-cylinder
Bore x stroke: 3.44 x 4.38 in.
Capacity: 162 cu. in.
Power: n/a
Transmission: Four-speed
Speeds: 2.2–10.1 mph
Wheelbase: 78 in.

HURLIMANN D100
[1946]

Switzerland may not be the first tractor-producing nation that springs to mind, but it has actually been home to several manufacturers. Buhrer of Zurich started building tractors in the 1930s, with advanced features like cabs, diesel engines, and three-range transmissions, before they entered the mainstream market. By the time production ceased in 1978, over 22,000 Buhrer tractors had been built.

The other major Swiss name is Hurlimann, based in St. Galen, which jumped into the tractor business in 1929. Like Buhrer, Hurlimann appears to have been a technologically advanced company —in 1939, it built what it claimed was the world's first four-cylinder direct-injection diesel tractor. The D100, introduced as the Second World War ended, was powered by that engine, adding a five-speed transmission, PTO, two-speed belt pulley, and differential lock. With 45 hp at 1,600 rpm, it was powerful enough, and also had a usefully low center of gravity, thanks to smaller than usual rear wheels.

Hurlimann was also one of the first manufacturers to build high horsepower tractors, with a 155 hp machine announced in 1966, powered by the company's own six-cylinder engine. From the late 1960s, Hurlimann increasingly used SAME components, and was later taken over by that company.

LEFT: *The D100 may have been the first four-cylinder direct injection diesel tractor in 1939, but this was the 1979 equivalent, the 5200. Although Hurlimann had diversified into producing high-horsepower tractors in the 1960s, the core of its range still consisted of compact, economical tractors like this one, which took their cue from the original D100. Until the 5200, with its new squared-off styling, 1970s Hurlimanns looked very similar to their predecessors of ten or even twenty years before—the D310 of 1975 was a good example. To go with its styling, the 5200 was a thoroughly modern tractor with a ten-speed transmission (five speeds in two ranges), and up to 52 hp. But despite its technical advances, Hurlimann was too small to survive on its own. For some time, it had been purchasing various SAME components, and it was later taken over by the Italian giant altogether. The Hurlimann range later became increasingly SAME dominated, and the current range includes the Prince compact tractors (25–42 hp), mid-range XE (50–76 hp), and big XB.*

HURLIMANN D100

Engine: Water-cooled, four-cylinder
Power: 45 hp @ 1,600 rpm
Transmission: Five-speed

OLIVER 66
[1947]

OLIVER 66 (1949)

Engine: Water-cooled, four-cylinder

Bore x stroke: 3.13 x 3.75 in.

Capacity: 129 cu. in.

PTO Power: 24 hp @ 1,600 rpm

Drawbar Power: 16.8 hp

Transmission: Six-speed

Speeds: 2.5–11.4 mph

Fuel Consumption: 9.89 hp/hr
  per gallon

Weight: 3,193 lb.

BELOW: *"Fleetline" was Oliver's new look for 1947, distinguished by the bold new seven-slatted grille.*

Nineteen forty-seven was a big year for Oliver. That year it renewed its entire tractor range, with the 70 becoming 77, 80 becoming 88, and so on. This went for the little four-cylinder 60 as well. Its major change centered around the engine, which was enlarged to 129 cu. in. thanks to a longer stroke of 3.75 in. Other than that though, this was still the same four-cylinder version of the 70's proven Waukesha-built six.

They also offered a diesel option for the first time, plus, of course, the usual kerosene-distillate. In the latter case a slightly larger bore gave 145 cu. in., to make up for kerosene's lower efficiency. Something the little 60 shared with the new generation of Olivers was "Fleetline" bodywork, which was a stylish, slightly more aggressive version of the original Oliver 70's look. The quickest way to spot a Fleetline Oliver is by the bold seven-slatted grille, which had replaced the old, unstylish, mesh grille.

The 66 was still Oliver's baby tractor, and it stayed in production for six years, until it was replaced by the Super 66 in 1954. Oliver was now making its own four-cylinder engine, which the 66 adopted, as well as a three-point hitch with Oliver's Hydra-Lectric hydraulic lift, and a three-speed governor. With a six-speed transmission, live hydraulics, and PTO, the 66 was very well equipped.

OLIVER 77
[1947]

Just as the Oliver 60 became a 66 in 1947, so the six-cylinder 70 became a 77. It was the first major update for the 70 since its introduction twelve years earlier.

The updated engines still had six cylinders, but juggling with bore and stroke dimensions (larger bore, shorter stroke) brought slightly less capacity, slightly higher engine speeds, and a little more power. Rated engine speed increased to 1,600 rpm, and there was a six-speed transmission. In gasoline and diesel form, the Waukesha-built power unit now came out at 194 cu. in., with a slightly larger 216 cu. in. for the kerosene-distillate version. But kerosene was becoming outdated—it

might be a cheaper fuel, but that didn't compensate for its lower efficiency. Instead, in 1952 Oliver unveiled a liquid petroleum gas (LPG) option, based on the standard gasoline engine. In fact, the 1950s were to be a virtual battleground of the various tractor fuel options. Kerosene/distillate was cheap but inefficient, and on the way out; gasoline gave best power, but was thirsty; LPG promised much of the power of gasoline with a cheaper fuel; and the new diesels cost more to make and buy, but they were most fuel-efficient of all. However, it would be another decade and a half before diesel emerged as the dominant fuel for all tractors.

OLIVER 77 (1952)

Engine: Water-cooled, six-cylinder
Bore x stroke: 3.31 x 3.75 in.
Capacity: 194 cu. in.
PTO Power: 34.5 hp
Drawbar Power: 25.8 hp
Transmission: Six-speed
Speeds: 2.5–11.6 mph
Weight: 4,670 lb.

BELOW: *Maybe not quite as sleek and streamlined as the 1937 model Oliver 70, but the new Fleetline 77 certainly stood out.*

MARSHALL SERIES II

[1947]

anz of Germany, SFV of France, Landini of Italy, HSCS of Hungary, and Marshall of Britain. Almost every European country seemed to produce their own variation on the classic early diesel tractor layout—a huge single-cylinder two-stroke mounted horizontally in the frame.

The Marshall tractor had its origins in the prewar 12-20, later renamed the M and reappearing after the Second World War as the Series I. Unlike its semi-diesel contemporaries, which used a hot spot in the cylinder head (the hot-bulb) to keep combustion going, the Marshall was a full diesel, relying on engine compression alone to generate the heat to cause combustion. But all of them were supremely simple machines, with no glow plug or a gasoline starting system.

As the new Series I for 1945, the prewar M was restyled for a more modern appearance, and the rated engine speed was increased from 700 rpm to 750, for more power. In fact, Marshall was to make valiant attempts to keep its big single competitive in the power stakes, but it was a losing battle against younger multi-cylinder rivals

But for the time being, the orange or green Marshalls sold to a dwindling but loyal band of owners, and their distinctive "duff-duff" exhaust note rang out across the valleys of Britain.

LEFT: *In Marshall's determined struggle to keep its single-cylinder diesel competitive against the multi-cylinder opposition in the late 1940s, they released the Series II in 1947. There were better brakes, new bearings, and improved cooling, plus larger rear tires. However, transmission failures continued to dog the latest Marshall, despite those new and larger bearings. This Achilles' heel was finally only solved with a substantially strengthened final drive in the Series III. There were lots of detail changes to the engine as well: piston, fuel pump, lubrication, and cooling all received attention, but although the Series III was able to achieve its rated 40 hp, it was unable to maintain this for long periods. Eventually, Marshall did persuade its tractor to produce a reliable 40 hp, but by then the era of the big single-cylinder diesel was rapidly drawing to a close.*

MARSHALL SERIES II

Engine: Water-cooled, single-cylinder diesel
Bore x stroke: 6.5 x 9.0 in.
Capacity: 298 cu. in.
PTO Power: 40 hp @ 750 rpm
Transmission: Three-speed
Speeds: 2.75–6.0 mph, 9 mph opt.
Weight: 6,500 lb.

MASSEY-HARRIS PONY

[1947]

Massey-Harris built very few tractors in Canada, despite being a Canadian company. In fact the little Pony was the only M-H to be produced on home soil in any numbers. Most of the Massey-Harris machines were actually manufactured in the U.S., Britain, or France.

Befitting its name, the Pony was a small single-plow tractor, aimed at small farmers, market gardeners, and tobacco growers. Weighing less than 1,900 lb., it produced 8 drawbar hp, and 10 at the belt. The U.S. market used a four-cylinder Continental engine of just 62 cu. in. It shared the same familiar styling of the bigger M-Hs and came with an adjustable front wheel width and high-clearance front axle options. What it didn't have until later was a hydraulic coupling, and apparently less than one hundred Ponys were so equipped.

Of course, it wouldn't have been a Massey-Harris without some sort of overseas connection, and later on the Pony was also assembled in France as the model 811, with a 78 cu. in. Simca engine replacing the Continental. The 811 in turn was replaced by the Pony 812 and 820, which used a 65 cu. in. Hanomag two-stroke diesel, as well as Simca or Peugeot gasoline engines.

LEFT: *Canadian-built Ponys were capable of hauling a 10-, 12- or 14-inch plow. There was some discrepancy in power figures, depending on whom one believed. Massey-Harris claimed 11.1 hp at the drawbar and 12.2 at the belt, but Nebraska testing (in September 1948) found only 8.4 and 10.4 hp respectively. Later French-made Ponys had more power (apart from a few early models, which still used the Continental). Powered by a 75 cu. in. Simca or 79 cu. in. Peugeot gasoline engine, the Pony 812 made 16 or 18 hp respectively. To suit the French market, a vineyard version was also offered, with adjustable tread down to less than a meter in width. Later still, the Pony 820 offered up to 20 hp from the Simca and Peugeot engines, thanks to an increased engine speed of 2,000 rpm. An interesting option was the 65 cu. in. twin-cylinder Hanomag two-stroke diesel. Some of these were badged as Massey-Ferguson, and sold through M-F dealers.*

MASSEY-HARRIS PONY

Engine: Water-cooled, four-cylinder
Bore x stroke: 2.38 x 3.5 in.
Capacity: 62 cu. in.
PTO Power: 10.4 hp @ 1,800 rpm
Drawbar Power: 8.3 hp
Transmission: Three-speed
Speeds: 2.7–7.0 mph
Fuel Consumption: 9.02 hp/hr per gallon
Weight: 1,890 lb.

FORD 8N
[1947]

It was almost too good to be true—and it was. On the basis of a simple handshake, Henry Ford and Harry Ferguson agreed on how the Ford 9N would come about. Basically, Ford would make it by the thousands, and sell them all to Ferguson, who would market and distribute them.

ABOVE: *The new model certainly did the trick. The 8N not only broke the link with Ferguson, it also made a profit for Ford and led to a whole new line of very successful Ford tractors.*

LEFT: *For Ford, the 8N's significance lay not in its four-speed transmission or the twenty-odd other minor changes, but that it was the first independently built and sold Ford tractor for nearly twenty years.*

That was fine when things were going well, but in 1945 Mr. Ford was eighty-two years old and in poor health. He retired, allowing his 28-year-old grandson Henry II to take over the massive Ford empire. The young Henry had some tough decisions to make. The company was losing money badly: over $25 million had been lost on the N series tractors alone, in six years.

The problem was that handshake agreement, which tied Ford into selling only to Ferguson, with no profit margin built in. As a result, Harry Ferguson was given nine months notice. From mid-1947, Ford would market and distribute the N series itself. Ferguson was furious, and took Ford to court, eventually winning over $9 million in compensation.

Part of the plan was an updated 9N—the new 8N (announced to coincide with the new Ford-only regime) had twenty design improvements over its predecessor, including a four-speed gearbox, better brakes, and a position control for the hydraulic lift. Ford needed to make a splash with the updated 9N, to underline that this was now an independent Ford operation. *Time* magazine reported that 300 guests, "quaffed beer and cocktails, munched cold meats and salads buffet-style then watched a new Ford tractor plow the hard clay of the soil outside." It was a huge success, and over 100,000 were sold in the first full year, outselling its nearest rival by ten to one. More to the point for Ford, every one of them made a profit.

FORD 8N

Engine: Water-cooled, four-cylinder

Bore x stroke: 3.19 x 3.75 in.

Capacity: 120 cu. in.

PTO Power: 21.1 hp @ 2,000 rpm

Drawbar Power: 13.6 hp

Transmission: Four-speed

Speeds: 2.8–10.2 mph

Fuel Consumption: 6.74 hp/hr per gallon

Weight: 2,714 lb.

MINNEAPOLIS-MOLINE UTC
[1948]

Minneapolis-Moline got very good value out of its U-series tractor. Announced in 1938 as the row-crop UTU, it was one of the new generation of Prairie Gold M-Ms—bright, up-to-date, and easy to maintain. It was styled along much the same lines as the little Z, but with 38 hp its 283 cu. in. four-cylinder engine was sixty-five percent more powerful. Why was it a good value? Because there were at least three variations on the theme. Apart from the original UTU, there was the infamous UDLX "Comfortractor."

In 1948 came this, the third U series variation. The UTC Cane tractor was specifically designed (as you might expect) for cane cultivation. There was an arched front axle and exceptionally high clearance —an essential for sugarcane work. With the five-speed transmission that was already an M-M trademark, the UTC cost $3,200 in 1954, its final year. Even allowing for the extra metalwork in the UTC's high-clearance chassis, that reflected a big increase since six years before, when the UTU cost just $1,586 on steel wheels.

LEFT: *For sugarcane cultivation, an ultra-high clearance was essential. Otherwise, the Minneapolis-Moline UTC was similar to the other U-series M-Ms.*

BELOW: *UTS, the standard-tread version of the U-series. In the M-M lineup, the U-series came one down from the big GTA, and one up from the Z.*

LPG (liquid petroleum gas) was just starting to replace kerosene as the cheaper alternative to gasoline, and in fact M-M had pioneered LPG power in 1941. It was not only cheaper than gasoline, but gave better economy and needed less maintenance, though a special tank was required. M-M must have had faith in LPG as the fuel of the future, as it didn't offer a diesel option on the U until the mid 1950s.

MINNEAPOLIS-MOLINE UTC

(Note: Specifications for mechanically identical UTS)
Engine: Water-cooled, four-cylinder
Bore x stroke: 4.25 x 5.0 in.
Capacity: 283 cu. in.
PTO Power: 36.1 hp @ 1,300 rpm
Torque: 247 lb. ft. @ 949 rpm
Drawbar Power: 26.8 hp
Transmission: Five-speed
Speeds: 2.5–14.0 mph
Fuel Consumption: 8.66 hp/hr per gallon
Weight: 5,905 lb.

GIBSON MODEL I
[1948]

Gibson tractors, built in Longmont, Colorado, were only sold for a few years after the Second World War. Wilbur Gibson formed the company in March 1946, as an offshoot from his father's railcar business, which had already begun experimenting with tractors.

The first tractor to roll out of Gibson's brand new factory was the little single-cylinder Model A (later SD), which was powered by a 6 hp Wisconsin AEH air-cooled engine. It was a tiny machine, weighing just 875 lb., and (unusually for a wheeled tractor) was steered by a lever as standard, although a conventional steering wheel was optional.

Gibson lost no time in developing bigger tractors. The slightly larger EF used another Wisconsin motor, a twin-cylinder this time, and was rated to pull one 14-inch plow. The full-size range commenced with the two-plow H, which started production in 1948. This was powered by a 133 cu. in. four-cylinder Hercules engine, rated at 25 belt hp. The biggest Gibson was the I model pictured here, with a six-cylinder Hercules. This one measured 149 cu. in. and was rated at 40 belt hp, allowing the I to pull a three-bottom plow. The I weighed around 4,500 lb., and three versions were offered: I with tricycle front end, IFS with fixed front axle, and IFA with adjustable front axle.

But despite the success of the smaller Gibsons (over 50,000, according to one estimate) the bigger ones only sold in small numbers. In any case, the company was now busy with a forklift contract for the U.S. Navy. Gibson was taken over by Helene Curtis Industries in 1952, by which time tractor production had already ceased.

LEFT: *Tested at Nebraska in May 1949, the Model I hit no problems in its forty-four hours of running time, although a smaller Model H tested in the same month was found to have faulty connected-rod bearings. The I produced 39.5 belt hp at maximum load—certainly respectable for the relatively small 149 cu. in. Hercules engine, probably the smallest six-cylinder unit available in a tractor at that time.*

GIBSON MODEL I
GASOLINE

Engine: Water-cooled, six-cylinder

Bore x stroke: 3.4 x 4.1 in.

Capacity: 149 cu. in.

PTO Power: 39.5 hp @ 1,800 rpm

Drawbar Power: 29.1 hp @ 1,800 rpm

Transmission: Four-speed

Speeds: 2.0–14.7 mph

Fuel Consumption: 10.0 hp/hr per gallon

Weight: 4,512 lb.

ALLIS-CHALMERS MODEL G
[1948]

Allis-Chalmers had the habit of coming up with the occasional technological milestone, from among what was otherwise a rather unadventurous range of tractors. It was the first manufacturer to offer pneumatic tires in the 1930s, and the first to offer a turbocharged diesel tractor in the early 1960s. But this miniature machine was Allis-Chalmers's 1940s innovation—the Model G.

Its radical design turned the traditional tractor layout on its head, with the engine at the back and the driver up front. In 1948, it probably seemed back to front, but there were plenty of advantages to this layout. Mounting the engine directly over the wheels placed eighty percent of the tractor's weight there, which was a great help to traction. Just as important, it gave the driver a completely unrestricted view of the work going on below, a particular boon when working on smaller, more delicate crops.

The little Model G was aimed specifically at nurseries and vegetable gardens, and at those farmers who couldn't even afford the bargain basement Model B, which was Allis-Chalmers's smallest conventional tractor.

LEFT: *Allis-Chalmers' "back to front" tractor, the little Model G, actually made a lot of sense. For market gardeners, it was easier to use than a conventional tractor, and not to mention a whole lot cheaper.*

BELOW: *This is what you call the bare bones. Bodywork was a luxury the little G did not pander too. The only concession was some sheeting to keep the rain off the engine, so the driver was somewhat exposed in all weathers!*

Allis didn't actually make an engine small enough to suit the G, so it bought in the 62 cu. in. four from Continental, which at 1,800 rpm gave 9 drawbar hp and 10.9 hp at the belt. Some people wanted more power, but A-C never responded, perhaps fearing that a 20 hp G would take sales away from the B Model.

Despite its small size the Model G was certainly well-equipped. Many of the other small tractors aimed at this market made do with single- or twin-cylinder motors, but the Model G's was actually a miniature four. It also had a four-speed transmission (with first gear low enough to allow 0.75 mph at part throttle) and an adjustable track between 36 and 64 inches. Customers were even able to specify an optional hydraulic lift for an extra $99, while a belt pulley would only cost the customer an extra $19. The Model G was assembled in Dieppe, France, as well as in the United States, in Gadsden, Alabama.

ALLIS-CHALMERS MODEL G

Engine: Water-cooled, four-cylinder
Capacity: 62 cu. in.
PTO Power: 10.9 hp @ 1,800 rpm
Drawbar Power: 9 hp @ 1,800 rpm
Transmission: Four-speed

FORDSON E27N DIESEL
[1948]

Just as it seemed that the elderly Fordson E27N was ready to be put out to pasture, it was given a final lease of life by Ford of England. The E27N was the English factory's update of the prewar Fordson Model N, which in turn was a mildly modernized 1917 Model F. The F's gasoline engine had never been designed to pull a three-bottom plow, and in its latest powered-up form, service life was limited.

The solution was a modern diesel. In Britain, diesel tractors were already far advanced. Frank Perkins (founder of Perkins Diesels, still supplying tractor engines today) had converted his own Fordson to diesel power. This was so successful that it went into production, using the Perkins P6 six-cylinder engine. This added 500 lb. to the weight of the Fordson, but with a meaty 45 hp at 1,500 rpm, transformed its performance. The rear axle was strengthened to cope with the extra power, while the standard transmission and clutch seemed happy enough to cope.

By 1952, when the E27N was replaced, 23,000 Perkins-powered versions had been built, all recognizable by the distinctive four-ringed Perkins badged on the front grille. With such solid sales figures it was hardly surprising that the Fordson's replacement, the New Major, had a diesel option from day one.

LEFT: *This was the ultimate Anglicized Fordson, one that could trace its roots right back to the original Fordson Model F of 1917. Production of the F was transferred to Ireland, then to Ford's Dagenham plant, near London, in the late 1920s. The British went on building and selling the F, gradually updating it as the E27N—it might have lost favor in the United States, but the old Fordson was still one of Britain's favorite tractors. But what it lacked for the postwar British market (and badly needed) was more power, and a diesel option. The Perkins P6 solved both these problems at a stroke, providing a huge power boost to 45 hp, along with diesel reliability and economy. Remarkably, the E27N's standard transmission and clutch were able to cope with this sixty-six percent power increase, though the rear axle was beefed up to suit. Today, a Perkins-powered Fordson, with that four-ringed badge on the grille, is a collector's item.*

FORDSON E27N DIESEL

Engine: Water-cooled, six-cylinder
Bore x stroke: 3.50 x 5.00 in.
Capacity: 288 cu. in.
Power: 45 hp @ 1,500 rpm
Transmission: Three-speed
Weight: 4,500 lb.

ALLIS-CHALMERS WD45

[1948]

This might look very conventional, but the Allis-Chalmers WD45 was in some ways just as radical as the little Model G, with lots of new features. Power shift wheels gave instant rear tread adjustment. It used the tractor's own power to move the rear wheels in or out on spiral rails, a simple but effective system which ranked alongside other milestones of tractor technology like the three-point hitch.

The two-clutch power control gave continuous power takeoff, and the oil-bath transmission clutch could take any amount of slippage. There was also traction booster, Allis-Chalmers's own version of hydraulic implement draft control. A new snap coupler allowed genuine in-seat hitching of implements.

The engine wasn't ignored, being larger than in the WC it replaced and with "Power Crater," a concave piston crown that was said to increase turbulence.

ALLIS-CHALMERS WD45

Engine: Water-cooled, four-cylinder
Capacity: 226 cu. in.
PTO Power: 40.47 hp
Drawbar Power: 30.18 hp
Fuel Consumption: 10.64 hp/hr
  per gallon
Speeds: 2.5–11.3 mph
Weight: 3,955 lb.

BELOW: *For the A-C owner who thinks he has everything—a monogrammed umbrella!*

LEFT: *The WD45D was A-C's first diesel tractor. Unlike John Deere and International who built their own, A-C bought one off the shelf from Buda.*

BELOW: *Postwar improvements included power-shift wheel adjustment, traction booster hydraulic draft control, snap coupler, and a live PTO.*

NUFFIELD UNIVERSAL
[1949]

A British success story. The Nuffield group (makers of Morris cars and MG sports cars) was encouraged, by the British government, to try and build a tractor immediately after the Second World War. Quite simply, Britain was bankrupt after six years of war, and desperately needed to export goods in order to earn foreign currency. It also needed tractors to increase food production—most tractors in Britain at this time were aging Fordsons, and horse teams were still a common sight.

Nuffield went to work immediately, and the Nuffield Universal was ready for production in 1946, though it didn't see production for another two years, thanks to steel shortages. When it finally appeared, the Nuffield came in M3 row-crop or M4 utility versions. You had to pay extra for a hydraulic three-point linkage or a PTO, but these were still rare on the cheaper tractors.

It worked well, but to overcome possible resistance to what was an unknown name in tractors, the Nuffield was was given a Fordson-esque appearance and painted Allis-Chalmers orange! The first engine was Nuffield's own 38 hp unit, but a Perkins diesel option arrived after two years. No British tractor maker could afford to be without a diesel, and by 1955 ninety-five percent of Nuffields were diesel powered. So the Nuffield tractor was a success, and not only for its maker—eighty percent of them were built for export, earning Britain that valuable foreign currency.

LEFT: *It may have benefited from a Ford-like appearance and Allis-Chalmers coloring, but the Nuffield would probably have succeeded anyway, thanks to its sturdy build and straightforward design. Developed with exports in mind, by the mid-1950s it was being sold in the U.S. in both gasoline PM-4 and diesel DM-4 form. The diesel was now Morris's own unit, in place of the Perkins, a 208 cu. in. engine that, produced 223 lb. ft. of torque at 1,329 rpm. At the rated engine speed of 2,000 rpm, according to Nebraska, it produced 45.3 hp at the belt with an impressive 15.3 hp/hr per gallon.*

NUFFIELD UNIVERSAL PM-4

Engine: Water-cooled, four-cylinder
Bore x stroke: 4.74 x 4.72 in.
Capacity: 208 cu. in.
PTO Power: 45.4 hp @ 2,000 rpm
Torque: 223 lb. ft. @ 1,329 rpm
Drawbar Power: 32.9 hp
Transmission: Five-speed
Speeds: 2.3–17.3 mph
Fuel Consumption: 13.77 hp/hr
 per gallon
Weight: 7,011 lb.

COCKSHUTT 40
[1949]

Cockshutt is best known for its smaller tractors, the little 20 and 30, but it offered bigger six-cylinder machines as well. The larger 40 and 50 were powered by Buda engines—Cockshutt never made its own power units, being too small for this to be economically viable.

The 40 shown here was the Canadians' biggest tractor at the time, and its Buda came in gasoline, distillate, or diesel. It didn't quite justify the "40" tag, producing just under 39 hp at Nebraska, at the rated 1,650 rpm. Cockshutt wasn't a big name like John Deere or IHC, but its tractors were

right up to date. The 40 came with a six-speed transmission, plus two reverse, while hydraulics and a live PTO were optional. There was a Cockshutt 50 as well, essentially exactly the same machine, but with a slightly larger version of the same Buda six engine.

All the Budas (20, 30, 40, and 50) were also sold under the Co-Op brand—Cockshutt had taken over the National Farm Equipment Co-Op in 1954. They later hired the famed industrial designer Raymond Loewy to redesign their tractors, but he was on a losing battle—the original Cockshutts were among the neatest-looking tractors ever made.

LEFT: *The good-looking Cockshutts of the late 1940s were actually the first tractors this Canadian company had built in-house. The Cockshutt Plow Company had been making implements since 1877, but in the 1920s began selling Hart-Parrs alongside its plows, painted and badged as Cockshutt machines. It wasn't until the end of the Second World War that Cockshutt decided to build its own tractors, launching the four-cylinder 30 in 1946. It was an attractive machine, but what really made it stand out was the continuously running PTO and hydraulics— that is, they kept operating if the transmission was declutched, a major step forward in tractor design. Within a few years all major manufacturers had followed the Canadians' lead, but the Cockshutt engineers came up with the term "live" PTO. All Cockshutts enjoyed this feature, the four-cylinder 20 and 30, and six-cylinder 40 (shown here) and 50. The company was later taken over by White.*

COCKSHUTT 40 GASOLINE

Engine: Water-cooled, four-cylinder
Bore x stroke: 3.4 x 4.1 in.
Capacity: 230 cu. in.
PTO Power: 38.7 hp @ 1,650 rpm
Drawbar Power: 30.3 hp
Transmission: Six-speed
Speeds: 1.6–12.0 mph
Fuel Consumption: 9.7 hp/hr per gallon
Weight: 5,305 lb.

JOHN DEERE MODEL R

[1949]

The Model R was a landmark machine for John Deere in three ways: it was the biggest tractor it had ever made to date, its first ever five-plow machine, and its first diesel. The latter was perhaps the most significant of all. Diesel development had been held back by the Second World War, but now the restraints were off. Its origins lay before the war, with the first signs of a horsepower war to cope with ever-larger farms. Fine, except that large, powerful gasoline engines use a great deal of fuel.

Even during the war, John Deere had its answer on the drawing board. The radical new R was no more nor less than a diesel version of the classic Deere twin-cylinder motor. At 416 cu. in., it was bigger than almost any previous JD, and more powerful, at 51 PTO hp. But it was more fuel efficient than any other big tractor, and that's what customers wanted. There were other innovations as well—a live power takeoff and a live Powr-Trol hydraulic system.

As salt in the wound for other manufacturers, the Model R was cheaper to run than any comparable rival. Tested at Nebraska in 1949, it set a new record for fuel efficiency, at 17.35 hp/hr per gallon, which was unbroken for six years. Even then, the new economy king was the John Deere 80, the Model R's successor!

Apart from a solitary Cockshutt (1958) and a Massey-Ferguson (1965) no modern tractor would surpass the Model R's efficiency (apart from other John Deeres) until 1973.

LEFT: *The Model R was a real departure for John Deere (its first diesel, and biggest-ever machine) yet it remained faithful to the twin-cylinder concept.*

ABOVE: *John Deere liked to promote its tractors as one of the family. It's a recurring theme in U.S. tractor advertising over the years.*

BELOW: *The R's cylinders measured over 200 cu. in. each, so a gasoline engine was provided to start it. The updated 80 used an electric starter and 24 volts.*

JOHN DEERE R DIESEL

Engine Type: Water-cooled twin-cylinder diesel
Bore x stroke: 5.75 x 8.0 in.
Capacity: 416 cu. in.
PTO Power: 51 hp @ 1,000 rpm
Drawbar Power: 46 hp @ 1,000 rpm
Transmission: Five-speed
Speeds: 2.1–11.5 mph
Fuel Consumption: 17.63 hp/hr per gallon

The 1950s:
AMPLI-TORC & MULTIPOWER

For almost all of the 1940s, tractor development had been put on hold. For the first half of the decade, the U.S. tractor industry was diverted by war; for the second half, it was too busy keeping up with a massive pent-up demand for new machines to worry too much about technical innovation.

But in the 1950s, normal competition was resumed. Customers were becoming more discerning—it wasn't enough to churn out aging machines into the eager embrace of a tractor-starved market. Hence the rapid development of diesel engines and more sophisticated transmissions during the 1950s, not to mention a resumption of long-term research and development projects—Oliver experimented with ultra high-compression gasoline engines, Ford with turbines, and Allis-Chalmers with fuel cells. It was also a time of relative prosperity for farmers—they could afford to spend more money on more complex machinery. Reflecting a faster, more competitive world, tractors had to offer more power, more gear ratios, more features every year, just to keep up. The pace of life was heating up.

Two factors in particular dominated U.S. tractor design in the 1950s—alternative fuels and multispeed transmissions. Since the first internal combustion engine tractors had chuffed their way into the fields in the early twentieth century, two fuels had been available—gasoline and kerosene. Gasoline produced more power, but kerosene was a cheaper fuel. During the 1920s, kerosene was gradually replaced by distillate, but eventually that too fell out of

use—not only were they more powerful, but gasoline engines were easier to start, diluted their lubricating oil less, and used the same fuel as the farm truck, so only one stock of fuel needed to be kept on tap.

The trouble with gasoline engines, and this was an increasing problem as tractors became ever larger and more powerful, was that they used a lot of fuel. Gas might be cheap, but it still cost money. In Europe (see Chapter 3) gasoline wasn't so cheap, and diesel tractors had been developed as an answer. Cubic inch for cubic inch, diesel was less powerful than gas, but far more fuel efficient, not to mention more reliable and longer lived. U.S. manufacturers took longer to take the diesel route, but encouraged by the success of Caterpillar, which pioneered U.S. diesels in the 1930s, they began offering diesel in the early 1950s.

There were a few exceptions, though. International introduced the diesel powered WD40 back in 1935, and the Farmall M four years later. As we've seen, John Deere launched its first diesel in 1949 (the big twin-cylinder Model R), and the same year Cockshutt of Canada began offering a Buda diesel engine on its mid-range 40 tractor. Then the floodgates opened. Some manufacturers followed Cockshutt's example and bought in diesels, others developed their own, either as all-new designs or based on existing gasoline engines. Within a few years, no major

RIGHT: *A simple, basic Minneapolis-Moline of the late 1940s. The following decade would make tractors more powerful, more capable, more complex, and more expensive.*

ABOVE: *The 1950s were the final decade for the twin-cylinder John Deere range. This 60 replaced the Model A, and remained JD's best-selling tractor.*

BELOW: *A family of six-cylinder engines (gasoline, LPG, and diesel) plus other changes transformed the Case LA into the very forward-looking 500.*

manufacturer was without a diesel option: Oliver offered its first diesel in 1950, Massey-Harris and Minneapolis-Moline followed in 1952, Case in 1953 with an all-new family of engines, and Allis-Chalmers in 1954. Ford is absent from this list, but for a good reason. Diesel power started at the larger end of the market, and Ford's

little N series was too small to qualify. In any case, the company was able to import the diesel-powered Fordson Major and Power Major from Britain, which filled the gap. The Europeans, of course, were already there, either with single-cylinder diesels from Lanz, Landini, Marshall, and others, or the new range of modern multicylinder engines from Perkins. The latter, in particular, was to become a major supplier of proprietary diesels throughout the tractor industry.

Although the International diesels had been on the market for some years, it was the John Deere R, with its new fuel-economy records, that drove home the message to U.S. farmers. The scale of this change is well illustrated by the Nebraska tractor tests of the time, an excellent pointer to what sort of tractors were on sale in the U.S. In 1950, only twenty-five percent of the tractors tested were diesels, and nearly seventy percent were gas. The following year, a flood of new models turned the tables, with nearly sixty percent

diesel and forty-five percent gas. But the turnaround wasn't as rapid as that implies. At the end of the decade, the figures were forty-five percent and thirty-five percent. It wasn't until 1979 that Nebraska tests were one-hundred percent diesel.

In fact, the 1950s and 1960s were something of a battleground between three alternative fuels: gasoline, diesel, and LPG (liquid petroleum gas). As far as mainstream manufacturers were concerned, Minneapolis-Moline was the pioneer of LPG. As early as 1941, it was selling an LPG-powered U model, with a higher compression version of the standard gasoline engine. In the U.S., LPG's main advantage was its cheapness, especially in oil-producing areas, as it was a byproduct of oil refining. Other manufacturers were slow to offer LPG, so there were numerous kits on offer to enable the conversion of existing tractors. The gasoline carburetor was modified, or a special LPG carburetor fitted, and the gasoline tank replaced by an LPG tank—sometimes an LPG cylinder was simply chained to the front of the tractor. As a tractor fuel, LPG was fairly popular through the 1950s and early 1960s, but by 1969 no new LPG tractors were being tested at Nebraska, a good indication that its days as an alternative fuel were over.

But the search for alternatives was ongoing. Remember how Oliver pioneered the use of high-compression gasoline in the 1930s? Its six-cylinder 70 used the high octane 68-70 gasoline. In 1954, it was still experimenting with higher compression and unveiled the XO-121 engine. This had a

ABOVE: *While its American rivals were developing their own diesels, Ford simply imported ready-made diesel Fordsons, such as this New Major.*

BELOW: *The early diesels of the 1950s led (eventually) to twenty-first century tractors like this, with electronic injection control, cleaner emissions, and high power.*

compression ratio of 12 to 1 (7 to 1 was a good average at the time) and produced forty-four percent more power than the standard model. Its 100 octane fuel was specially supplied by the Ethyl Corporation.

Ford was looking further ahead with its Typhoon experimental tractor, revealed in 1957. This used a gas turbine engine of great smoothness and high power. At the time, interest was high in gas turbines, which were being seriously considered by many car manufacturers. International Harvester built a turbine tractor, too, powered by a derated helicopter engine. But for tractors, turbines were a dead end. Gas turbines might be compact, smooth, and powerful, but they lacked the low-speed torque so essential to tractor operation. And, the ultimate killer, they used more fuel than a gasoline engine, let

alone diesel. We heard no more about gas turbine tractors.

In some ways, the Allis-Chalmers fuel cell tractor of 1959 was more promising. Fuel cells produce electricity by a chemical reaction of a variety of fuels—hydrogen, oxygen, and methane are examples, though the A-C machine used propane. And electric motors are ideal for tractors, giving linear torque from very low speeds. Fuel cells have the added advantage of being very clean in operation, compared to fossil fuels such as diesel and gasoline. The A-C fuel cell tractor, revealed to the press in 1959, certainly worked. Its 1,008 fuel cells powered a 20 hp electric motor, enough to pull a two-furrow plow with up to 3,000 lb. at the drawbar. It never entered production, but work on fuel cells continues—if nothing else, their ability to run on renewable fuels could mean their

ABOVE: *Ferguson merged with Massey-Harris in 1953, and from 1957 all their tractors were badged as "Massey-Fergusons" in the new corporate colors of red over gray.*

time will come when oil becomes scarce. Whatever their fuel—diesel, gasoline, LPG—production tractors were getting more powerful by the year. Before the Second World War, 30–40 hp at the PTO was the top power class. In 1949, the John Deere R produced just over 50 hp. Then sixty became the new target, and by 1955 the Oliver Super 99, powered by a GM two-stroke supercharged diesel, produced 72 hp. The 100 hp tractor wasn't here yet, though it was on the way.

But all this extra power would be of little use without a transmission that could take advantage of it. Through the 1920s and 1930s, tractors had gradually acquired

ABOVE: *Orchard tractors, with their streamlined metalwork to prevent damage to valuable trees, were an important part of the tractor market. This is a Case 400, all new for 1955.*

BELOW: *Case's new engine family could be produced in four- or six-cylinder form, and as either gasoline, LPG, or diesel. This is the 377 cu. in. six-cylinder diesel in the 500.*

more transmission ratios in their simple, car-type gearboxes: from two, to three, to four, and Minneapolis-Moline was offering five speeds by the time war broke out. However, powerful tractors needed a wider range of speeds to cover everything from field work at a slow walking pace to fast hauling on the road. Simple transmissions couldn't provide this. Worse still, shifting down a gear in the field entailed stopping the tractor and restarting, the last thing drivers wanted when hitting a sticky patch of soil. Faster road speeds were sought after (saving fuel as well as time) in a high gear. Some companies offered bolt-on devices to increase the road speed, such as the M-W gear conversion for Farmall H and M tractors—it provided nine forward speeds and up to 16 mph.

In short, the time was right for the tractor manufacturers themselves to come up with a solution. International got there first, with the "Torque Amplifier" in 1954. This was a two-speed planetary transmission mounted in front of the standard five-speed. It thus gave two ranges, doubling the ratios to ten forward and two reverse. In low range, ground speed was reduced by thirty-two percent and pulling power

increased by forty-eight percent. Better still, the driver could shift between ratios on the go, without having to stop, which was a great boon for field work. So successful was the "TA," as it was known, that it was fitted to some International machines up to 1980.

International's rivals soon responded. Minneapolis–Moline's similar "Ampli-Torc" appeared a couple of years later, but Case took a different route. "Case-O-Matic" (1957) replaced the conventional clutch with a torque converter, which allowed easier starting with heavy loads, and could be switched in to increase pulling ability in sticky patches. When the going was easier,

RIGHT: *International's Torque Amplifier pioneered a new form of transmission, adding a dual range to the existing unit, to double the number of ratios available, and allowing the driver to shift gears on the move.*

BELOW: *Flying the Farmall banner in the mid-1950s was this Super M-TA, well equipped with Torque Amplifier (for ten forward speeds), 264 cu. in. diesel, and live PTO.*

the torque converter could be locked out to give direct drive. Actual transmission ratios were four- or six-speed, depending on the model, but in 1959 Case-O-Matic was updated with eight-speed dual range and eight-speed shuttle options. Meanwhile, Allis-Chalmers unveiled "Power Director," a twin clutch setup (one foot, one hand operated) which could be used to reduce speed and increase pulling power. Massey-Ferguson offered "Multipower" and Oliver the "Power Booster" (both twelve speeds with shift on the go), while Ford's version (announced in 1959) was the clutchless "Select-O-Speed"—if nothing else, these developments kept copywriters in work!

Other technical developments reflected the increasing sophistication of tractors. Power steering was

increasingly common—as with multispeed transmissions, this was presaged by several aftermarket kits. Disc brakes were another advance, giving a longer life than the old contracting band brakes, and being less prone to fade. But driver comfort was still fairly rudimentary, apart from some seat improvements, with no cabs available—even as an option. Nor was there any attempt to provide rollover protection for the driver, and so fatalities continued each year. Most tractors were now using a variation of the Ferguson three-point hitch, simply because it was the best solution. There was an urgent need for standardization, so that a range of implements from different manufacturers could be easily fitted to any tractor and swapped around. Finally the American Society of Agricultural Engineers (ASAE) and the Farm and Industrial Equipment Institute (FIEI) laid down an industry standard, which made life much simpler for the implement manufacturers, not to mention farmers.

Diesel power, multispeed transmission, and widespread use of the three-point hitch—in a single decade, many U.S. tractors had come to adopt the basics of the modern farm tractor.

ABOVE: *Six-speed gate for a John Deere, and the age of the multispeed transmission, with ten, twelve, and more ratios, was here.*

BELOW: *Neat electrical box on the Farmall Super M-TA, housing the ammeter, ignition switch, light switch, and fuse.*

MINNEAPOLIS-MOLINE V

[1950]

With its big U series and the bigger still GTA, Minneapolis-Moline had worthy contenders in the big and mid-range tractor markets. What it lacked was a sub-20 hp machine to rival the Allis-Chalmers B, John Deere H, and smallest Farmalls. The demand for these little single-plow tractors was growing, but M-M's own two-plow R was too heavy and expensive to compete. The company had toyed with the idea of a miniature version of the R, and twenty-five prototype YTs were built, with a twin-cylinder engine based on an R power unit cut in half. They were not a success, and all were eventually recalled by the factory.

In 1950 a solution presented itself—a ready-made small tractor and a dealer network in the southeastern U.S., where M-M's coverage was weak. The B. F. Avery Company of Louisville, Kentucky, had both of these, and when it came up for sale, M-M bought it.

There were two well-established tractors that were part of the deal. The single-plow V (pictured here) weighed just 1,612 lb. and was powered by a 65 cu. in. Hercules engine—it was already popular with vegetable and tobacco farmers. And the light two-plow BG (132 cu. in. engine, 2,880 lb.) allowed M-M to move its own R up as a heavy two-plow machine. It all sounded ideal, but for whatever reason it didn't work—M-M dropped the little Averys after only two years.

LEFT: *The Model V pictured here was a single-plow machine, powered by a tiny Hercules four-cylinder engine of 65 cu. in. The year before the takeover, this was joined by the larger BF, again Hercules four-cylinder powered, but of 133 cu. in. producing 22 hp at the drawbar and 27 hp at the PTO—rated speed was 1,800 rpm. There was a four-speed transmission, giving 2.4 to 13.1 mph. The two-plow BF had hydraulic controls and adjustable rear tread, while three front ends were available.*

MINNEAPOLIS-MOLINE V

Engine: Water-cooled, four-cylinder Hercules ZXB-3
Bore x stroke: 2.6 x 3.0 in.
Capacity: 65 cu. in.
Weight: 1,612 lb.

MINNEAPOLIS-MOLINE BG

Engine: Water-cooled, four-cylinder Hercules 1XB-3
Bore x stroke: 3.25 x 4.0 in.
Capacity: 132 cu. in.
Weight: 2,880 lb.

OLIVER 88
[1950]

This was the biggest of Oliver's new Fleetline range, announced in 1947 to celebrate the marque's centenary. Sharing new modern styling, the 66, 77, and 88 replaced the 60, 70, and 80 respectively.

These three tractors looked similar and shared many parts in order to cut costs. But while the 66 and 77 were updates, the 88 was a new machine. Out went the 80's old four-cylinder motor, which could trace its lineage back to the days of Hart-Parr. In came a modern 231 cu. in. Waukesha six in gasoline or diesel forms. With over 43 hp at the PTO, this was a powerful machine for its time, and according to author P. W. Ertel, "The first combatant in a row-crop tractor horsepower war that would last into the 1970s." The 88 could still be had in kerosene form, in which case a rather bigger bore Waukesha of 265 cu. in. was offered. All 88s had a six-speed transmission (with two reverse ratios) and a thermostatically controlled cooling system. Rated as a four-plow tractor, it came in three row-crop versions: dual narrow-front, single front wheel, and adjustable wide-front. Standard-tread, orchard, industrial, and high-crop versions were available as well. More power came in 1954 with the Super 88, but Oliver's high-horsepower tractor remained the big 99.

As for the 88, although launched in 1947, this was very much Oliver's upper mid-range tractor of the 1950s—updated as the Super 88 and later the 880, it bequeathed some parts to the 1962 1800.

LEFT AND ABOVE: *The 88 was a radical update on the old four-cylinder 80. With a six-cylinder engine in gasoline, diesel, or kerosene form, it marked a decisive break with the Hart-Parr-inspired 80, which could trace its roots back to the 1920s.*

OLIVER 88 DIESEL

Engine: Water-cooled, six-cylinder
Bore x stroke: 3.5 x 4.0 in.
Capacity: 231 cu. in.
PTO Power: 43.5 hp @ 1,600 rpm
Drawbar Power: 29.4 hp
Transmission: Six-speed
Speeds: 2.5–11.8 mph
Fuel Consumption: 12.9 hp/hr
   per gallon
Weight: 5,680 lb.

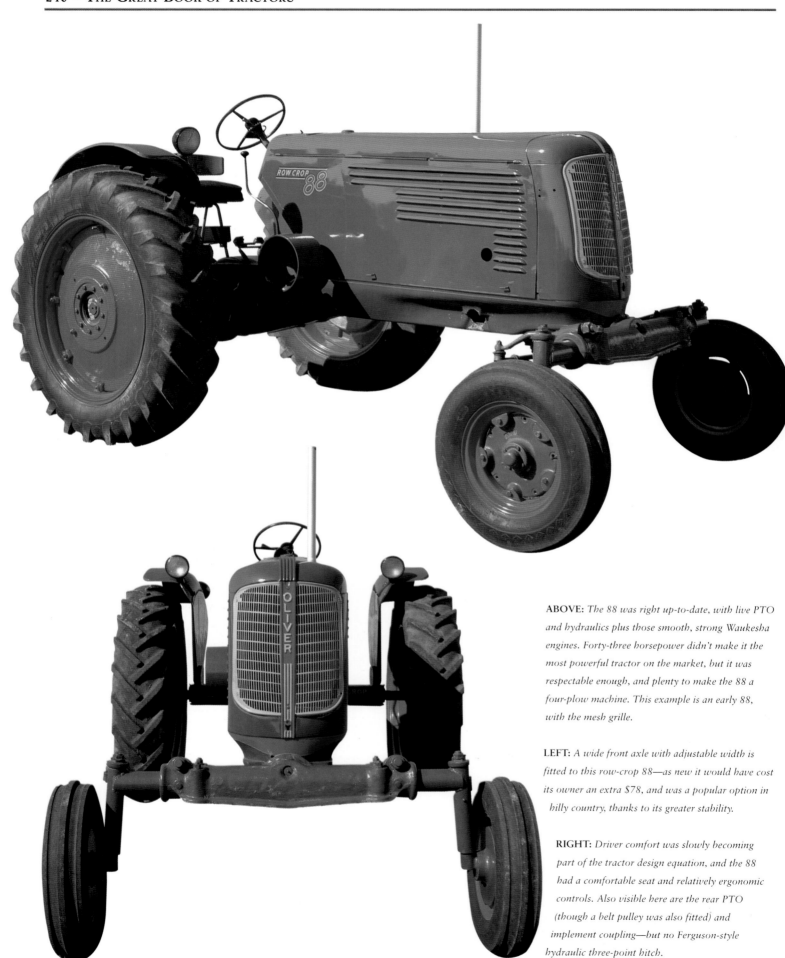

ABOVE: *The 88 was right up-to-date, with live PTO and hydraulics plus those smooth, strong Waukesha engines. Forty-three horsepower didn't make it the most powerful tractor on the market, but it was respectable enough, and plenty to make the 88 a four-plow machine. This example is an early 88, with the mesh grille.*

LEFT: *A wide front axle with adjustable width is fitted to this row-crop 88—as new it would have cost its owner an extra $78, and was a popular option in hilly country, thanks to its greater stability.*

RIGHT: *Driver comfort was slowly becoming part of the tractor design equation, and the 88 had a comfortable seat and relatively ergonomic controls. Also visible here are the rear PTO (though a belt pulley was also fitted) and implement coupling—but no Ferguson-style hydraulic three-point hitch.*

TURNER V4
[1950]

TURNER V4

Engine: Water-cooled, V-4

Bore x stroke: 3.75 x 4.5 in.

Capacity: 207 cu. in.

Drawbar Power: 32 hp

PTO Power: 40 hp

Transmission: Four-speed

The Turner V4 tractor—"The Yeoman of England"—looked very good, sounded unique, and according to its maker, would give the pull of a crawler with the economy of a wheeled tractor. The reality turned out to be very different.

Turner, based in Wolverhampton in the English Midlands, was a newcomer to the tractor business in 1949, looking for a new outlet for its established range of industrial diesel engines. A family of three was offered: a single-cylinder, a V-twin, and V-4, all with the same 3.75 in. bore and 4.5 in. stroke. It was the 4V95 V-4, with its 68 degree cylinder angle, that formed the basis of the Turner tractor. Rated at 40 hp with good fuel economy, it looked like a useful power unit for a utility tractor.

Sadly, it proved not quite powerful enough, and the Turner tractor itself was woefully unreliable. The engine often overheated, the automotive steering box wasn't up to rugged farm use, and the transmission had some serious weaknesses, especially in third gear and the final drive.

All these problems could have been overcome with time, but the Turner was selling too slowly. It was too expensive, and even after the price was cut, it still cost considerably more than a Fordson Diesel Major. Sales dwindled, and less than 2,500 Turners found homes in eight years. Turner sensibly decided to concentrate on transmission manufacture, and still produces them today.

LEFT: *A promising design that failed to deliver in practice. Nuffield and David Brown had already shown that British tractors could be competitive, saleable, and exportable. Unfortunately, the Turner wasn't in that league. Its 68-degree V4 diesel had an impressive exhaust note, but in practice it overheated and in any case just wasn't powerful enough. The Marles steering box proved unreliable, as did the transmission, especially in third gear. To add to the tractor's problems, it was far more expensive than a Nuffield or Fordson, despite lacking such items as a hydraulic lift, power takeoff, lights, and differential lock equipment (these all cost extra). Turner did make a determined attempt with the Yeoman—a Mark 3 was more reliable—and slashed the price. But it was too late and Turner moved on.*

MINNEAPOLIS-MOLINE
MODEL UTS [1951]

Remember the Minneapolis-Moline U series? It was launched in 1938 as the row-crop UTU, closely followed by the ill-fated UDLX Comfortractor. It was basically a much bigger version of the all-new Z series, resplendent in M-M's trademark Prairie Gold paintwork, and powered by the company's very own beefy four-cylinder engine.

The trouble was, by the early 1950s, most of the other major manufacturers were quickly moving on to six cylinders for tractors in this class. John Deere was the honorable exception—sticking to two cylinders—but the Allis-Chalmers's WD45, the Case 500, and Oliver 88 all now boasted the smoothness and sophistication of six cylinders. Also, 39 hp had been impressive enough in 1938, but it just wasn't a class leader any more. Still, the UTS—the standard-tread version of the U series—

remained a solid, 5,000 lb. tractor that could very comfortably pull a four-bottom plow all day.

M-M's own 283 cu. in. engine was available in gasoline, kerosene, or distillate versions. The latter gave less power than gasoline—7 hp less, on the U series—but was cheaper to buy, and avoided the pre-ignition problems of kerosene. But the power loss, plus the fact that over time distillate would dilute the oil and thus shorten engine life, led many farmers to invest in gasoline. A diesel option arrived in 1952 with the UB, using a diesel version of that same 283 cu. in. motor.

**MINNEAPOLIS-MOLINE
MODEL U (1954)**

Engine: Water-cooled, four-cylinder

Bore x stroke: 4.25 x 5.0 in.

Capacity: 283 cu. in.

PTO Power: 36.1 hp @ 1,300 rpm

Torque: 247 lb. ft. @ 949 rpm

Drawbar Power: 26.8 hp

Transmission: Five-speed

Speeds: 2.5–14.0 mph

Fuel Consumption: 8.66 hp/hr per gallon

Weight: 5,905 lb.

RIGHT: *Minneapolis-Moline's long-lived big four, the U series, whose 283 cu. in. power unit saw service from 1938 right up to the late 1960s, in the M670. By then it was in enlarged 336 cu. in. form in diesel, gasoline, or LPG form—the company was a staunch proponent of LPG power right up to the early 1970s. Meanwhile, while all its rivals were going the six-cylinder route, M-M stayed faithful to its four, both on the U series and big GT/GTA. But it wasn't blind to progress, and in 1952 unveiled a diesel version of the 283 cu. in. engine, in the UB. This was tested at Nebraska in May/June 1954, recording over 300 lb. ft. of torque at the low speed of 920 rpm—the equivalent gasoline UB made that 247 lb. ft. at 949 rpm. For power, the diesel 283 was rated at 1,300 rpm, so it was slower revving than its six-cylinder rivals. It produced 42.9 hp at the belt (which made it competitive with the Oliver 88, another four-plow tractor), and gave 33.7 hp at the drawbar. (Pictured here is the 1954 Model U.)*

MARSHALL SERIES III
[1951]

Marshall's big single-cylinder diesel, with its prewar roots, was coming under pressure from younger multicylinder rivals, more powerful and flexible than a single could be.

But the last few years saw intense effort from Marshall to cure its tractor's faults and keep it up-to-date. One problem was cracked transmission housings, addressed for the 1951 Series III with a beefed-up final drive—there was a double crown wheel, with reduction gearing now taken care of in housings on either side of the main transmission. These housings also acted to strengthen the casing, in a bid to defeat the cracking problem. There were engine improvements too—more fuel and coolant capacity, and changes to lubrication, piston, and fuel pump.

But the big single still had trouble maintaining its rated 40 hp, which was finally cured by the Series IIIa Marshall of the following year. A pressurized cooling system, more efficient fuel pump, and injectors and wide piston top ring now made the rated power sustainable. An electric start was offered, as well as an Adriolic hydraulic lift and three-point linkage. Marshall even planned a Series IV, and supercharging was considered to keep the big single competitive. But it was not to be, and Marshall dropped this distinctive tractor in 1957.

LEFT: *One by one, the European single-cylinder diesel tractors were killed off in the 1950s: SFV in France, the German Lanz Bulldog, Landini in Italy, and this, the British Marshall. Despite its problems in keeping up with the multicylinder opposition (particularly when maintaining full power for long periods), Marshall made strenuous efforts to update the single. The ultimate development was this, the Series IIIa, which finally produced a strong, reliable 40 hp, thanks to a pressurized cooling system and several detail engine changes. There was electric start and a three-point hitch, and Marshall even considered supercharging for a planned Series IV, but none of these updates were enough to sell the single in large enough numbers, and later in the 1950s Marshall pulled out of the tractor business, to concentrate on crawlers.*

MARSHALL SERIES III

Engine: Water-cooled, single-cylinder diesel
Bore x stroke: 6.5 x 9.0 in.
Capacity: 298 cu. in.
PTO Power: 40 hp @ 750 rpm
Transmission: Three-speed
Speeds: 2.6–4.9 mph, 6–11.3 mph opt.
Weight: 6,650 lb.

FARMALL BMD
[1952]

Not all Internationals were American made. International Harvester's factory at Doncaster in England produced tractors for many years. The BMD shown here was a British version of the Farmall M—basically identical to the U.S. original, except for an improved front axle assembly, which mounted the tie bar behind the axle. Otherwise, it was powered by the same 264 cu. in. four-cylinder engine, set up to run on British TVO (tractor vaporizing oil). The Farmall was already a very familiar sight in Britain, as many had been imported before the war, so the tractor had no trouble gaining acceptance with British farmers.

At first, engines were sent over from America, but in early 1951, the first Doncaster-built engine was completed, and the tractor itself was renamed the BM. A diesel variant was essential for the economy-conscious British farmers, and the following year they got it, the BMD shown here. The engine was a diesel version of the 264 cu. in. unit, though with a slightly larger bore. Nor was it the same as International's U.S. diesels. The CAV injection equipment included glow plugs, so there was no need for a gasoline start from cold. The tractors were a great success, and were soon being exported to other parts of Europe. In 1953, they were joined by the BT6 and BT6D crawlers, and in 1954 by the Super BW6 and BWD6 tractors (British versions of the W6). The Super BM and BMD superseded them, with live hydraulics. As for Doncaster, it still produces tractors today, under the McCormick name.

LEFT: *At first, British-built Farmalls were U.S. models assembled in a different factory. Eventually the Internationals built in England were adapted to British and European needs, specifically with a diesel version of International's 264 cu. in. four-cylinder engine. It was unrelated to the company's American-made diesels and thousands of diesel-powered Internationals were built. The plant almost closed in 2000, following Case-IH's merger with New Holland, but it was bought by Argo, the Italian owner of Landini, to produce Case-based McCormick tractors.*

FARMALL BMD

(Specifications for Farmall M)
Engine: Water-cooled, four-cylinder
Bore x stroke: 3.9 x 5.25 in.
Capacity: 264 cu. in.
PTO Power: 33 hp
Drawbar Power: 24 hp
Transmission: Five-speed
Fuel Consumption: 11.8 hp/hr
  per gallon

CASE MODEL 500
[1952]

This Case, the Model 500, was very outdated and very forward-looking, both at the same time. Outdated because it was basically an updated version of the LA, which could be traced back to the L of 1929. It still used the roller-chain final drive which the original LA had featured,

and retained its hand clutch—the final drive ratio was higher, but that was all.

So why forward-looking? The 500 was Case's first production diesel machine, with an all-new six-cylinder unit of 377 cu. in. Seven main bearings (one between each connecting rod, as well as each end) made it

an immensely strong and durable motor—it was also one of the most powerful diesels on offer to American farmers in the 1950s. It had indirect injection (the fuel was injected into the inlet tract, not directly into the cylinder) and used the Lavona "power-cell"-type combustion chamber, the same as used on the Oliver 88 and 99 machines, and by Mack trucks. It was just as well for Case that its diesel had its good points, as it was a latecomer—John Deere and International Harvester had long since been offering a big diesel to farmers.

The 500 had been worth the wait—Nebraska tests showed that it could develop 7,400 lb. of drawbar pull and 64 hp at the belt. Now all it needed was gear final drive and a modern transmission.

LEFT: *It used underpinnings dating back to 1929, but the Model 500 was a big step forward for Case, thanks to its all-new six-cylinder diesel engine. With seven main bearings, this was a strong unit that promised long life, which was just as well, as Case had planned it as the first of a whole family of four- and six-cylinder engines, all based around the same twin-cylinder block units with 4-inch bore and 5-inch stroke. Gasoline, LPG, or diesel cylinder-heads could be fitted as appropriate. The plan worked, with the 500 followed up in 1955 by the four-cylinder 400, with 49 hp from its smaller 251 cu. in. cousin to the 500's six. The difference between the two tractors was that the mid-size 400 was genuinely new. It had bevel-gear final drive, not a roller-chain like the 500, and an eight-speed transmission. The 500 was updated as the six-speed 600, but it still had chain-drive.*

CASE MODEL 500

Engine: Water-cooled, six-cylinder
Bore x stroke: 4.0 x 5.0 in.
Capacity: 377 cu. in.
PTO Power: 63.8 hp @ 1,350 rpm
Torque: 411 lb. ft. @ 1,050 rpm
Transmission: Four-speed
Speeds: 2.7–10.1 mph
Fuel Consumption: 15.8 hp/hr per gallon
Weight: 8,128 lb.

COCKSHUTT 20
[1952]

COCKSHUTT 20 GASOLINE

Engine: Water-cooled, four-cylinder

Bore x stroke: 3.2 x 4.4 in.

Capacity: 140 cu. in.

PTO Power: 27.4 hp @ 1,800 rpm

Drawbar Power: 20.2 hp @ 1,800 rpm

Torque: 186 lb. ft.

Transmission: Four-speed

Speeds: 2.5–13.3 mph

Fuel Consumption: 10.5 hp/hr
per gallon

Weight: 2,813 lb.

This was the smallest Cockshutt, designed by the Canadian company to rival the successful Allis-Chalmers B. The Canadians never built their own engines, so power came courtesy of a 124 cu. in. Continental unit which was soon dropped in favor of a 140 cu. in.—both were four-cylinder engines with 4.4 in. strokes, and both came in gasoline or distillate form. Compression ratios were quite high for the day (5.0:1 distillate, 6.75:1 gas), and at the rated 1,800 rpm, the bigger-engined 20 produced just over 27 PTO hp at tests in Nebraska.

The Cockshutts were quite advanced little tractors for their time. The company pioneered a live power takeoff and hydraulics in 1947—both could be used even if the drive wheel clutch was disengaged. It was such a leap forward that other tractor companies followed suit, and live hydraulics and PTO soon became standard practice. Both were optional on the 20, whose standard transmission was a four-speed. Like other Cockshutts, it was also sold under the Co-Op brand name, in this case as the Co-Op E2.

According to American author Robert Pripps, the smallest Cockshutt was "one of the cutest and best performing little tractors ever made." He's quite right, don't you think?

BELOW: *The early 1950s Cockshutts were neat, good-looking little tractors, and advanced for their time, thanks largely to the Canadians' pioneering work with a live PTO and hydraulics. Sadly, later in the decade, the entire range was restyled. As before, there was a full range, now using engines from Hercules, Perkins, or Continental, as Buda, Cockshutt's long-standing supplier, had been taken over by Allis-Chalmers. The 540 was a 26-31 hp utility tractor; the 550 a 26-34 hp, in row-crop or standard-tread forms; the 560 a 35-43 hp; and the 570 a 40-54 hp.*

FORDSON MAJOR ROADLESS
[1953]

Roadless made its name with half-track truck conversions, and tractors from the late 1920s. Based in England, its Fordson conversions were popular for a variety of uses—the prototype was demonstrated hauling a lifeboat up a beach!

It was inevitable that full-track conversions would follow, and the Roadless Model E was one such, based on the Fordson E27N with a choice of TVO or diesel power. The later J17 seen here was a conversion of the English Ford-designed Major Diesel. Both of these were steered by levers—Roadless half-tracks, with their conventional front wheels, retained the standard tractor's steering wheel.

Roadless crawler conversions looked like production line machines, so complete was the transformation. Ford's English tractor arm had finally replaced the elderly E27N in 1952, with the New Major. It was an all-new design, powered by a family of four-cylinder engines in diesel, gasoline, and TVO (tractor vaporizing oil) forms. All were based on the same cylinder block and crankshaft, but the gasoline/TVO versions were 199 cu. in. against the 220 cu. in. diesel. By 1958, the Power Major had brought a hefty twenty-two percent power increase, not to mention a live PTO and power steering, though there was still no differential lock or draft control.

FORDSON MAJOR ROADLESS

Engine: Water-cooled, four-cylinder
Bore x stroke: 3.74 x 4.52 in.
Capacity: 199 cu. in.
Rated Speed: 1,600 rpm
Transmission: Six-speed
Weight: 5,100 lb.

BELOW: *British-built Fordsons were the tractor of choice for a Roadless—like this J17 Major Diesel. Fordson Majors proved to be an ideal base for Roadless crawlers.*

FORD NAA/600 SERIES

[1953/54]

After its split from Harry Ferguson, Ford was determined to stay in the tractor business and do things its own way. It was also clear that Ford wouldn't repeat the Model F story, and neglect a good-selling tractor until it became outdated. So the 8N was replaced in 1953 by the NAA.

This wore Golden Jubilee badges, celebrating Ford's fifty years in the transport business. Although superficially similar to the 8N, the NAA was heavier and more powerful. It was the first Ford tractor (or Fordson) with an overhead valve engine—more powerful and fuel-efficient than side valves. There was new sheet metal, but no diesel option, one reason why Ford of America imported the British-built diesel Fordson to sell alongside it.

The following year saw a new transmission when NAA was replaced by the 600 and 800 series. The new 640 had a four-speed transmission; the 650 was a five-speed; and the 660 added a live PTO. Engine-wise, the 600s used the NAA's 134 cu. in. engine, with an enlarged 172 cu. in. version in the 800.

In 1955, they were joined by the 700 and 900 series, basically row-crop versions of the same tractors. But there was no diesel option until 1959.

LEFT: *The neat NAA bore a family resemblance to the 1939 9N, and not just in the sheet metal work. The driver was sat low, astride the transmission, a position used by the 9N, and every Ferguson-influenced tractor.*

BELOW: *"Workmaster" was right. The small Ford tractors remained as tough and useful as the 9N, or for that matter the Fordson F, had ever been. High-horsepower Fords were still years away though.*

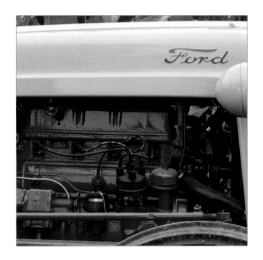

ABOVE: *For the first time on a Ford tractor, there was an overhead valve engine, which was used in both the 600 and 800 series. Ford America didn't make a diesel version as the demand for small diesel tractors in the U.S. was still relatively low, and it could easily import a ready-made diesel Fordson.*

FORD NAA (1953)

Engine: Water-cooled, four-cylinder
Capacity: 134 cu. in.
PTO Power: 27.6 hp @ 2,000 rpm
Drawbar Power: 22.4 hp @ 2,000 rpm
Torque: 198 lb. ft. @ 1,125 rpm
Transmission: Four-speed
Speeds: 3.1–11.6 mph
Fuel Consumption: 10.7 hp/hr per gallon
Weight: 3,031 lb.

MARSHALL MP6
[1954]

Marshall of England had made its name, reputation, and business by producing single-cylinder diesel tractors in the classic European mold. But by the mid-1950s these were looking increasingly out-of-date, particularly because a new breed of multicylinder diesels had entered the field by then. Smoother and more powerful, the diesels soon outclassed the big singles.

Marshall didn't have the resources to develop a brand-new multicylinder diesel of its own, so it did what many tractor manufacturers of the time were doing—bought someone else's. The machine it chose was a six-cylinder unit, the UE350, produced by the British truck manufacturer Leyland.

The Leyland-engined MP6 was unveiled in 1954, all new from stem to stern and having nothing in common with the old Marshall tractors. On paper, it all looked promising. To go with the brawny Leyland engine, there was a six-speed transmission, and the MP6 had an impressive drawbar pull of 10,000 lb.

But in practice it was too big, powerful, and expensive for the British home market—it was better suited to the American prairies than the small fields of Britain—and all but ten of the 197 MP6s manufactured were exported. Many went to the West Indies for sugar cultivation, or to Australia to take part in a government-sponsored land-clearance program.

Perhaps with a determined push, the 70 hp Marshall could have sold by the boatload to Midwest farmers, as an alternative to a big John Deere or Minneapolis-Moline. Still, history is full of might-have-beens, and the eventual reality was that the MP6 was dropped in 1957, allowing Marshall to concentrate on its crawler business.

LEFT: *No one could accuse Marshall of ignoring the trend toward multicylinder tractors. While persevering its long-running single, the company also produced this, the all-new MP6. It was modern, powerful, and very strong. The problem was, in size it was more suited to the American prairies than the smaller-scale British fields, and sales were disappointing at home. Most MP6s were exported to the West Indies or Australia, and even then, less than 200 were produced in all.*

MARSHALL MP6

Engine: Water-cooled, six-cylinder diesel
Power: 70 hp
Drawbar Pull: 10,000 lb.
Transmission: Six-speed

JOHN DEERE 80 DIESEL
[1955]

Early John Deere diesels were all about big, beefy dimensions. Take this 80, a 1955 update on the R, JD's first diesel which had appeared in 1949. The engine was JD's biggest ever—each piston measured over six inches across, running up and down a bore of eight inches, to give 475 cu. in. To the casual observer, such massive cylinders might look like a desperate attempt to squeeze competitive power from an outmoded design. But the 80 Diesel was efficient, and its sister model 70 Diesel set a fuel consumption record at Nebraska that was unbeaten for ten years.

The 80 was also twin-engined, with John Deere's first-ever four-cylinder donkey motor! The Model R had been equipped with an electric start, but the 80's massive cylinders were simply too big for such a system. Instead, it had a small donkey engine—a 60 cu. in. V4 gasoline, which ran up to 5,500 rpm just on starting duties. The little V4's exhaust was routed so that it would help to warm up the big diesel before attempting to start it. Still, it was a rather complex way of starting up each morning, and a heavy-duty 24-volt electric starting system later superseded the V4. The 80 was mildly updated into the 820 and 830 later in the 1950s, before giving way to the all-new multicylinder Deeres in 1960.

LEFT: *This was the tractor that broke the John Deere Model R's fuel efficiency record, its replacement! In 1955, the new 80 recorded 15.96 hp/hr per gallon at rated belt load. The greater efficiency came came from a bigger engine—it was basically similar to that of the R, but with a greater 6.125-inch bore (R, 5.75-inch) to give a capacity of 475 cu. in. Power was boosted substantially, and Nebraska recorded the torque as a massive 424 lb. ft., with that giant twin-cylinder engine ticking over at just 768 rpm—rated power was at 1,125 rpm. Interestingly, the little donkey engine was one of John Deere's first-ever multicylinder units, after thirty-five years of making twins! The experience with this V4 led JD to experiment with V4 and V6 units to power its new generation of tractors, though the idea was later abandoned.*

JOHN DEERE 80 DIESEL

Engine type: Water-cooled twin-cylinder
Bore x stroke: 6.125 x 8 in.
Capacity: 475 cu. in.
PTO Power: 65 hp @ 1,125 rpm
Drawbar Power: 60 hp
Transmission: Six-speed
Speeds: 2.5–12.5 mph
Fuel Consumption: 15.96 hp/hr
  per gallon
Weight: 8,511 lb.

OLIVER SUPER 99 GM
[1955]

Two-stroke engines and tractors don't often go together, but the Oliver Super 99 GM was the exception to this rule. With over 70 hp at the PTO, this was the largest, most powerful tractor of its day.

Determined to stay ahead in the power race, Oliver decided to offer an interesting

LEFT: *Lateral-thinking from Oliver (buying in a supercharged truck engine to power its top tractor) resulted in the most powerful field tool you could buy.*

ABOVE: *The Super 99 shared the very bold Fleetline styling of the other, much smaller Olivers, though everything was on a rather bigger scale.*

power option on its Super 99. In place of the company's own conventional six-cylinder diesel, from 1955 buyers could specify a General Motors 3-71 two-stroke. Designed for trucks, this was a super-charged two-stroke diesel, with three cylinders, though rated at the same 1,675 rpm as the four-stroke sixes. Unlike conventional two-strokes, this one had poppet valves to control the gases, plus a Roots-type blower to purge exhaust gases and supercharge the fresh mixture. The compression ratio was 17:1. It produced a unique wailing exhaust note, and unlike ordinary diesels, needed to be kept revving to produce power.

The tractor it transformed, the 99, was Oliver's biggest of the time, and one of its most successful, staying in production for twenty years. It started life as an industrial tractor, but was soon available in farm form. Initially, it used the same 443 cu. in. four-cylinder engine as the 90, albeit in high-compression form, but six-cylinder 302 cu. in. motors soon followed, in both gasoline and diesel forms. Still, it's this hot rod supercharged two-stroke that excites most interest today. This was the start in

earnest of the tractor power race—just look at the difference between the Super 99 and the plain-Jane gasoline-powered 99 of 1950. That produced 41 hp at the drawbar, the Super churned out an extra forty-three percent over and above that, not to mention over 500 lb. ft. of torque. That made the super-charged Oliver more torquey than John Deere's mighty diesel twin. In short, it was quite a tractor.

OLIVER SUPER 99 GM

Engine: Water-cooled, three-cylinder two-stroke
Bore x stroke: 4.5 x 5.0 in.
Capacity: 213 cu. in.
PTO Power: 72 hp @ 1,675 rpm
Torque: 504 lb. ft. @ 1,309 rpm
Drawbar Power: 59 hp
Transmission: Six-speed
Speeds: 2.6–13.8 mph
Fuel Consumption: 12.4 hp/hr per gallon
Weight: 10,155 lb.

MINNEAPOLIS-MOLINE 335
[1955]

Minneapolis-Moline had ended the 1930s with a strong range of up-to-date tractors. But by the mid 1950s it was lagging behind. It was a pioneer of LPG on its larger machines, but wasted time and effort on the Uni-Tractor, an innovative three-wheeler machine that was designed to be a piece of cut-price equipment that could free up the conventional farm tractor for other work. Unfortunately, it also needed a unique set of implements, so it wasn't cut-price at all—few were sold.

Meanwhile, the smaller tractors had been somewhat neglected, though M-M answered this in 1955 with two brand-new designs, the small-medium 335 and 445. Both were modern and up to the minute, bristling with the latest features. Ampli-Torc for example, which gave the option of a two-speed planetary gear set between clutch and gearbox. It effectively doubled the choice of ratios (to ten forward and two reverse), and being hydraulically operated, could shift between ranges without stopping the tractor or even declutching. Both 335 and 445 were also available with a Ferguson three-point hitch and live PTO.

The 335 shown here was one of the new "utility" tractors, with adjustable treads but no high clearance. Powered by a 165 cu. in. four-cylinder engine of 24-30 hp, it came in gasoline form only. The bigger 445 had a wider choice of fuels: LPG, gasoline, or diesel, all based on the same 206 cu. in. four.

LEFT: *Driver seated low, astride the transmission, with adjustable axles and standard clearance. This was the new breed of utility tractor popularized by the Fergusons and Ford 9N, and one that would eventually help make the distinction between row-crop and standard-tread tractors obsolete. The utility had elements of both, and in the 1950s most major manufacturers were offering one. Minneapolis-Moline was not before its time in launching its utility 335. Concentrating on its big four-cylinder tractors, it had allowed the smaller ones, the R and Z models, to fall behind. These were both of prewar origin, so the 335 and its big brother, the 445, were welcome additions to the range.*

MINNEAPOLIS-MOLINE 335

Engine: Water-cooled, four-cylinder
Bore x stroke: 3.63 x 4.0 in.
Capacity: 165 cu. in.
PTO Power: 31.8 hp @ 1,600 rpm
Drawbar Power: 24.1 hp
Transmission: Five-speed
Speeds: 2.7–15.1 mph
Fuel Consumption: 9.99 hp/hr per gallon
Weight: 3,707 lb.

JOHN DEERE 420

[1956]

For tractor spotters, the John Deere 20 series of the 1950s is easy—it was the first Deere to use that yellow stripe on the hood. But there was more to it than that.

Harry Ferguson had finally come to a less-than-amicable legal settlement with Ford, which meant that patent restrictions on his three-point hitch were finally off. Now every other rival could produce their own version. JD's take on Ferguson's automatic draft control was something called the Powr-Trol. Just like the original, this automatically raised the implement a little when it hit heavy ground, to maintain speed. Once the going was easier, the draft went back to its preset level. Within a few years, any tractor that didn't have a variation on the Ferguson system would be sadly lacking. The 20 series was John Deere's attempt at a final update on its twin-cylinder range, before the all-new multicylinder tractors were ready. But in 1956 they were still four years away, so the whole range got the 20 series treatment. The 420 shown here, which replaced the Model 40, received a bigger engine with new pistons and cylinder heads, for more power and lower fuel consumption. Similarly, the 520, 620, and 720 took over from the 50, 60, and 70 respectively, while a new, smaller general purpose tractor, the 320, was added to the range.

LEFT: *Not long now. The 20 and 30 series John Deeres of the 1950s were the final updates on the long-running twin-cylinder range. The new generation JDs were on target for a 1960 launch, but in the meantime, the faithful "Johnny Poppers" had to go on selling. These had been mildly updated in 1952 with a live PTO plus some detail changes, and most of the range given numbers in place of letters: the Model M became the "40," the B "50," A "60," and G "70." The big R diesel wasn't renamed "80" until 1955. All were updated as the 20 series the following year, signifying the introduction of "Powr-Trol," John Deere's version of the Ferguson three-point hitch. Two years later, the 30 series was a very minor update, and in 1959 the 435 was a GM two-stroke powered utility tractor. In 1960 the new generation was launched, and things were never the same again.*

JOHN DEERE 420

Engine Type: Water-cooled, twin-cylinder
Bore x stroke: 4.25 x 4.0 in.
Capacity: 113 cu. in.
PTO Power: 29.2 hp @ 1,850 rpm
Drawbar Power: 27 hp @ 1,850 rpm
Transmission: Four-speed (five-speed opt.)
Weight: 3,250 lb.

MASSEY-FERGUSON 95 SUPER
[1956]

Massey-Harris and Harry Ferguson's companies had merged in 1953, and for a time, Massey-Ferguson would become the world's dominant tractor manufacturer. But in the meantime they needed a complete range of tractors. The small and medium end were taken care of by rationalizing, rebadging, and repainting various M-H or Ferguson models. What M-F needed was something bigger than the 50 hp M-F 65, and quickly.

So they went to Minneapolis-Moline and bought in the big Gvi. With new bodywork, repainted and rebadged, this was marketed as the Massey-Ferguson 95 Super, and was very successful. With a five-speed transmission, 75 hp at the belt, and weighing around 8,000 lb., it gave the company the right sort of machine for the American wheatlands. The plan worked, as M-F also went on to buy five hundred Model 990 tractors from Oliver, which were sold as Massey-Ferguson 98s. When the Gvi was replaced by M-M's new G705, that too got the same treatment, as the 100 hp M-F 97. Buying someone else's tractors is more expensive than building your own, and while it was selling rebadged Olivers and Minneapolis-Molines, M-F was designing its own high-horsepower contender. It came in 1959, as the 60 hp 88, a genuine 4-5 plow tractor. For Massey-Ferguson, the 95 Super had served its purpose.

LEFT: *The newly merged Massey-Ferguson bought in the Minneapolis-Moline Gvi and rebadged it, because it lacked a big wheatlands tractor of its own. The Ferguson end of the operation had a suitable machine under development—the five-plow LTX 60—but control now lay with the Canadian owners and U.S. sales force. Neither wanted the LTX, so it was killed off, and M-F continued to buy in big tractors until an American-built design of its own was ready. At first, the marriage of Ferguson and Massey-Harris looked fairly equal—both were medium-sized manufacturers that together made a very large one. But Harry Ferguson quickly became very disillusioned when he realized that he was being sidelined into a mere figurehead role. He soon sold his share of the business to Massey-Harris, which then assumed complete control.*

MASSEY-FERGUSON 95 SUPER

Engine: Water-cooled, four-cylinder
Bore x stroke: 4.25 x 5.0 in.
Capacity: 426 cu. in.
PTO Power: 75 hp @ 1,300 rpm
Drawbar Power: 67 hp
Transmission: Five-speed
Speeds: 3.1–17.1 mph
Weight: Approx. 8,000 lb.

ALLIS-CHALMERS D14
[1957]

Allis-Chalmers was having a busy decade. Late 1950 saw a much-improved C Model, the CA, with many of the advanced features seen in the bigger WD—Traction Booster, a transmission clutch, and power-adjust wheels. Three years later, the WD itself got a twenty-five percent power boost, followed by a six-cylinder diesel version. And from 1957, a rolling program saw A-C replace its entire range over the following three years.

The D series—D10, 12, 14, and 17—replaced A-C's complete lineup of B, CA, WD, and really the long-dead E and A as well. It was a big and varied range, with over fifty models available once the little D10/12 came into production, reflecting the fact that tractors were becoming more specialized, and the only way to keep up was to offer one for every job.

The WD was actually replaced by two tractors: the bigger D17, and the mid-range three-plow D14 pictured here. This had an all-new Allis-designed engine, a 149 cu. in. four, though it was derived from WD experience, with Power Crater pistons. It came in gasoline or LPG form, with 32.6 belt hp at 1,650 rpm. A diesel option didn't arrive until 1960 with the updated D15.

There was a new transmission as well. Power Director doubled the number of ratios available (to eight forward on the D14) thanks to a second clutch that ran at seventy percent of engine speed. Every major manufacturer introduced some sort of double-range transmission in the 1950s—A-C wasn't about to be left behind.

LEFT: *A new generation for the 1960s, the D series was introduced progressively over 1957–59. This D14 was the first, and along with the bigger D17 it replaced the successful WD-45. Power Director was A-C's take on the dual-range transmission, doubling the ratios to eight forward. It wasn't before its time either, as International's pioneering Torque Amplifier had been on the market for three years by the time Power Director was launched. The three-plow D14 sold reasonably well, but the little D10 and D12 machines were never as popular as the Model B they replaced.*

ALLIS-CHALMERS D14 GASOLINE

Engine: Water-cooled, four-cylinder
Capacity: 149 cu. in.
PTO Power: 32.6 hp
Drawbar Power: 24.5 hp
Fuel Consumption: 12.01 hp/hr
  per gallon
Speeds (high range): 2.2–12.0 mph
Weight: 3,623 lb.

MERCEDES-BENZ UNIMOG

[1957]

Truck or tractor? People have been asking that question about the Mercedes Unimog for nearly half a century. The German manufacturer of trucks and luxury cars actually has a long association with tractors. As far back as 1919, it unveiled two "Land Traktors" of 40 and 80 hp. The 30 hp twin-cylinder S7 of 1922 was the world's first diesel-engined tractor. Initially a tricycle tractor (with outriggers to improve stability), it was soon replaced by the four-wheel BK. But the company seemed sold on diesel power, producing the single-cylinder OE diesel in the 1930s.

Production ceased during the 1930s Depression, but Mercedes-Benz returned to tractors in 1957 with the Unimog. It wasn't actually an M-B design—German specialist Boehringer had produced the Unimog in small numbers for a few years. M-B bought it up, fitted its own 25 hp engine, and marketed the 'Mog as a cross between a truck and farm tractor, which is exactly what it was. A multispeed transmission allowed walking pace in the fields and over 30 mph on the road, while four-wheel drive, high ground clearance, and impressive towing capacity underlined the Unimog's multipurpose nature. Its relatively small wheels proved a limitation in field work, but the Unimog's strength lay in its sheer versatility. Over fifty years on from its first appearance, Unimog is still in production, though the latest 200 hp model is a far cry from the original.

LEFT: *Not actually a Unimog, but a much later development of the same concept, though the MB-Trac was closer in concept to a pure tractor than the tractor/truck hybrid that was the Unimog. It had bigger, tractor-sized wheels/tires, with more attention paid to implement hauling that stowage space. Mercedes stopped building the MB-Trac in the early 1990s, but it was revived by German manufacturer LTS and a consortium of Unimog dealers, who realized the continuing demand for this unique machine. It was relaunched, in updated form, with 99 hp, 110 hp or 160 hp Mercedes engines, a ZF transmission, and electronic control of the hydraulics.*

MERCEDES-BENZ UNIMOG 30 DIESEL

Engine: Water-cooled, four-cylinder
Bore x stroke: 2.95 x 3.94 in.
Capacity: 108 cu. in.
PTO Power: 27.3 hp @ 2,550 rpm
Drawbar Power: 20.6 hp
Speeds: 0.72–33.0 mph
Fuel Consumption: 11.42 hp/hr
  per gallon
Weight: 4,979 lb.

MASSEY-FERGUSON 50
[1957]

It took Massey-Harris-Ferguson four years to properly rationalize its range. The two companies had merged in 1953, both of them with a complete range of small tractors. There was some attempt at rationalization—Massey-Harris Ponys, for example, were repainted gray and sold as Fergusons. But M-H-F attempted to keep two tractor lines and two separate dealer networks going, while not taking advantage of the newly merged M-F-H's economies of scale.

It all changed in 1957. Now, the whole lineup was badged as Massey-Fergusons, in the new corporate colors of red bodywork with a metallic gray chassis, colors which everyone now associates with M-F. The tractor range was rationalized, using existing parts to produce a single unified range. So the M-F 30 was really a Ferguson in TO-30 in the new color scheme. The 50 pictured here was a stretched version of Ferguson's TO-35, which initially had been sold as an all-red Massey-Harris 50 or all-gray Fergsuon 40. A 2-3 plow tractor, it started off with a Continental 134 cu. in. gasoline engine, later adding LPG and diesel options, the latter being a 38 hp three-cylinder Perkins. The standard transmission was a dual-range, giving six forward and two reverse speeds, but a 12-speed multipower was optional. Power steering, dual rear wheels, and 88 in. rear tread were other options.

LEFT: *One of the first tractors to be badged as a Massey-Ferguson, and carry the now familiar red and gray color scheme. The 50 owed more to the Ferguson side of the family than the Massey-Harris, being an enlarged Ferguson TO-35 with more power and the option of a 38 hp Perkins and 12-speed multipower transmission. At the same time, the bigger MF65 offered the same transmission options with a 50 hp Continental engine. For the next couple of years, MF's bigger tractors were taken care of by bought-in M-Ms and Olivers, but in 1959 the company launched its own 60 hp machine, the 88 and row-crop 85. A 68 hp 90 followed in 1962.*

MASSEY-FERGUSON 50 DIESEL

Engine: Water-cooled, three-cylinder
Bore x stroke: 3.6 x 5.0 in.
Capacity: 153 cu. in.
PTO Power: 38.3 hp @ 2,000 rpm
Drawbar Power: 32.4 hp
Transmission: Six-speed
Speeds: 1.3–14.6 mph
Fuel Consumption: 13.42 hp/hr
   per gallon
Weight: 3,933 lb.

CASE 910B
[1958]

The biggest Case, which could trace its lineage through the L, LA, 500, 600, and 900, was out on a limb by the late 1950s. By then, the rest of the range had been renewed or substantially updated, as Case fought to catch up to its more go-ahead rivals. The new 400, 300, and 200, and the new family of gas, diesel, and LPG engines which powered them, were the fruit of this change. But the big 900 was really little more than a revamped version of the original Model L of 1929, though it was re-engined with the new six-cylinder diesel in 1953, and became the 500.

Since then, there had been a couple of updates. The Case 600 replaced the 500 in 1957, though it was only produced in that year. Two extra speeds were added to the gearbox, giving six forward ratios in all, and Flambeau Red gave way to a two-tone Desert Sunset/Red color scheme. But really that was it. The same year, the short-lived 600 was itself replaced by the 900, which again was hardly changed apart from a taller, squared-off grille that incorporated the headlights. This was the new Case corporate look.

Case's three-digit numbering system looked complicated, but had a logic to it, and was a way of keeping track of an increasingly complex range. The first number denoted the size of tractor, the second the engine type (gas, diesel, or LPG) and the third, standard tread or row crop. Diesel was already the dominant choice though, and in the Case 900 was outselling LPG by four to one.

LEFT: *Chain drive, hand clutch—in some ways, the big Case 900 was sadly outdated by the late 1950s and almost ignored while the smaller Case tractors were updated and renewed. In 1958, Case spent a million dollars on a lavish dealer launch program, flying every single Case dealer and spouse to Phoenix for a three-day program of wining, dining, and trying the latest tractors. No one had spent that sort of money on a dealer presentation before, at least in the tractor industry, but it was characteristic of Case's flamboyant boss of the time, Marc Rojtman. In any case, 30,000 tractors were sold as a result.*

CASE 910B LPG

Engine: Water-cooled, six-cylinder
Bore x stroke: 4.0 x 5.0 in.
Capacity: 377 cu. in.
PTO Power: 71.1 hp @ 1,350 rpm
Drawbar Power: 62.1 hp @ 1,350 rpm
Transmission: Six-speed
Speeds: 2.5–12.5 mph
Fuel Consumption: 8.8 hp/hr per gallon
Weight: 8,625 lb.

OLIVER 770
[1958]

Allis-Chalmers had the "Power Director;" Minneapolis-Moline opted for "Ampli-Torc," and International Harvester the more straight-laced "Torque Amplifier;" Case favored the "Case-O-Matic" and Oliver the "Power Booster." By the late 1950s, when Oliver's 770 replaced the Super 77, no major manufacturer could afford to be without a dual-range transmission of one sort or another.

In the previous couple of decades, tractor transmissions had gradually acquired an increasing number of ratios—three, four, five, and six—but this was different. All those fancy names referred to a more sophisticated transmission that allowed ratio changes on the go, whether by an extra clutch or additional two-range facility. Oliver favored the latter, which was mounted in front of the standard six-speed box. When the going got sticky, the driver could get a half-step downshift without loss of power—the actual ratio was 1.32:1. The Power Booster operated on all of the 770's gears, effectively giving it twelve forward speeds.

That was the 770's most significant new feature, although it also had the Power Traction hitch—the lower links were mounted quite far forward, to even out the weight distribution (although still with a distinct rearward bias). A ten percent power increase—from the same six-cylinder diesel as its predecessor—capped off the Oliver 770's improvements.

LEFT: *In the late 1950s, Oliver's entire lineup moved up to three figures, to signify the arrival of Traction Booster, the company's dual-range transmission. So 44, 55, 66, 77, 88, and 99 became 440, 550, 660, 770, 880, and 990 with Power Booster standard on the 770 and 880. The Hundred Series also had new colors and styling, while the 550 received a more powerful 155 cu. in. engine. You could still buy a hot rod supercharged Oliver, with that GM two-stroke diesel, and the renamed 990 got a power boost to 84 hp. There was also a less frenetic 67 hp 990, with conventional six-cylinder four-stroke diesel, and the torque converter-equipped 995 Lugmatic.*

OLIVER 770 DIESEL

Engine: Water-cooled, six-cylinder
Bore x stroke: 3.5 x 3.75 in.
Capacity: 216 cu. in.
PTO Power: 48.8 hp @ 1,750 rpm
Drawbar Power: 34.9 hp
Transmission: Six-speed
Speeds: 2.1–10.8 mph
Fuel Consumption: 12.9 hp/hr per gallon
Weight: 5,565 lb.

ALLIS-CHALMERS D12
[1959]

ALLIS-CHALMERS D12 GASOLINE

Engine: Water-cooled, four-cylinder

Capacity: 139 cu. in.

PTO Power: 28.6 hp

Drawbar Power: 23.6 hp

Fuel Consumption: 10.73 hp/hr per gallon

Speeds (high range): 2.0–11.4 mph

Weight: 2,945 lb.

BELOW: *The D10 and D12 were neat, lightweight, and well equipped, but they never recaptured the popularity of the Model B they had replaced.*

Allis-Chalmers's little Model B had been a great success in its heyday, but by the late 1950s its sales had dwindled to the point where it was dropped from production altogether, two years before its updated replacements were ready. These were the D10 and D12, smallest of the new D series range.

Both models used a 139 cu. in. version of the D14's four-cylinder engine, with Power Crater pistons, but the D10 was set up as a single-row machine, the D12 as a two-row. Tests of a D10 at Nebraska produced 28.5 PTO hp and 25.7 at the drawbar, and the D12 was almost identical.

In keeping with the D series philosophy, most of the features found on Allis-Chalmers's bigger tractors were also offered on the smaller ones. So the D10 and 12 could come with Traction Booster, Power Shift rear wheels, and independent PTO, but not the Power Director transmission. For the time being, customers had to make do with plain four speeds. There was a seventeen percent power boost in 1961 though, when the 10 and 12 were fitted with the 14's bigger 149 cu. in. engine.

However, there was never a diesel option on the smallest D series machines, and perhaps this is one reason why they were never very successful—in nearly a decade, their combined sales were a little over 9,000. Over an admittedly longer period, Allis sold ten times as many Model Bs.

ALLIS-CHALMERS D272
[1959]

Just as International Harvester built a factory in Britain, so did Allis-Chalmers. The new A-C plant began assembling Model Bs in 1948. As demand grew, the factory was quickly outgrown, so a bigger factory was opened. At first, both were pure assembly operations, but as with IHC's BM Farmalls, the content of these Allis-Chalmers gradually changed as the factory redesigned the B to suit British conditions. It was updated into the D270 in 1955, adding a live PTO (which was needed for work with a Roto-Baler); a four-speed transmission replaced the three-speeder; and there was a diesel option. Perkins provided the P3/143 three-cylinder. It had actually offered more power than the original gasoline version, though it

cost an extra $145. Four years later, the D272 (pictured here) was announced, with another power boost (30 hp from gas) and improved hydraulics.

Alongside the D272, English Allis offered the bigger ED-40 in 1960. This used a 138 cu. in. Standard-Ricardo diesel of 38 hp (later 41) and was exported to Canada. But unlike IHC, Allis-Chalmers was unable to make a success of its British operation. Sales of the ED-40 were disappointing.

Catering to a wide range of A-Cs both old and new, over the whole of Europe, was a big operation, though it was simplified by a telegraphic code for ordering parts. If the spares men at A-C America received the message "AIRYX," it meant that the part was

needed by air express delivery. "SOOTY" was "ship by express" and "STAUB" was a cancelled order. If all else failed and the part failed to turn up, the message "when and how did you dispatch the order?" came up as "SPLAT!"

BELOW: *The D272 below had improved hydraulics and a gas power boost.*

ALLIS-CHALMERS D272

Engine: Water-cooled, four-cylinder
Power: 30 hp
Transmission: Four-speed

FORDSON POWER MAJOR
[1959]

Ford, of course, had been building tractors in Britain long before either Allis-Chalmers or IHC, and the British arm had been developing its own machines for many years, still under the Fordson name.

This was particularly true of diesels, in which Britain was forging ahead. Ford U.K. designed its own 220 cu. in. diesel for the New Major of 1952, which replaced the venerable E27N. Larger and heavier than the tractor it replaced, the New Major weighed over 5,000 lb. It came with a two-range shifter in addition to the standard three-speed transmission, which provided six forward speeds in all, and if you weren't quite ready for diesel, there were also 199 cu. in. gasoline or TVO alternatives, based on the same cylinder block.

Seven years on, a comprehensive update resulted in the Power Major pictured here. There was twenty-two percent more power from the diesel, thanks to a modified fuel injection system, camshaft, cylinder-head, and rocker arms. The differential was uprated to cope, producing a genuine five-plow machine. There were other improvements too: live power takeoff and optional power steering. The Super Major was the same tractor with disc brakes, a differential lock, and draft control. All were built in Britain, but as part of Ford's move to produce a unified tractor range, the Super Major was exported to the U.S. as the 5000 Diesel until 1964.

LEFT: *The Power Major was one of the last independently produced Fordsons from Britain. Just like Massey-Ferguson and other companies that had factories in different parts of the world, it made more sense to rationalize what these factories were doing, to prevent duplication of effort, and maximize economies of scale. That was the thinking behind the unified Ford tractor range from 1961, all with the same corporate colors and carrying the same badge. Ford already imported some British-built Fordsons, but in Fordson blue and orange, not U.S. Ford colors. Under the new regime, the four-plow Super Major became the Ford 5000 Diesel while the little Fordson Dexta was renamed the 2000 Diesel.*

FORDSON POWER MAJOR DIESEL

Engine: Water-cooled, four-cylinder
Bore x stroke: 3.94 x 4.52 in
Capacity: 220 cu. in.
PTO Power: 47.7 hp @ 1,700 rpm
Drawbar Power: 42.6 hp
Transmission: Six-speed
Speeds: 1.9–13.8 mph
Fuel Consumption: 14.2 hp/hr per gallon
Weight: 5,445 lb.

The 1960s: POWER GAMES

The 1960s may have been a decade of social revolution, but for tractors, the times weren't a-changing quite so much. Instead, we had more of everything. More power, more weight, more features. The giant super-tractors from Steiger and Big Bud began to gain widespread acceptance, and there was more attention paid to safety.

But the decade saw no great leaps forward in tractor technology. Instead, existing technology was applied to tractors for the first time (turbocharging and hydrostatic drives), or old technology finally came of age, such as four-wheel drive. It was as if, after the major advances of the previous couple of decades (the three-point hitch, diesel engines, and multispeed transmissions), the industry was consolidating instead of experimenting. In fact, economics seemed to play as great a role as engineering. The 1960s saw several examples of badge engineering, as manufacturers sought to cut development costs by bolting their own badge onto someone else's tractor, while companies like Ford and Massey-Ferguson became global in outlook, producing a single range of tractors from plants situated all over the world.

The U.S. tractor power race that gathered pace in the 1950s was still going strong, and the new decade would see 100 hp as the new target for top-power row-crop machines. Oddly, it was Allis-Chalmers that led the way. Odd, because A-C had rarely been at the cutting edge of technology before (pneumatic tires excepted). It was actually first with a 100 hp row-crop tractor, the big D21 of 1963. Powered by a new direct injection diesel six of 426 cu. in., the D21 was so massive a new range of implements had to be designed specifically for it, including a seven-furrow plow. As the decade wore on, A-C's rivals all stepped into the 100 hp class—International's offering was the 1206 of 1965. The tractor market was more competitive than ever before, and where one manufacturer went, the others had no choice but to follow. By the end of the decade, 130 hp was the new target, and the Ford 9000 and International 1256 were both examples.

These high-power outputs would never have been practical without turbocharging, and here again A-C was first. It was not a new technology—U.S. diesel trucks had been using turbochargers for a decade—but caused considerable excitement at the time. For A-C, it was an eleventh hour decision, when it realized that the proposed 60 hp D18 wouldn't impress a marketplace that already had 70 hp machines. A turbocharger boosted power by twenty-five percent, and the renamed D19 entered the history books in 1961. Again, by the end of the decade, they were commonplace, particularly in the 70 hp+ class.

But even the new 100 hp flagships weren't the most powerful tractors you could buy. A new class of super-tractor was pioneered by the Steiger brothers from the late 1950s. All the ingredients of a super-tractor were there from the start: four same-size wheels, all of them driven, an articulated drive shaft, and

RIGHT: *Twin-wheel, turbocharged 122 hp six-cylinder diesel: this Ford 9000 typified the new breed of power-tractor which appeared in the 1960s.*

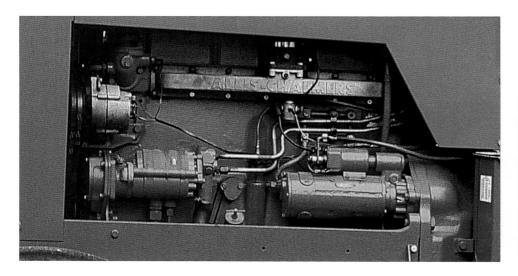

BELOW: *Turbocharging the D19's diesel engine was actually a late decision, once it was realized that 60 hp wasn't enough for a high-horsepower tractor.*

ABOVE: *It might not look glamorous, but this was Allis-Chalmers's 426 cu. in. direct injection engine, which powered the first 100 hp row-crop tractor in 1963.*

a massive diesel engine. Power outputs climbed as super-tractors grew larger, to 200 hp, then 300. The Steigers went on to build 120 giant tractors on their Minnesota farm during the 1960s, before joining forces with a business consortium and moving to a factory in Fargo, North Dakota. Their name became a byword for the type, but other specialists soon joined in, like Wagner and Big Bud.

The Steigers also made a good living out of selling their super-tractors to the mainstream manufacturers, such as Ford and Allis-Chalmers. They were later bought out altogether by J. I. Case. But International chose to build its own super-tractor, the 4300 in 1961. It was reportedly even more powerful than a Steiger, with 300 hp from its 817 cu. in. turbocharged diesel, which International made itself. With the help of an eight-speed transmission and seventeen-inch air-assisted clutch, it could pull a ten-furrow plow with ease. It also featured something else that was ahead of its time—the front and rear wheels could be steered independently, which allowed crab-style maneuverability. In 1964, Case also unveiled an in-house super-tractor, the 1200 Traction King. It used a 451 cu. in.

turbo diesel with oil cooler, and hydrostatic power steering. As with the International, front and rear wheels could be steered independently.

All these super-tractors had four-wheel drive. Like turbocharging, four-wheel drive was anything but new, and in fact all-wheel drive had been tried and put into production by a few tractor manufacturers right from the very early days, on machines like the 1910 Heer and 1912 Olmstead. But the 1960s saw four-wheel

drive enter the mainstream. The previous decade had seen several specialists grow up to convert standard tractors to four-wheel drive. Many of them were British: County and Roadless concentrated on Ford and Fordson tractors, while Bray converted the Nuffield machine.

BELOW: *Allis-Chalmers was first with turbocharging as well, with the 1961 D19. It was exciting stuff at the time, though the D19 was by no means the most powerful tractor on the market.*

A more formidable four-wheel-drive device was the Doe Triple-D. Ernest Doe, a British Fordson dealer, built up a business out of linking two Fordson Major tractors in tandem. The driver sat on the rear machine, controlling both via one set of controls! The Doe Triple-D was large and unwieldy, but for bigger farms it provided four-wheel drive and 100 hp, not available in any other wheeled tractor in Britain at the time. Other tandem conversions were built in the U.S., Australia, and France. Later, the mainstream manufacturers such as Ford and Massey-Ferguson were to introduce their own four-wheel drives, which effectively killed off the specialists.

But away from super-tractors, four-wheel drive, and four-wheel steering was something far more radical—John Deere abandoned the twin-cylinder Johnny Popper. In one fell swoop, the entire lineup of old JDs was dropped in favor of an all-new range of fours and sixes. They had a

huge impact. After all, Deere had been faithful to twin horizontal cylinders since the 1920s, and had inherited that layout from the 1914 Waterloo Boy. It was like Harley-Davidson announcing that it had ceased production of its famous V-twin cruisers, replacing them with a range of four-cylinder Japanese look-alikes.

ABOVE: *M670, the final 1964 update on Minneapolis-Moline's mid-size tractor, and still using the 336 cu. in. four-cylinder motor descended from the 1938 U series!*

BELOW: *At a stroke, John Deere dropped its entire twin-cylinder range in 1960, replacing it with an all-new lineup of threes and fours.*

Here's what the new 5020 can do for you

LEFT: *More power meant more furrows, and so more work done in less time. The new power-tractors were expensive to buy and maintain, but cheaper in the long run.*

BELOW: *"34 to 143 horsepower" for the John Deere 20 series, the first update on the new generation. Seven years' development ensured success for a new generation of JDs.*

BELOW: *ROPS (rollover protection system) first appeared in the 1960s, as can be seen on this International. For the first time, safety was being taken seriously by the industry.*

Eleven models – 34 to 143 horsepower...

But John Deere pulled it off. The new lineup of four-cylinder 1010, 2010, and 3010 four-cylinder machines, and the 4010 six, was very well received, even by John Deere traditionalists. In every way, they were a great advance on their twin-cylinder predecessors. More power, more comfort, and a wider choice of both ground speeds and transmission speeds. All but the smallest came in gasoline, diesel, or LPG form and all had three-point hitches with hydraulic load and depth control. The two largest models had power brakes and hydrostatic power steering as well.

Deere's research and development department must have been very busy, for it appears to have taken a lead in safety research too. It was the first to fit ROPS (rollover protection system) to its tractors, and took the unusual step of offering its patents to the rest of the industry. The company also developed Power Gard, designed to keep feet and hands out of swiftly rotating power takeoff shafts. Again, Deere made its patents generally available. Of course, John Deere wasn't the only company working hard to improve tractor safety, and its work merely reflected a growing awareness within the industry as a whole.

Meanwhile, small technical advances were going on all the time. Three-point hitches had long since become the industry standard, but that didn't mean it wasn't possible to improve on Harry Ferguson's original. In 1960, International introduced the first American-made three-point hitch with hydraulic draft control, using a torsion bar for the top link sensing. Massey-Ferguson, too, made its own improvements. Its Pressure Control hitch was claimed to bring hydraulic weight transfer to pull-type implements. The idea was to make tractor and implement work more as one unit, and a pressure control lever allowed the driver to transfer weight from the tractor's front wheels and the implement itself to the driving wheels.

Hydrostatic drive was another new feature that would become common in years to come. International had already developed a hydrostatic transmission in its experimental gas turbine tractor, the HT-340, so naturally it was first on the market with a production version, in 1967. The idea was simple. Instead of driving through a conventional geared transmission, the engine drove a hydraulic pump. This in turn drove a hydraulic motor which was connected to a high-low transmission. There was no clutch, as the hydraulic motor acted as a torque converter, but the main advantage was a very precise control of speed with no need for gear changes—speed control was actually infinite within the ranges. Final drive and rear axle were as on a conventional tractor. International launched the hydrostatic system on its bigger six-cylinder machines, in diesel or gasoline form.

Behind the technical advances, the tractor industry was changing as well. Companies like Ford and Massey-Ferguson had factories on both sides of the Atlantic, as well as other parts of the world, and decided to maximize their economies of

scale by having a single unified range, with each factory specializing in one size of machine. So the smaller Massey-Fergusons were built in England and France, the larger ones in Canada and the U.S. Ford began working toward its unified range in 1961, making use of British expertise in smaller diesel tractors to dovetail with its American experience in larger ones. But whichever continent they came from, these tractors carried the same corporate color scheme. It was really the start of a global economy in tractors, a process that continues today, when only specialist manufacturers can afford to survive with one factory in one country.

Associated with this trend, the 1960s saw increasing numbers of manufacturers buy in machines from outside to fill gaps in their own range. It was a much quicker and cheaper alternative to developing machines in-house, though something that carried its own dangers—becoming too dependent on outside technology, instead of developing one's own, could leave a manufacturer

ABOVE: *Fiat made inroads into the U.S. tractor market from the late 1960s onwards, as U.S. manufacturers began to find it increasingly difficult to make low-price tractors economically.*

vulnerable. This didn't bother Oliver, with its own well-established range of mid-size machines. It lacked a smaller tractor though, so it bought one in from David Brown of England in 1961—this was repainted in Oliver colors and badged the Oliver 500. It later bought Fiats as well, as did Minneapolis-Moline and Allis-Chalmers. Before it brought out its own big tractors, Massey-Ferguson sold Minneapolis-Molines under its own name —the M-F 97 was an M-M G705, 706, 707, or 708.

The world was changing, and no tractor manufacturer could afford to ignore the trend toward globalization. However, the next two decades would see tougher times, with echoes of the 1920s, as some long-established names were taken over, or closed down altogether.

MINNEAPOLIS-MOLINE M-5
[1960]

For nearly twenty years, Minneapolis-Moline's long-running U series had represented the company in the 40 hp class. Even the 5-Star that replaced it in 1957 used the same 283 cu. in. engine in gasoline and LPG form, though the diesel was upped in size to 336 cu. in. M-M was persevering with long-stroke, low-revving four-cylinder engines while many rivals were moving on to smoother, more powerful sixes. The 5-Star was a more comfortable ride than its predecessor, placing the driver ahead of the rear axle and astride the transmission.

The company welcomed the 1960s with another update, the M-5. This stuck with the tried and trusted 336 cu. in. four-cylinder diesel, though it did follow the smaller M-Ms in adopting Ampli-Torc, the dual range transmission that gave ten forward speeds. There were live hydraulics as well, plus power steering.

Perhaps bigger news came with the four-wheel-drive M504 in 1962. Basically an M-5 with mechanical front-wheel drive, Minneapolis claimed it was the industry's first sub-100 hp four-by-four tractor. Meanwhile, the 30 hp 335 and 38 hp 445 had been replaced by the Jet Star and 4-Star respectively, while the six-cylinder Gvi had built a good reputation in the big tractor class. But this range also revealed M-M's fundamental weakness—they had no sub-30 hp machine at all. This weakness meant that its days as an independent manufacturer were numbered.

LEFT: *Minneapolis-Moline had good value out of its long-running U series. Launched in 1938 (with a blaze of publicity, thanks to the sleek, attention-grabbing Comfortractor) it was in production for nearly twenty years. Even its 1957 replacement, the 5-Star, was more of an update of the same tractor. It also acquired some of the features of M-M's smaller, younger 335 and 445, with new squared-off styling and a new lower seating position that placed the driver astride the transmission—the latter position was fast becoming popular, as what the driver lost in visibility, he gained in comfort.*

MINNEAPOLIS-MOLINE M-5 DIESEL

Engine: Water-cooled, four-cylinder
Bore x stroke: 4.63 x 5.0 in.
Capacity: 336 cu. in.
PTO Power: 58 hp @ 1,500 rpm
Drawbar Power: 51.4 hp
Transmission: Five-speed
Speeds: 3.1–17.4 mph
Fuel Consumption: 13.3 hp/hr per gallon
Weight: 6,965 lb.

CASE 930
[1960]

J. I. Case & Co. had been very busy in the 1950s, playing catch-up after a decade or so of falling behind the competition. Technological improvements included the new diesel engine, Case-o-matic transmission (which added a torque converter to the existing eight-speed transmission), and

You'll handle more acres per day with **CASE** HI-TORQUE POWER

Two new *Comfort King* Tractors

a whole new range of tractors. Hardly surprising, then, that by the early 1960s they had run out of money, and so settled down to a few years of consolidation and marketing, rather than engineering.

Therefore there was no major new model launch until 1969, with the 70 series. In the meantime, the 30 series of 1960 brought little real change. Every tractor in the range acquired the new number, from the 30 hp 230 and 330, to the 37 hp 430 and 50 hp 530, not to mention the 630, and 50 hp 730/830. It all looked very neat, but its introduction did make a nonsense of the previous numbering system, in which each of the three digits told you something about the tractor.

Meanwhile, the new 930 was little more than the old 900, which was originally based on the 1929 Model L. However, the 930 did get a more substantial update as the Comfort King, in 1965. This model isolated the driver's platform by moving it up, away from the chassis, and mounting it on rubber. As farmers were never ones to prioritize comfort over economy, Case's marketing team attempted to push the potential profitability of a smoother, more comfortable tractor—less fatigue meant longer working hours, and therefore more profit. It worked well, so well in fact that Case extended rubber mounting to the 730 and 830 as well.

ABOVE: *"You'll handle more acres per day with CASE hi-torque power." Early tractors were sold on their simplicity, reliability, and ease of maintenance, a marketing plan aimed at farmers who had never owned a tractor before and needed convincing. But the 1960s consumer had very different priorities. In fact, there were three of them—power, power, and more power.*

LEFT: *It looked modern, thanks to that aggressive new styling, but the Case 930 still owed something to its predecessor, the 500, or for that matter the original foundation for that machine, the Model L of 1929. One big advance was the Comfort King's rubber mounting for the driver's platform. The rubber helped to isolate the driver's seat from much of the vibration and, according to the copywriters, helped reduce fatigue and increase working hours and profitability—a cab was an option as well.*

CASE 930 DIESEL

Engine: Water-cooled, six-cylinder
Bore x stroke: 4.125 x 5.0 in.
Capacity: 401 cu. in.
PTO Power: 80.7 hp @ 1,600 rpm
Drawbar Power: 70.9 hp @ 1,600 rpm
Transmission: Six-speed
Speeds: 2.5–13.6 mph
Fuel Consumption: 15.2 hp/hr per gallon
Weight: 8,845 lb.

ALLIS-CHALMERS D19/D21
[1961]

If the 1950s had seen the beginnings of a horsepower race in the U.S. tractor market, the 1960s saw a full-blown Grand Prix. Forty-five horsepower, once seen as the big, heavyweight class, now powered no more than a middleweight row-crop. Soon the target was 50 hp, then 60, then 70, then 100. There were various means of searching for more power, and two Allis-Chalmers machines of the early 1960s—the D19 and D21—illustrate this perfectly.

Take the D19, originally intended as a 60 hp D18, a modest step up from the 53 hp D17, then A-C's most powerful tractor. But

ABOVE: *Allis-Chalmers's logo depicted a gearwheel, a suitably simple engineering theme for the time. Many tractor manufacturer logos got a makeover in the 1960s—even Old Abe the eagle gave way to CASE, in bold, simple capital letters.*

LEFT: *You had to hand it to Allis-Chalmers. Before the Second World War, it was just a mid-size player in the tractor market. Its pioneering work with pneumatic tires put them ahead of the competition, but it still wasn't in the Ford or John Deere league. But postwar, A-C fought its way up among the big boys, thanks to a string of technical advances on the 1948 WD45, and the publicity garnered from two special tractors of the early 1960s: the D19 was America's first turbocharged tractor, and this D21 was the world's first 100 hp row-crop.*

ALLIS-CHALMERS D19

Engine: Water-cooled, six-cylinder, turbo
Bore x stroke: 3.6 x 4.4 in.
Capacity: 262 cu. in.
PTO Power: 67 hp @ 2,000 rpm
Drawbar Power: 62 hp @ 2,000 rpm
Transmission: Eight-speed
Fuel Consumption: 12.84 hp/hr
  per gallon
Weight: 6,835 lb.

when the development was quite far advanced, it was realized that 60 hp wouldn't be enough in 1961. What to do? The 262 cu. in. diesel could have been enlarged to 290 cu. in., until someone pointed out that a turbocharger would give the same power boost, and be quicker to develop. It worked, liberating an extra twenty-five percent power, to give 67 PTO hp and 62 hp at the drawbar. There was a 70 hp gasoline D19 as well, and for 1961, these were impressive figures.

It's a measure of how fast the power race was going that only two years later, A-C was ready to launch its first 100 hp tractor. After the success of the D19, it seemed likely that the company would opt to turbocharge the new D21 as well. In the end they actually created a massive new direct-injection diesel engine which relied on cubic inches, rather than a turbo, to get results. With 426 cu. in. and 103 hp, it again took A-C into new markets, and the D21 was so big it needed an all-new transmission and new range of implements to suit, including a seven-bottom plow. The D21 stayed in production for six years, and by the end of the decade it too had been turbocharged, taking them on another step in the horsepower Grand Prix.

BELOW: *A comfortable perch for the driver. The seat was well padded, and note the large spring supporting it. Combined with the ergonomic controls, these comforts were provided to encourage longer hours with less fatigue.*

RIGHT: *An eight-speed Power Director transmission permitted on-the-go clutchless shifting between two speeds (1/2, 3/5, 4/6, or 7/8, as here).*

BELOW: *Ammeter, oil pressure gauge, speed and engine revs, but the other gauges are beyond reading on this well-used D19, which has evidently spent much of its life outdoors.*

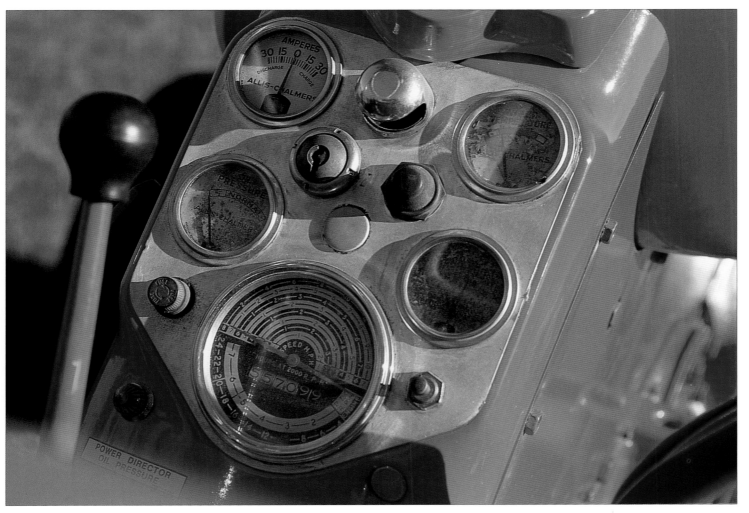

FORD 6000
[1961]

Until 1961, there were two Ford companies building tractors. One in the U.S., one in England. The split came about because Ford of Dagenham had declined the chance to built the new Ford-Ferguson 9N, preferring to carry on with its own development of the old Model N. That led to a new range of modern diesel tractors that were suited to British conditions, some of which were exported to the U.S. and sold through Ford dealers. Ford U.S. meanwhile, followed its own path, to suit their market.

But there was no attempt to coordinate the two tractor ranges. They even came in different colors—blue/orange British tractors sat alongside their gray/red stablemates in Ford dealers. But as Massey-Ferguson had already realized, rationalization was the only sure way to economies of scale, so in 1961 Ford established its "World Tractor" program. From now on, all Ford tractors—wherever they were made—would be part of a unified worldwide range, and all would come in the same corporate colors.

The 6000 pictured here was the first fruit of that change. It was a mid-range row-crop machine, using a 223 cu. in. six-cylinder gasoline engine or 242 cu. in. diesel. Unfortunately, it also used the troublesome Select-O-Matic transmission, which Ford had introduced a couple of years before. This allowed the driver to shift through all ten gears without stopping the tractor, but out in the field it just wasn't durable enough. However, despite various recalls and updates, it remained in production until 1967. It didn't matter though—Ford's career as a worldwide tractor manufacturer was underway.

LEFT: *Until the 1960s, Ford and Fordson concentrated exclusively on small, lightweight tractors. It wasn't until 1961, with the launch of the unified tractor range, that Ford finally began to make bigger tractors, of which this 6000 was the first. Implicitly, the company had realized that no mainstream manufacturer could survive by restricting itself to just one part of the market.*

FORD 6000 GASOLINE

Engine: Water-cooled, six-cylinder
Bore x stroke: 3.62 x 3.60 in.
Capacity: 223 cu. in.
PTO Power: 66.7 hp @ 2,400 rpm
Drawbar Power: 63.1 hp
Transmission: Ten-speed
Speeds: 1.2–18.2 mph
Fuel Consumption: 10.32 hp/hr
    per gallon
Weight: 7,225 lb.

URSUS C-325
[1961]

European farmers, and many in the U.S., associate Ursus with tractors. But this long-lived Polish engineering company has made a huge variety of products over the years. It was established in 1893, in Warsaw, to produce fittings for the sugar and food industries. By 1913, it was producing internal combustion engines, and built a total of 6,000 before the outbreak of the First World War, some of up to 450 hp. It soon turned its attention to tractors, building a prototype engine as early as 1918, though the first complete machine wasn't finished for another four years. It was a small-scale operation—just one hundred Ursus tractors were assembled over the next seven years, by which time the company was busy making buses and trucks as well.

Ursus collapsed in 1930, but it was saved by nationalization and went on to do very well during the Second World War, building cars, motorcycles, buses, and tanks, plus about 700 military tractors. It also continued to produce engines for planes and agriculture, and as stand-alone units.

Mass production of tractors finally began after the war, when Ursus started churning out a copy of the German Lanz Bulldog. As in many other industries, certain German designs were acquired as reparations. Ursus built 60,000 Bulldog copies between 1947 and 1959, but went on to develop its own machine, the C-325. This twin-cylinder diesel tractor was the first of a long line of light tractors from the Ursus factory.

LEFT: *This early Ursus owed a great deal to the Lanz Bulldog, one of the European single-cylinder diesel tractors that were so ubiquitous in the 1930s, 1940s, and early 1950s, when they gave way to multicylinder machines. Market conditions were different behind the Iron Curtain however, and Ursus was able to carry on making its Bulldog clone for a while. Even here though, the limitations of a single-cylinder became apparent, particularly for export markets. Hence the twin-cylinder C-325, which was tested at Nebraska in June/July 1961, and was the first Polish tractor to undergo the tests.*

URSUS C-325

Engine: Water-cooled, twin-cylinder
  diesel
Bore x stroke: 3.9 x 4.7 in.
Capacity: 111 cu. in.
PTO Power: 24.6 hp @ 2,000 rpm
Drawbar Power: 18 hp
Transmission: Six-speed
Fuel Consumption: 14.78 hp/hr
  per gallon
Weight: 4,849 lb. (incl. test ballast)

MASSEY-FERGUSON 97
[1962]

Massey-Ferguson badge, but a Minneapolis-Moline tractor. Look closely at one of these, and you find the famous "M-M" trademark stamped on the cylinder block. The M-F 97 was really a G705 Minneapolis in Massey-Ferguson colors. M-M had been here before.

Minneapolis Steel & Machinery was actually kick-started into the tractor business by building machines under contract for J. I. Case and the Bull company—these valuable contracts helped the company keep afloat while its own Twin City machines were established. The

M-F connection came much later, with the 95 Super, which was really a rebadged M-M Gvi. Nor was this Massey-Ferguson's only foray into badge-engineering—the M-F 98 of 1960 was really an Oliver 990.

The 97 came about for the same reasons. The newly unified Massey-Ferguson desperately needed a high-horsepower tractor to sell in the Midwest, and a rebadged Minneapolis-Moline was the quickest route. So the 97 was based first on the M-M G705 and four-wheel-drive G706, later on the updated 707 and 708. Only 429 M-F 97s were actually sold, but they did help establish the company as a seller of big tractors as well as small ones.

In any case, the company soon came up with its own big wheatland machine, the 88, a 60 hp tractor that also came in 4–5 plow row-crop form as the M-F 85.

LEFT: *In two ways, this Massey-Ferguson 97 gives away its Minneapolis-Moline heritage. M-M was a strong proponent of LPG fuel as an alternative to gasoline or diesel. LPG wasn't as economical as diesel, but was a cheaper fuel than gasoline, and many manufacturers offered it as an option in the 1960s. The LPG tank just in front of the steering wheel is the giveaway here. Spotted the second one yet? Drive-tread front wheels to match the rears denote a four-wheel-drive version, and here again Minneapolis-Moline was one of the first tractor makers to offer a four-wheel-drive option.*

MASSEY-FERGUSON 97 DIESEL

(Using G705 basis)

Engine: Water-cooled, six-cylinder
Bore x stroke: 4.63 x 5.0 in.
Capacity: 504 cu. in.
PTO Power: 101 hp @ 1,600 rpm
Drawbar Power: 90.8 hp
Transmission: Five-speed
Speeds: 3.3–18.3 mph
Fuel Consumption: 12.35 hp/hr
  per gallon
Weight: 8,155 lb.

JOHN DEERE 20 SERIES
[1963]

JOHN DEERE 4320 SYNCRO-RANGE DIESEL

Engine: Water-cooled, six-cylinder

Bore x stroke: 4.25 x 4.75 in.

Capacity: 404 cu. in.

PTO Power: 108 hp @ 2,200 rpm

Drawbar Power: 102 hp @ 2,200 rpm

Transmission: Eight-speed

Speeds: 2.0–18.9 mph

Fuel Consumption: 15.4 hp/hr per gallon

Weight: 10,675 lb.

In 1960, the sky fell in for John Deere enthusiasts. In one fell swoop, the entire range of old twin-cylinder machines was swept aside in favor of an all-new lineup of four- and six-cylinder tractors.

They were the result of a seven-year development program, ranged from 35 to 80 hp, and came with new styling to underline the transformation. Ninety-five percent of the parts were new—rumor has it the other five percent was probably accounted for by those JD badges and color scheme, the only things that hadn't changed! To arrive at this radically new range, the company had asked farmers what they wanted from a tractor. The answers were clear: more power, bigger fuel tanks, better transmissions and hydraulics, and extra comfort. With the new 10 series, they got it.

The new range was well received, but this didn't mean John Deere was going to rest on its laurels—the New Generation would receive regular updates in the coming years. So 1963 saw the arrival of the 20 series. The four-cylinder 3020 and six-cylinder 4020 had Power Shift shift-on-the-go transmission (with eight forward speeds), and were soon joined by a more powerful 5020. The 4020 in particular was a great success, accounting for nearly half of JD's entire sales in the U.S. and Canada in 1966. From that year it also had the option of front-wheel drive, offering a twenty percent boost to traction.

Generation II, the 30 series, was to come in the early 1970s, but the policy of constant updates didn't let up. In the meantime, the 4320 pictured here was uprated to 115 hp, from the standard 94 hp, and alongside it was the 4620, with a turbo-intercooled version of the same engine giving 135 hp. In a single decade, John Deere had come a very long way indeed.

LEFT: *John Deere's New Generation of 1960 (this is one of the subsequent updates) caused something of a stir. The company received a flood of letters from owners of faithful "Johnny Poppers," who couldn't understand why this long-running design had been abandoned overnight. However, once they tried the new four- and six-cylinder machines, most of them soon came around—the New Generation proved to be just as economical and (mostly) reliable as the old twins, but with new convenience features like power steering. The gamble of replacing its entire range paid off, and John Deere entered a new era.*

MINNEAPOLIS-MOLINE G705

[1963]

Minneapolis-Moline had renewed its mid-range tractors in the mid-1950s, with the 335 and 445. But its big machines had to wait until 1963, when the Gvi was finally replaced by the G705, first of the M-M G series tractors. For the first time, there was no gasoline option, just diesel or LPG, both based on the same 504 cu. in. six-cylinder engine which M-M built itself. There was a 706 as well, which had four-wheel-drive, but was otherwise mechanically the same as the 705. Both LPG and diesel were rated by the company with 105 hp at the flywheel at first, though this was later revised to 112 hp. Nebraskan tests on the diesel however, suggested just 101 hp. Whatever the power, four-wheel drive was an expensive option, adding $2,000 to the G705 Diesel's basic price of $6,725, but it was a sign of things to come—as power increased, four-wheel drive became the only practical means of applying it without losing traction. Both 705 and 706 used the latest squared-off but slightly rounded styling, and were finished in yellow with white highlights. They were superseded in 1965 by the 707 and 708.

BELOW: *This is a G705 Rice Field Special, one of thirty-one converted by a specialist company.*

MINNEAPOLIS-MOLINE G705 DIESEL

Engine: Water-cooled, six-cylinder

Bore x stroke: 4.63 x 5.0 in.

Capacity: 504 cu. in.

PTO Power: 101 hp @ 1,600 rpm

Drawbar Power: 90.8 hp

Transmission: Five-speed

Speeds: 3.3–18.3 mph

Fuel Consumption: 12.35 hp/hr per gallon

Weight: 8,155 lb.

MINNEAPOLIS-MOLINE G706
[1963]

MINNEAPOLIS-MOLINE
G706 LPG

Engine: Water-cooled, six-cylinder

Bore x stroke: 4.63 x 5.0 in.

Capacity: 504 cu. in.

PTO Power: 101 hp @ 1,600 rpm

Drawbar Power: 86.2 hp

Transmission: Five-speed

Speeds: 3.3–18.3 mph

Fuel Consumption: 7.82 hp/hr per gallon

Weight: 9,165 lb. (diesel model)

Four-wheel-drive tractors were nothing new—some steam traction engines had offered it in the 1880s, and several tractor manufacturers were building four-by-fours before the First World War. In the 1920s and 1930s, Lanz of Germany, Pavesi of Italy, and Massey-Harris all built four-wheel-drive tractors, and after the Second World War a whole raft of specialist companies in the U.S. and Britain offered four-by-four conversions of existing tractors.

But as the 1960s progressed, the demand for four-by-fours grew, not least because tractors were getting more powerful by the year. Once over 100 hp, all-wheel drive was the most efficient means of transmitting all that power to the ground. Much of this demand was for much larger super-tractors, which had been captured early by specialists like Steiger.

The Minneapolis-Moline was not one of these. The company was actually a pioneer of four-wheel drive in smaller machines, unveiling the G706 in 1963. It would be another decade before four-wheel drive—whether full four-wheel drive or the cheaper front-wheel assist—became a common feature on this class of tractor.

Not that being a pioneer helped M-M very much. The same year as the 706 was announced, it was taken over by White Motors, and in 1974 the name was dropped altogether, after a decade of badge engineering. But the G706 wasn't M-M's last four-by-four. The articulated A4T was launched in 1969, using the company's own 504 cu. in. engine and ten-speed transmission.

LEFT: *In the early 1960s, the G705 and G706 were the biggest tractors offered by Minneapolis-Moline, powered by their own six-cylinder power unit, which itself shared bore and stroke dimensions with the much older four-cylinder 336 cu. in. unit. As was the pattern in bigger M-M machines, it was offered in low-compression LPG as well as high-compression gasoline form, and as a diesel. It was replaced in 1965 by the G1000, though still with the same 504 cu. in. six- and five-speed transmission plus the Ampli-Torc dual range. In 1967, this was supplanted by the G900, with a 425 cu. in. version of the same engine, and the same gasoline, LPG, or diesel options. Minneapolis-Moline was unusual in persevering with a gasoline alternative on such a large tractor—diesel was increasingly dominant at this level, to cut fuel costs.*

MINNEAPOLIS-MOLINE M670
[1964]

This was the last gasp of Minneapolis-Moline's homegrown mid-range tractors, the M series, which had begun with the M-5 in 1960 but whose roots went back much further. After the takeover by White Motors in 1963, the company increasingly specialized in much larger machines, all powered by its own 504 cu. in. six-cylinder engine.

But through the 1960s, the M670 carried on, still powered by M-M's faithful 336 cu. in. four-cylinder engine, in gasoline, LPG, or diesel form. This motor had been used in the M670's predecessor, the M-5, and the Five-Star before that, and was basically a bored-out version of the 283 cu. in. U series motor of 1938!

The M-5 had been superseded by the short-lived M602 (plus an M604 four-wheel-drive variant), which was offered in 1963–64. The M670 lasted longer; it was launched in 1964 and featured in the M-M lineup right through to 1970. They also offered the smaller U302 alongside it, announced the same year. This shared styling with the big G705 and G706, and was a four-bottom plow machine.

BELOW: *Final update on the midsize M-M, the M670 was in production for six years.*

MINNEAPOLIS-MOLINE M670 GASOLINE

Engine: Water-cooled, four-cylinder
Bore x stroke: 4.63 x 5.0 in.
Capacity: 336 cu. in.
PTO Power: 73 hp @ 1,600 rpm
Drawbar Power: 62.2 hp
Transmission: Ten-speed
Speeds: 1.6–17.2 mph
Fuel Consumption: 9.89 hp/hr per gallon
Weight: 7,395 lb.

MASSEY-FERGUSON 135
[1964]

At the London Smithfield Agricultural Show in 1964, Massey-Ferguson unveiled its most important tractor line to date. The 100 series Red Giants represented a complete renewal of the M-F range, as they replaced the old 35, 40, and 50 in one fell swoop.

Just as Ford had initiated its worldwide unified range of tractors a few years earlier, so was this for Massey-Ferguson. The 100 series was built to a worldwide specification, with only minor differences between different national markets. The smaller tractors were built in Britain and France, the larger ones in the U.S., with exports both ways. That suited the tractor expertise on each side of the Atlantic, as well as the dominant market.

Baby of the British-made Red Giants was this, the little 135, which was to become a familiar sight on British farms for the next twenty years. But though the Red Giants looked completely new—and they were the result of a major R&D program—some components were carried over from

previous Massey-Fergusons. The 135 offered the same power options as its 35 predecessor: Continental 134 cu. in. gasoline or Perkins 152 cu. in. three-cylinder diesel. The gasoline option was mainly for the benefit of U.S. farmers, as in Europe diesel was now the norm for farm tractors. Whatever its power unit, the 135 also retained the 35's beam front axle, though the larger 150 and 165 had a different front end to accommodate row-crop equipment. However, there was a new six-speed transmission, or twelve-speed with the optional multipower.

LEFT: *Spiritual successor to the original little gray Fergie, the Massey-Ferguson 135 was the smallest of the new 1964 Red Giants, though M-F's French arm later built a smaller still 130.*

BELOW: *Engine choices for the 135 were carried over from the Ferguson 35—Continental gasoline or Perkins diesel, the Continental in place with an eye on exports to the U.S.*

MASSEY-FERGUSON 135 GASOLINE (1965)

Engine: Water-cooled, four-cylinder
Capacity: 152 cu. in.
PTO Power: 35.4 hp @ 2,000 rpm
Drawbar Power: 30.5 hp
Transmission: Twelve-speed
Speeds: 1.4–19.8 mph
Fuel Consumption: 9.02 hp/hr per gallon
Weight: 3,565 lb.

MASSEY-FERGUSON 150
[1964]

This, the 150, was the mid-range model of the Red Giants, though in reality it was very similar in specification to the 135 —the engine and transmission options were identical.

Just as the 135 was a straight replacement for the M-F 35, so the 150 did the same for the old Model 50. It used the same hydraulics as the 50, but the control was repositioned on the right side of the transmission. There was also a new feature named Pressure Control, which allowed for weight transfer from implements, plus auxiliary hydraulics for operating equip-

ment off the tractor. This was soon made standard on the 165 and 175, though it remained an option on the smaller machines. As with the 135, the Continental gasoline engine was kept on for the benefit of U.S. farmers, though in 1969 this was dropped in favor of a gas version of the Perkins diesel.

The 150 itself was later dropped, being so similar in specification and performance to the cheaper 135. There were in any case plenty of other M-Fs to choose from, such as the 165 and smaller 130. The latter was made in France, and the smallest M-F sold in Britain, using a Perkins 107 cu. in. four-cylinder diesel. The French arm of M-F also produced vineyard and orchard versions of both this and the 135. Again, M-F was building these tractors close to their biggest markets—vineyard models in France, small utility tractors in Britain, and high-horsepower machines in the U.S.

LEFT: *An early cab on this Massey-Ferguson 152— cabs would rapidly progress in comfort and sophistication as the 1960s gave way to the 1970s. Better still, they began to incorporate rollover protection, a protective frame built strong enough to protect the driver if the tractor turned over. Over the years, hundreds of tractor drivers were killed, and many more injured, when their machines turned over—the Ferguson hitch had made the old problem of a tractor turning over backward far less likely, but they could still topple sideways when traversing a slope.*

MASSEY-FERGUSON 150 DIESEL (1965)

Engine: Water-cooled, three-cylinder
Bore x stroke: 3.6 x 5.0 in.
Capacity: 152 cu. in.
PTO Power: 37.8 hp @ 2,000 rpm
Drawbar Power: 33 hp
Transmission: Twelve-speed
Speeds: 1.4–18.6 mph
Fuel Consumption: 15.4 hp/hr per gallon
Weight: 4,805 lb.

MASSEY-FERGUSON 165
[1964]

This was the Red Giants' flagship, powered by the same 50 hp 203 cu. in. Perkins as the Massey-Ferguson 65, or a 176 cu. in. gasoline engine. But it didn't stay top dog for long, soon being joined by a more powerful 175. This too was powered by a Perkins four-cylinder diesel, but of 236 cu. in. capacity—it was an engine designed specifically for this tractor. In 1971, the 175 was itself replaced by the more powerful still 178, this time with a 248 cu. in. Perkins.

The Red Giants had their first major update later that year, when the range diverged into two separate lines. For budget customers, M-F produced the no-frills value-for-money tractor: the "Standard Rig" 135, 165, and new 185, with no multipower or power steering. But if you could afford it, the "Super Spec" 148, 168, and 188 (based on the 135, 165, and 185 respectively) came with a whole raft of new features.

The wheelbase was longer, which allowed the fitting of a more spacious safety cab—the first cabs had restricted access—and also brought better weight distribution, so that heavier implements could be used without the need for front weights. Super Spec tractors also had the twelve-speed multipower transmission as standard, plus independent PTO, a suspension seat and high capacity hydraulic pump. The top 188 added power steering and power-adjusted wheel tread.

LEFT: *In Europe, Massey-Ferguson is often perceived as a British manufacturer, though in reality it was Canadian owned, and highly dependent on the huge U.S. tractor market—this was the biggest in the Western world, and no mainstream manufacturer could afford to ignore it. Massey-Ferguson's range reflected this, with row-crop versions of the 150 and this 165, aimed at American farmers. These were still small tractors by American standards, but M-F also built high-horsepower machines for the American prairies, such as the 90 hp 1100 and 120 hp 1130. The 1968 1150 used a 135 hp Perkins V8 diesel.*

MASSEY-FERGUSON 165 GASOLINE (1965)

Engine: Water-cooled, four-cylinder
Bore x stroke: 3.58 x 4.38 in.
Capacity: 176 cu. in.
PTO Power: 46.9 hp @ 2,000 rpm
Drawbar Power: 39.9 hp
Transmission: Twelve-speed
Speeds: 1.3–18.5 mph
Fuel Consumption: 9.43 hp/hr per gallon
Weight: 5,005 lb.

FORD 3000

[1965]

FORD 3000 DIESEL

Engine: Water-cooled, three-cylinder

Bore x stroke: 4.2 x 3.5 in.

Capacity: 155 cu. in.

PTO Power: 38 hp @ 2,000 rpm

Drawbar Power: 33 hp @ 2,000 rpm

Torque: 118 lb. ft. @ 1,150 rpm

Transmission: Ten-speed (optional)

Speeds: 1.0–16.4 mph

Weight: 3,790 lb.

For Ford, the mid-1960s was a time of busily building up its unified world-wide range of tractors. The big 6000 had been the first, in 1961, and in that same year the British-built Fordson Super Major was renamed the Ford 5000 to slot in underneath it—part of the rationalization involved the final pensioning off of the Fordson name. Meanwhile, the old 800/900 series was now the 4000 and the 600/700 became the 2000. The Dagenham-built Dexta, a well thought of little tractor, became the 2000 Diesel while Ford U.S.'s own small diesel was dropped.

Four years later, the gap between 2000 and 4000 was filled by . . . you guessed it, the 3000. With modern squared-off styling to match the bigger tractors, this was powered by a three-cylinder gasoline or diesel engine. The little 2000 was updated at the same time. The 3000 also came in narrow form, for orchard work and vine-yards, with an overall width of just 52 in., ten inches less than the standard 3000. A downswept exhaust, new rear mudguards and new seat completed the package. There was even a four-wheel drive 3000, though this was built by English conversion specialist Roadless—their Ploughmaster 46, launched in 1966 was built in small numbers, using an Italian Selene front axle.

BELOW: *The 3000 utility tractor, powered by a 37 hp three-cylinder diesel, neatly filled the gap between 2000 (an updated 600/700) and 4000 (800/900). But it was a small machine, and meanwhile the high-horsepower Grand Prix was forging ahead. Ford responded in 1968 with the 8000, its first tractor to break the 100 hp barrier.*

RENAULT SUPER D

[1965]

Renault—the dominant French tractor manufacturer—was a pioneer car manufacturer, but didn't build its first tractor, a crawler based on a wartime tank, until 1919. A wheeled version soon followed, and from the start, Renault tractors used their distinctive curved hood with the radiator mounted well back, out of harm's way. Unlike other European manufacturers that built semi-diesel tractors, Renault stuck with gasoline-kerosene spark-ignition engines at first, though it did experiment with diesels from 1931, and launched a production diesel tractor, the VY, two years later. A 45 hp machine was the first French diesel tractor, but the company also experimented with gas power from the 1920s and used methane during the Second World War.

After the war, Renault built 7,500 gasoline-kerosene types in 1947–48 alone. The 3040 formed the core of its tractor range, and was its first with a full electrical system. It also had a two-speed PTO, hydraulic lift, and adjustable tread. The D series of 1956 was unusual in offering air-cooled as well as water-cooled diesels, and the rest of the tractor—differential lock, syncromesh transmission, and 540 rpm PTO—was fully up-to-date. All it lacked was the three-point hitch, but that arrived with the Super D pictured here. Launched in 1965, this was the pinnacle of the D series, equipped with Tracto Control hydraulics. Launched in 1965, the Super D was the pinnacle of the D series, equipped with Tracto Control hydraulics. Although the Super D was a great advance on the

RENAULT 3045 (1955)	
Engine: Water-cooled, four-cylinder	
Bore x stroke: 3.3 x 4.1 in.	
Capacity: 144 cu. in.	
Power: 22 hp	
Transmission: Four-speed	

Renault tractors of a decade earlier, there was a direct link between it and Renault tractors of the 1950s. Specifications for the 1955 3045 are given above.

BELOW: *France proved a receptive market to small, maneuverable tractors, and Renault blossomed as the major independent French manufacturer of up-to-date, high-tech tractors.*

LAMBORGHINI
[1965]

Lamborghini is a name associated with luxury sports cars, but Senior Ferruccio Lamborghini was making tractors long before he built cars. In fact, the story goes that he only turned to sports cars after a dismissive remark by Enzo Ferrari—"You should stick to tractors!"

Lamborghini was a farmer, born in 1916, though he also studied mechanical engineering at Bologna University and found his niche after the Second World War with a real swords-into-plowshares operation, concerned with converting surplus military hardware into agricultural machinery. In 1949, the Carioca model used a British Morris engine, converted from gas to diesel.

But the following year saw the first all-Lamborghini tractor, the L33, though this too used a Morris-based engine, with the addition of Lamborghini's patented hot-bulb. When the supply of Morris engines dried up, Lamborghini turned to MWM and Perkins diesels before developing his own air-cooled engines in 1954. The company was already making its own transmissions, and much later (in 1966) Lamborghini tractors were the first in Italy to be sold with a synchromesh transmission.

All went well until a large order from Bolivia for 5,000 tractors fell though. This, plus an economic slump in the early 1970s, led Snr. Lamborghini to sell his tractor business to SAME. Since then, the line has flourished, producing thousands of high-tech tractors a year. (Due to a paucity of information on earlier models, specifications given here are for the Lamborghini 1056 DT, tested at Nebraska in March/April 1978.)

LEFT: *After Lamborghini sold out to SAME, his workers could have been forgiven for fearing job losses. But under SAME ownership, Lamborghini tractors did well. A big range of two-, three-, four-, and six-cylinder air-cooled diesels was available in the 1970s, with 10,000 a year (both wheeled tractors and crawlers) rolling off the line by 1980. This sprayer-equipped 674 is typical of the later modern Lamborghinis.*

LAMBORGHINI 1056 DT
(1978)

Engine: Air-cooled, six-cylinder diesel
Bore & stroke: 3.86 x 4.72 in.
Capacity: 331 cu. in.
PTO Power: 92 hp @ 2,220 rpm
Drawbar Power: 75 hp @ 2,220 rpm
Transmission: Twelve-speed
Speeds: 0.9–16.1 mph
Weight: 10,350 lb.

CASE 1030 DIESEL
[1966]

It might have caught up in other ways, but Case was in danger of getting left behind in the power race. Even the 80 hp 930, using the company's now well-established 401 cu. in. six-cylinder diesel, wasn't powerful enough any more. Now 100 hp was the aim.

LEFT: *High seat, high power. Complete with the Comfort King rubber-mounted operator platform, the 1030 was Case's most powerful tractor for the mid-1960s.*

ABOVE: *Instead of turbocharging, Case chose to increase its engine capacity to produce its first 100 hp tractor. Adding a quarter-inch to the bore of the six-cylinder diesel did the trick.*

It wasn't power for its own sake. Instead, the search for more tractor power was all about exacting a higher rate of work. If a tractor had, say, a twenty percent power boost, that could turn it from a four-plow into a five-plow machine. Assuming the same speed, that meant twenty-five percent more acres worked in a day. So the tractor power race wasn't simply a marketing man's tool, though there's no denying that it was a gift to tractor salesmen.

Case's first response was the 930GP, which combined the 930's big diesel engine with the smaller 730 row-crop chassis. But that on its own wasn't enough—the flagship tractor needed to have that magic "100" figure in the horsepower column of its specification sheet. Case could have decided to turbocharge its diesel, but it chose instead to take the cubic-inch route.

The bore was increased by a quarter-inch to give a capacity of 451 cu. in., though the

five-inch stroke was unchanged. Combined with a new rated speed of 2,000 rpm, that gave 102 hp, breeching the magical "100" barrier, the most powerful Case tractor yet. However, it wasn't long before turbocharging came along as well—there seemed to be no end to the horsepower war.

CASE 1030 DIESEL

Engine: Water-cooled six-cylinder
Bore x stroke: 4.375 x 5.0 in.
Capacity: 451 cu. in.
PTO Power: 102 hp @ 2,000 rpm
Drawbar Power: 88 hp @ 2,000 rpm
Transmission: Eight-speed
Speeds: 2.0–16.2 mph
Fuel Consumption: 13.24 hp/hr
  per gallon
Weight: 9,335 lb.

LEFT: *Now measuring 451 cu. in. the Case straight six produced 102 hp at 2,000 rpm, according to Nebraska. Not that this put it ahead of the game— Allis-Chalmers had offered a 100 hp row-crop three years earlier. Still, turbocharging the 451 would boost that to 120 hp.*

BELOW: *As power increased, year on year, the problem of transmitting it to the ground without excessive wheelspin became ever greater, in the days before four-wheel drive became common for 100 hp+ machines. Twin rear wheels (not shown on this Case) were a popular solution.*

ABOVE: *The 1030 presented a bold front, but Case itself was running out of money in the mid-1960s. It had invested a great deal in renewing and updating its entire range in the 1950s, thanks in part to the exuberant leadership of Marc Rojtman, but now the company just didn't have the financial muscle to survive independently. A partial takeover by Tenneco in 1967 gave the stability it needed.*

RIGHT: *Case tractors were still wearing the aggressive twin headlight front end introduced in 1960, but this would change.*

ALLIS-CHALMERS ONE SEVENTY [1967]

Fashion affects tractors as much as it affects almost anything else. The Allis-Chalmers D series, which seemed so fresh and clean in the late 1950s, was beginning to seem outdated by the mid-1960s. Not so much in their technical specification, but the way they looked.

The new look, from the mid-1960s, right through the 1970s and beyond, was a severe, squared off appearance that all tractors eventually adopted. Allis had already hinted at this with the giant, square-rigged D21 of 1963, but now the entire range was going that way. A-C introduced the new 100 series gradually. A One Ninety appeared in 1965, to replace the turbocharged D19. The One Ninety didn't offer a turbo at first, until it became clear that the standard 301 cu. in. six-cylinder engine just wasn't powerful enough to keep up with its 90 hp rivals.

The engine was part of a new family of power units for the 100 series. There were six of them, of either four or six cylinders, but all sharing many components to maximize economies of scale. Gasoline, LPG, or diesel versions were offered. Two years later, the big One Ninety was followed by the One Seventy (pictured here) and One Eighty, which jointly replaced the D17. Under the skin, they carried over plenty of D17 parts as well: the Power Director, Traction Booster, and four-speed transmission were unchanged.

But there were some new features—a safety cab was offered for the first time, reflecting increasing concern about roll-over accidents. And the One Seventy could be had with a Perkins diesel of 236 cu. in., which produced just over 50 PTO hp, 39 hp at the drawbar. It was the first time A-C had bought in an engine for many years. Both tractors were soon uprated as the 175/185, which in diesel form were available for another twelve years.

LEFT: *Allis-Chalmers re-skinned and re-engined the D series from the mid-1960s. This One Seventy, and a new One Eighty, jointly replaced the D17.*

ALLIS-CHALMERS ONE SEVENTY

Engine: Water-cooled, four-cylinder
Capacity: 236 cu. in.
PTO Power: 54 hp
Drawbar Power: 39.4 hp
Fuel Consumption: 16.38 hp/hr
  per gallon
Transmission: Eight-speed
Speeds: 2.0–13.3 mph
Weight: 5,950 lb.

INTERNATIONAL 1256

[1967]

Remember the power race that gathered pace after the Second World War? By the late 1960s, it was running full speed ahead. Allis-Chalmers had been the first mainstream manufacturer with a 100 hp machine, in 1963. International's answer arrived two years later, though its devel-opment may have been prolonged by lack of experience with such high-horsepower machines. Even in 1965 most tractors were in the 40–70 hp class and 100 hp was rare.

The 1206 used a turbocharged version of International's existing D361 six-cylinder engine which was already used in the 806 tractor. The transmission was beefed up to suit, with hardened gears, heavier pinions, and final drive gears. It certainly needed to be—the prototype 1206 had so much power that conventional tires buckled their sidewalls or simply span off the rim. A new tire had to be designed specifically for the 1206, one that could cope with its pro-digious power output.

In 1967, the 1206 was updated as the 1256 (as pictured here), which was part of a whole new range of 56 series Inter-nationals. In the quest for yet more power, the turbo diesel was enlarged to 407 cu. in. Driver comfort and safety was getting a higher billing now, too, and a "Deluxe" two-door cab was optional on the 1256, as was two-post ROPS (rollover protection system) and the amazing luxury of air-conditioning. But the power race carried on, and just to illustrate the pace of change, specifications are given below for the 1973 International 1466, which just a few years after the 1256 was offering over 140 hp in standard form.

LEFT: *With 100 hp as the latest power target, most manufacturers responded with bigger six-cylinder diesel engines. Allis-Chalmers had led the way with its all-new 426 cu. in. direct injection unit in 1963. Ford managed the magic three figures with its 401 cu. in. six, while Minneapolis-Moline upsized its long-lived engine to 504 cu. in. International chose the turbo route instead, basing its 100 hp engine on its existing 361 cu. in. unit. It certainly did the trick.*

INTERNATIONAL 1466 (1973)

Engine: Water-cooled, six-cylinder turbo-diesel
Bore x stroke: 4.3 x 5.0 in.
Capacity: 436 cu. in.
PTO Power: 146 hp @ 2,600 rpm
Drawbar Power: 123 hp @ 2,600 rpm
Fuel Consumption: 15.31 hp/hr per gallon
Weight: 13,670 lb.

URSUS 4514
[1967]

Ursus of Poland was a well-established tractor maker by the 1960s. It had built many thousands of semi-diesel machines based on the German Lanz, and developed its own twin-cylinder machine. But as the decade progressed, it became increasingly dependent on Zetor of Czechoslovakia. It wasn't completely one-way—Ursus built front axles and hydraulics for Zetor, but about half the components of Ursus tractors came from Czechoslovakia, and there's little doubt that technically the Czechoslovakians were far ahead of Ursus.

According to one anonymous writer (in the book *Vintage Tractor Album*) this sometimes led to foreboding on the Zetor side: "The quality of the metal in both Ursus and Zetor gears has sometimes given ample grounds for criticism and caused Zetor men in unguarded moments to mutter that they wish they could return to producing the whole tractor themselves."

So close was the relationship with Zetor, that the "new" Ursus 4011 of 1965 was, according to one writer, no more than the already-obsolete Zetor 4011. The 4514 (pictured here) was a development of that machine, though it went on to be updated, and as the C-355 and C-360 was actually produced up to 1992. By then, Ursus had already come a long way, after a licensing agreement was signed with Massey-Ferguson in the early 1970s.

LEFT: *Don't be fooled by the "Lightforce Deluxe," this really is an Ursus. From producing outdated single-cylinder machines in the late 1950s, Ursus developed its own twins and fours in the 1960s, some of which were also exported to the U.S. The C-350 Diesel was tested by Nebraska in July 1968, and produced 43 hp at the PTO from its Ursus-built 190 cu. in. power unit. Ten forward gear ratios allowed a slow crawl of 0.9 mph up to nearly 16 mph on the road. The mid-size Ursus only needed a small amount of attention during its fifty-five hours of testing: the throttle lever friction brake had to be adjusted and the plastic fuel sediment bowl replaced.*

URSUS C-350 (1968)

Engine: Water-cooled, four-cylinder diesel
Bore x stroke: 3.7 x 4.3 in.
Capacity: 185 cu. in.
PTO Power: 43 hp
Drawbar Power: 37 hp
Transmission: Ten-speed
Speeds: 0.9–15.9 mph
Fuel Consumption: 14.6 hp/hr per gallon
Weight: 4,880 lb.

BIG BUD 525/50 DIESEL
[1968]

Super-tractors, the 500 hp four-wheel-drive monsters that roam the wheat prairies of the Midwest, are a peculiarly American invention. It's only on these really big acreages that such expensive machines make any kind of economic sense. But they weren't pioneered by Case-International, or Allis, or John Deere. Instead, small independents like the Steiger brothers or Big Bud got there first.

When it was launched in 1968, the Big Bud was the biggest tractor in the world, powered by a 250 bhp six-cylinder diesel. Big Buds used truck engines married to tractor type transmissions and four-wheel drive. Quite appropriate, as the machine looked like a mutant truck with some tractor overtones. It was evidently a success, for a second series of Big Buds was announced in 1977. The power options now extended from 320 to 525 bhp, while the cab was widened to 60 in. though otherwise much of this Big Bud was similar to the original.

A third series went on sale in 1979, now with up to 650 bhp and mostly using Twin Disk Power Shift transmissions. A ROPS safety cab was later added, before the fourth series Big Bud arrived in 1986. This had a new oscillation system and used mainly twelve-speed power shift transmissions. Power was up to 740 bhp. More recently, the Big Bud 16V-747 boasted a V16 Detroit Diesel two-stroke, with twin turbochargers and 760 bhp at 2,100 rpm.

LEFT: *They don't come much bigger than this. Big Buds reflected the giant farms of the Midwest, where the acreage made super-tractors like this viable, despite their sky-high prices and scary running costs. All followed the formula established by the Steiger brothers in the late 1950s: articulated chassis, four-wheel drive through equal-size wheels, and a massive diesel engine. The latter was generally bought off the shelf from a non-tractor source, for the simple reason that these super-tractors required more power than any existing tractor. Double or triple wheels were used to maximize traction.*

BIG BUD 525/50 DIESEL

Engine: Water-cooled, six-cylinder, turbo intercooled
Bore x stroke: 6.25 x 6.25 in.
Capacity: 1,150 cu. in.
PTO Power: Not measured
Drawbar Power: 406 hp @ 2,100 rpm
Transmission: Nine-speed
Speeds: Not measured
Fuel Consumption: 14.9 hp/hr per gallon
Speeds: Up to 25 mph
Weight: 51,920 lb.

MINNEAPOLIS-MOLINE G1050
[1969]

Minneapolis-Moline, which started the 1960s with a complete range of tractors built in-house, ended it heavily dependent on badge-engineering—that is, selling someone else's machine with its own badge and paintwork. The M-M G350 and G450 were imported Fiat tractors, repainted in M-M colors. But there were still some new M-M's in the late 1960s, albeit with a strong contribution from existing parts bins. The G1050 (pictured here) started out as the G1000 in 1965, a new big row-crop tractor which used the now familiar 504 cu. in. six-cylinder engine in diesel or LPG forms. As with the rest of the range, transmission was five-speed plus two-speed Ampli-Torc.

It was updated as the G1000 Vista a couple of years later. As befitted its name, the Vista had a higher, and further forward driving position, which gave much better visibility for the driver. Specifications for the Vista are given below, for the LPG model that was tested by Nebraska in 1968.

There were further variations on the same theme. A G900 appeared in 1967, based on the same chassis but with a smaller 425 cu. in. engine in diesel, LPG, or (increasingly unusual) gasoline forms. All were available as wheatland tractors in two-wheel-drive form.

But 1969 saw the introduction of new sheet metal to produce the G1050 (shown here), plus a similar G955. The final new M-M was the G1355 of 1973, with an enlarged 585 cu. in. engine and Oliver transmission, before the name was finally dropped the following year.

LEFT: *This is the LPG-fueled Minneapolis-Moline G1050, which gives its power source away by the two big tanks, with one on the nose, and the other squeezed between engine and cab. The G1050 wasn't massively powerful at 111 hp, but this one still has twin rear wheels fitted. Note the large, spacious cab—prior to the option of air conditioning, tinted glass was a very desirable fitment, which helped to lessen the greenhouse effect of those big windows on a hot summer's day.*

MINNEAPOLIS-MOLINE G-1000 VISTA LPG

Engine: Water-cooled, six-cylinder
Bore x stroke: 4.63 x 5.0 in.
Capacity: 504 cu. in.
PTO Power: 111 hp @ 1,800 rpm
Drawbar Power: 96.6 hp
Transmission: Ten-speed
Speeds: 2.3–18.0 mph
Fuel Consumption: 8.33 hp/hr per gallon
Weight: 11,960 lb.

The 1970s:
BIG IS BEAUTIFUL

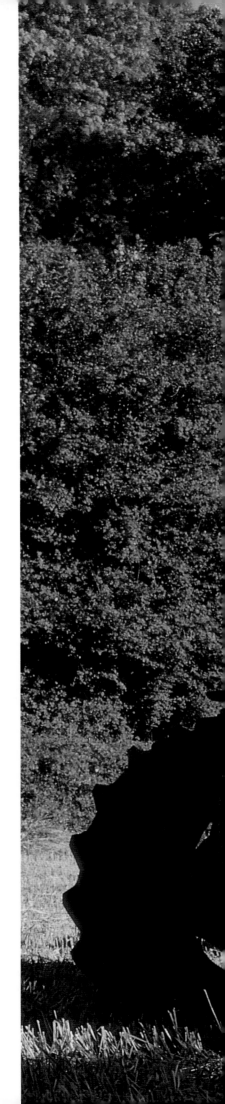

In the 1970s, the world suffered its first oil crisis. Some knew it as the "oil shock," and for a good reason—it was a wake-up call to the Western world, that cheap, plentiful oil could no longer be depended on, whether for political reasons, for economics, for the simple fact that sooner or later oil wells run dry. An outsider to the tractor industry might therefore ask, Why did the power race continue almost without pausing for breath? Surely bigger, more powerful tractors guzzle more fuel?

They do, of course, but in the process they often do proportionately more work. Bigger tractors can pull bigger plows, and pull them faster. So if farmers could afford to pay for ever more expensive, complex, and powerful tractors, they would (eventually) save money. But an interesting aside was some research at the time which found that drivers of the new breed of high-power tractors, of 90 hp or more, weren't making use of all that extra power, so work rates weren't improving. In fact, close examination revealed that high-power tractors were only achieving around half their potential work rates. The reason was something tractor manufacturers hadn't given much thought to—driver comfort. With more power came more noise and vibration, so drivers were naturally holding back. What a factory's test driver might find acceptable for short stints was too much for the farmer spending ten hours a day at the wheel.

So the 1970s saw great improvements in this area—quieter, safer, and more comfortable cabs were a key step forward at this time. Aftermarket cabs had been available in the 1960s, but they were often crude things that allowed dust in and made noise levels worse. Nebraska began to include noise tests from 1970, reflecting increasing concern about this issue—there was now plenty of evidence that prolonged tractor driving led to occupational deafness. The only answer was purpose-designed cabs from the tractor manufacturers. And that's exactly what happened. Nebraska's noise figures through the 1970s paint a dramatic picture. In 1970, the average noise level was 95 dB(A)—in 1978, it was down to 85.2 dB(A). Splitting cabbed and non-cab tractors made it obvious where most of the improvement had come from. Non-cab tractors fell from an average 95.4 dB(A) to 92.6—for cab tractors, the figures were 93.7 dB(A) and 80.9! And a reduction of 10 dB(A) is equivalent to halving of noise for the human ear. Of course, these were average figures covering whatever machines happened to be on test that year, but the trend is clear.

Typical of the new generation of cabs was the Sound-Gard, which was part of John Deere's "Generation II" 30 series tractors of 1972. This was actually the first major update of Deere's 1960 new generation machines, and the cab was certainly a big step forward. A huge glass area maximized visibility, and underlining how quiet it was, a stereo radio was optional. You could also specify air-conditioning, or a pressurizer to

RIGHT: *Oil crisis or no, many farmers wanted bigger tractors to cope with the competitive 1970s—this Ford TW-15 is typical, with four-wheel drive and a 121 hp turbo-diesel.*

keep the dust out, while the cab had Deere's patented ROPS built in. Allis-Chalmers unveiled the "Acousta-Cab" in 1975. Rubber isolation mounts, flexible control cables, fiberglass, and open cell foam padding all featured, and this attention to detail resulted in just 78.5 dB(A) for the new high-power two-wheel-drive 7040 and 7060. A-C claimed this was the quietest cab on the market, and it was.

Meanwhile, in the endless quest for more power, intercoolers were being added to existing turbo diesels. These were simple devices to cool the intake air, after it had been compressed (and therefore heated) by the turbocharger. Cooler air is denser, so can therefore mix with more fuel and create more power. The turbocharged JD 4320 of 1971 produced 117 PTO hp in Nebraskan tests. Its turbo-intercooled cousin, the 4620, managed 136 hp, a sixteen percent increase.

LEFT: *Four-wheel drive was an expensive option, but the next best thing was twin rear wheels, to help get this John Deere's 108 drawbar hp to the ground.*

ABOVE: *This 4040 John Deere has the optional four-wheel drive, plus, of course, the Sound-Gard cab, which set new standards of comfort and low-noise for tractor cabs.*

RIGHT: *If the 1960s had been the decade of the turbo, in the 1970s tractor manufacturers began adding an intercooler as well, to keep up in the horsepower race.*

These were two-wheel-drive tractors—four-wheel drive was still restricted to the top end of the market, and in the meantime, power levels continued skyward. Take the International 1468 (145 hp V8) or the Allis-Chalmers 7080 (180 hp turbo intercooled) or Massey Ferguson's 2805 (195 hp turbo V8). This sort of power had been restricted to four-wheel-drive super-tractors only a decade earlier. Nor were high-power tractors restricted to a small, exclusive

segment of the market—in the U.S. in 1975, 64,000 tractors were sold in the 40–99 hp class, and 65,000 in the 100 hp+ class.

Now the problem was how to get all this power to the ground without resorting to full four-wheel drive. Twin drive wheels were the simplest solution, and many manufacturers began offering front-wheel assist as well—the latter used hydrostatic or mechanical drive to the front wheels, but only a limited amount, and retained smaller front wheels. It was cheaper than full mechanical four-wheel drive and kept most of a two-wheel-drive machine's maneuverability.

But just as important as making best use of all this power was continued advances in transmission design. At the start of the decade, the typical transmission gave twelve forward speeds—a six-speed unit with two-speed power shift. Oliver announced its eighteen-speed Hydraul-shift in 1972, and the following year, Allis-Chalmers's new range of 7000 series (the "Power Squadron") could be had with twenty speeds. Power shifting—that is, being able to shift on the move without

using the clutch—moved from covering two ratios to each gear to three or even four. Eventually, full power-shift transmissions made every change possible on the move, and shuttle systems allowed quick and easy forward/reverse selection. Electronics had yet to find their way into transmission control, but the emphasis was now firmly on ease of use and convenience.

Two-wheel-drive mainstream tractors engaged in their own power race—the four-by-four super-tractors were getting larger by the year. So big in fact, that in 1979 the Nebraska test laboratory had to be rehoused in a new 30,000 square foot building. The original, built eighty years earlier, was just too small to house modern large tractors. Such as? Well Steiger launched its Tiger III in 1977, its biggest yet. The ST-470 model was rated at 450 hp, with 372 hp at the drawbar, making it the most powerful tractor yet tested at Nebraska. That same year, Versatile produced a prototype named Big Roy. All eight of its wheels were driven and the 1,150 cu. in. Cummins produced 600 hp. And it weighed over 54,000 lb. Big Roy was exhibited at shows in 1977, but never went into production.

At the other end of the scale, a market was emerging for mini-tractors of 10 hp upward. Many of the American manufacturers found they had left the sub-40 hp market behind, as power ratings inexorably rose. None of them attempted to design their own mini-tractors—they imported them from Japan instead. The Kubota was sold in the U.S. under its own name, but the Toyosha was imported in both Allis-Chalmers and Massey-Ferguson colors, while Deere signed a joint venture with Yanmar. And from 1973, Ford also made a success of importing mini tractors.

Other rebadged imports were brought in for cost reasons alone. Certain Olivers and Minneapolis-Molines were really Fiats, while the Allis-Chalmers 160 was built in France by Renault, using some A-C parts. Rather more intriguing was the Long Manufacturing company of Tarboro, North Carolina, which created a business by simply importing tractors from Italy, Poland, and Romania, and giving them an American gloss. This involved fitting American wheels, tires, batteries, cabs, and wheel weights, as well as a repaint and new "Long" badges. A range of five models was available, from 32 to 98 hp.

ABOVE: *The 1655 pictured here was one of the last Olivers to bear that badge, before the parent company dropped the name in 1974 in favor of its own White badge.*

RIGHT: *Super-tractors like the Steiger were in a class of their own from that of conventional machines. It was still a limited market, which they served well.*

ABOVE: *John Deere was the only major American manufacturer to survive the troubled 1970s and 1980s without merger or takeover.*

This was all part of the developing global economy in tractors, as referred to in the last chapter. But those manufacturers who already owned plants in more than one continent—John Deere, International, and Ford, for example—were in a better position to take advantage of this than those who didn't. Despite the success of independents like the Steigers, the American farm equipment industry was still dominated by big concerns—in 1976 it

was estimated that seven companies controlled almost eighty percent of the business. John Deere, International, Massey-Ferguson, and Ford were said to make up the "Big Four," while Case, Allis-Chalmers, and White were the "Little Three." Outside the U.S., Fiat and Kubota were viewed as significant world players as well. Records of the sales turnover in 1979 appeared to confirm these rankings, with John Deere heading the list—with a sales income of over $3.9 billion—followed by International with $3 billion. Then came Massey-Ferguson, Ford, J. I. Case, Allis-Chalmers, White, Versatile, and Steiger.

White was a new badge in the tractor business, though White Motors had taken over Oliver, Cockshutt, and Minneapolis-Moline in the early 1960s. In 1974 it dropped all these famous old names, and brought all its tractors together under its own name, with a brand-new silver color scheme. There was a range of models sold under the Field Boss name, from the two-wheel-drive 2-60 to the four-by-four 4-180. White sold off its tractor interests in 1980, though the name continued to live on, and is currently owned by AGCO. Incidentally, another famous name also disappeared from the market in the mid-1970s—International finally dropped the Farmall name, which had been in continuous use for fifty years and had almost become a marque in its own right.

But the 1970s wasn't just about more power and transmission speeds—there were some genuinely new ideas as well. Versatile launched its bidirectional Model 150 in 1977. As the name suggests, it was designed to work equally well forward or backward. The driver's seat and controls could be swiveled through 180 degrees—

BELOW: *Allis-Chalmers, like many of its rivals, attempted to keep a toehold in the market for small tractors with the use of imports. This A-C 6140 is actually a Japanese-built Toyosha.*

forward if the tractor was pulling an implement, backward if it was using a loader. The 150 wasn't a big tractor, with a 71 hp diesel engine and hydrostatic drive to all four wheels, but it did introduce a new concept that enhanced tractor versatility. Bidirectional tractors were later produced by converting conventional models from manufacturers such as Fendt, SAME, and Massey-Ferguson, among others. Versatile itself went on to develop higher-powered versions of the 150 and became the leading manufacturer of bidirectional machines.

Another new idea of the time was the systems tractor, which had implement mounts and power takeoffs both front and rear, plus four-wheel drive. Two German

tractors of this type were launched independently in 1972, the Mercedes-Benz MB-Trac and Deutz Intrac. Mounting different implements front and rear allows the tractor to do two jobs at the same time, for example with a front-mounted rake and rear-mounted baler. Elements of these two tractors were later taken up by other manufacturers, and the systems tractor is now an established piece of equipment.

So the 1970s saw many technical changes, but the American industry was still dominated by the same few companies which had been at the top for over forty years. In the 1980s and 1990s, the industry would see some serious structural changes —things would never be the same again.

OLIVER 1655

[1970]

OLIVER 1655

Engine: Water-cooled, six-cylinder
Bore x stroke: 3.75 x 4.0 in.
Capacity: 265 cu. in.
PTO Power: 70 hp @ 2,200 rpm
Drawbar Power: 57.4 hp
Transmission: Eighteen-speed
Speeds: 2.2–17.0 mph
Fuel Consumption: 12.54 hp/hr per gallon
Weight: 7,780 lb.

White Motors made trucks but was determined to break into the tractor industry. So, rather than set out to design its own machines from scratch, it decided to take a shortcut—it simply took over existing tractor makers with a ready-made range. Oliver was the first, in November 1960, followed by the Canadian Cockshutt company in 1962 and Minneapolis-Moline the year after that.

Oliver and Cockshutt already had a long history of cooperation, but under the White regime they increasingly shared components. In an effort to maximize sales, Cockshutt dealers in Canada were given Olivers to sell, repainted and badged as Cockshutts. In fact, this was only a temporary arrangement and later all White's tractors were sold with its own badge, under the Field Boss name.

In the meantime, Oliver tractors in the traditional green and cream went on selling.

The 1655 pictured here was a competitive 70 hp machine, though not in the prime of life, with roots stretching back to the 1962 1600, a four-plow machine with a 58 hp six-cylinder engine. But there had been useful updates, and the 1655, as well as having extra power, offered three auxiliary transmission options (Hydra-Power Drive, Over/Under Hydraul-Shift, or Creeper Drive) plus front-wheel assist.

BELOW: *The identity of Olivers became confused in the 1960s as models were repainted and rebadged. This 1655 really was an Oliver born and bred, though it was getting a little elderly by the early 1970s, despite new transmission options and extra power. Front-wheel assist was available too, though this example is plain two-wheel drive.*

OLIVER 1855

[1970]

Like the 1655, the bigger 1855 started out in 1962, as the 1800. That year had brought up-to-date squared-off styling, a far cry from the streamlined "Fleetline" look that Oliver had pioneered twenty-five years before. As a big six-plow tractor, the 1855 fulfilled the same role as the earlier Oliver 80 and 90, though with six cylinders. It didn't have the supercharged two-stroke GM diesel of the almost legendary Super 99, but that was still available in the higher-powered 1900. In four-cylinder 212 cu. in. form, that produced 90 hp at the drawbar and made the 1900 an eight-plow machine—the later 1950 made that 106 hp at 2,400 rpm. It was later replaced by a 105 hp turbo diesel version of Oliver's own six-cylinder diesel.

The 1800 was more conventional, actually using the same 265 cu. in. six-cylinder engine as the 880 it replaced, but with rated speed increased to 2,000 rpm. The diesel version was slightly larger at 283 cu. in. As the 1850 in 1964 it got a power boost to 92 hp in gasoline form. There were still some old 1800s in stock, so Oliver cunningly renamed them 1750s and sold them off as mild updates.

In 1970, another update resulted in the 1855 (which is pictured here), with an engine upsize to 310 cu. in. With Oliver's own 283 cu. in. six-cylinder diesel, it was still strong enough to haul a six-bottom plow, despite lacking a turbocharger. The home-built Olivers now had only a few years to run.

OLIVER 1855 DIESEL

Engine: Water-cooled, six-cylinder
Bore x stroke: 3.875 x 4.375 in.
Capacity: 310 cu. in.
PTO Power: 99 hp @ 2,400 rpm
Drawbar Power: 82.7 hp
Transmission: Eighteen-speed
Speeds: 1.4–18.6 mph
Fuel Consumption: 12.2 hp/hr per gallon
Weight: 11,140 lb.

BELOW: *The square-rigged "industrial" look of this 1855 originated in the early 1960s, when it was decided that the Oliver lineup should abandon the more curvy "Fleetline" styling.*

VOLVO BM T650

[1970]

As a tractor manufacturer, Volvo of Sweden is inextricably linked with Bolinder-Munktell of Finland. Already a well-established maker of cars and trucks, Volvo decided to enter the tractor market in 1943. From the start, it signed an agreement with Bolinder Munktell—Volvo and BM machines would differ in engine, color, and the badging only. So the new five-speed BM GBMV-1 of 1943 also formed the basis of the Volvo T40 series.

After the Second World War, the red BM10 and green Volvo T21 were identical apart from their power units: a two-stroke diesel for the BM, and a four-cylinder four-stroke gasoline for Volvo. Volvo bought BM in 1950.

The company also pioneered the use of rollover protection for tractors. This was partly of necessity, as the Swedish government made this mandatory from July 1959, years before many manufacturers even thought of it. But it gave Volvo BM a head start in safety cab design.

The successful T350 Boxer of that year was joined by the larger T470 Bison and six-cylinder T800, while 1969 saw Trac-Trol, Volvo's take on a two-speed power shift. The T650 shown here was the 1970 replacement for the Boxer, with updates including a new 73 hp four-cylinder diesel and all-new cab made up of stamped pieces of steel, spot-welded together. There was also hydrostatic power steering, and with the optional Trac-Trol, sixteen forward speeds. A turbocharged T700 with 90 hp was added to the line-up in 1976.

LEFT: *Reflecting their record in car occupant safety, Volvo of Sweden also pioneered protection sytems for tractor drivers, driven by the Swedish government, which made rollover protection mandatory on tractors from 1959. This caused the relatively small Volvo BM concern additional research expense, but turned out to be a real advantage, giving the company a significant head start on its big U.S. rivals. This T650 (pictured here) was Volvo BM's upper mid-size tractor of the early 1970s, part of a complete range at that time, which ranged from the 40 hp Buster to the 100 hp T800. In 1979, Volvo BM agreed to develop a tractor jointly with Valmet of Finland—the Finns later bought out Volvo's share in the project.*

VOLVO BM T650

Engine: Water-cooled, four-cylinder, diesel

Capacity: 258 cu. in.

PTO Power: 78 hp @ 2,600 rpm

Transmission: Sixteen-speed

Weight: 8,580 lb.

JOHN DEERE 830
[1972]

JOHN DEERE 830 DIESEL

Engine: Water-cooled, three-cylinder
Bore x stroke: 3.86 x 4.33 in.
Capacity: 152 cu. in.
PTO Power: 35 hp @ 2,400 rpm
Drawbar Power: 28 hp @ 2,400 rpm
Transmission: Eight-speed
Speeds: 1.4–15.9 mph
Fuel Consumption: 14.3 hp/hr
   per gallon
Weight: 4,376 lb.

ABOVE: *Awaiting restoration . . . Maybe one day someone will beautify this late 1960s 820, but in the meantime it still looks ready for work.*

LEFT: *This is the three-cylinder 820, introduced to the 20 series range in 1967; it was subsequently upgraded in the new 30 series as the 830. The tractors were mechanically very similar and the new 30 series retained the 20's styling, rather than adopt the new look of the bigger New Generation tractors. The idea was to save money, as it wasn't cheap to build small tractors in the U.S. or Germany, compared to Italy or Japan. The 830 was powered by Deere's own three-cylinder diesel of 152 cu. in. This was JD's budget tractor, so you wouldn't find front-wheel assist, four-wheel drive, or power shift—the standard transmission was an eight-speed manual. In Nebraska's 1973 test, it gave no trouble in over forty-six hours of running time. A range of JDs were built in Germany, culminating in the 71 hp 2030, 79 hp 2130, and 97 hp 3130 (all engine hp).*

RIGHT: *The 820-3120 was John Deere's first worldwide tractor (preceding the 30 series), designed to be acceptable on both sides of the Atlantic.*

No American tractor manufacturer who wanted a true worldwide presence could afford to be without a European factory. John Deere had had a base in Mannheim, Germany, since 1959, when it took over Lanz. From here, tractors were made to suit European conditions, though there was plenty of crossover—some Mannheim tractors used American-made engines, for example, while some U.S. tractors were exported to Europe complete. The 830 (not to be confused with the American-made 830 of the late 1950s, a very different machine) was part of the 30 series unveiled in 1972. It replaced the 1967 20 series, which encompassed a complete range, from the three-cylinder 34PS 820, to the 64PS four-cylinder 2020. Bigger machines—the 3020, 4020, and 5020— were imported from the Waterloo factory. Mannheim's first six-cylinder tractor, the 2120, was added to the range a year later.

The 30 series of 1972 was mechanically similar to these, with the 830 the smallest of the range, featuring two-wheel drive and four-post ROPS rather than a full cab. All other 30 series had mechanical four-wheel drive, apart from the top model 2130 and 3130, which featured hydrostatic front-wheel drive.

ALLIS-CHALMERS 440
[1972]

Before Allis-Chalmers came up with its own four-wheel-drive super-tractors, it rebadged those of other manufacturers. So the Allis-Chalmers's 440 was no more or less than a Steiger Bearcat in Allis-Chalmers colors. It was a sensible move, giving A-C dealers something to sell in this growing market, and quickly, while the company continued to work on its own homegrown four-by-four.

Steiger never built its own engines, and the Bearcat was powered by a Cummins V8 diesel of 555 cu. in. and coupled a 10-speed transmission. In A-C colors, about a thousand of them were sold between 1972 and 1976.

The Steiger brothers, of course, were good people to buy from. They had been pioneers of the super-tractor, and were now well established as the leading American make. Originally, they just built a big tractor for themselves, only to find that neighbors were asking for copies. The business grew from there, though the first tiller-steered Steiger ("a powerful beast, but a numb lump," according to tractor historian Peter Simpson) soon gave way to smaller, more manageable machines—with steering wheels.

LEFT: *In the early 1980s, Allis-Chalmers designed, built, and powered its own big four-by-four super-tractors. But well before then, it had twice attempted to enter this market, first with a modified version of the Deerfield T16 loader, fitted with an Allis-Chalmers engine. This proved a failure for farm work, not being reliable enough for long stints in the fields. However, it did find a niche in the sugarcane industry. For its second attempt, A-C turned to a manufacturer with long experience of building giant tractors for field work—Steiger. So the Allis-Chalmers 440 of 1972 was built for A-C by Steiger, though it wasn't identical to Steiger's own machines, using a smaller 555 cu. in. Cummins V8 in place of the 636 cu. in. Caterpillar and 903 cu. in. Cummins favored by Steiger itself. Although not many 440s were built—only about one thousand over four years—it paved the way for Allis-Chalmers's homegrown super-tractors in the 1980s.*

ALLIS-CHALMERS 440

Engine: Water-cooled V8 Cummins
Bore x stroke: 4.6 x 4.1 in.
Capacity: 555 cu. in.
PTO Power (claimed):
 208 hp @ 2,800 rpm
Drawbar Power (claimed):
 165 hp @ 2,800 rpm
Transmission: Ten-speed
Speeds: 2.3–18.8 mph
Weight: 17,500 lb.

CASE 2670
[1972]

To meet the growing demand for massive four-wheel-drive super-tractors, some companies bought in models from specialists like Steiger and Versatile, rebadged and repainted. Case built its own, the first being the 1200 Traction King of 1964, making it a pioneer of this market.

The Traction King was powered by a turbocharged version of the 451 cu. in. diesel first seen in the 1030. It produced 120 hp, and powered a massive machine with four-wheel drive, four-wheel steering, and an all-up weight of 16,500 lb. And it went a long way to help "[reestablish] Case as the pre-eminent builder of big wheat-land tractors," according to tractor historian P. W. Ertel.

After five years, the 1200 was updated as a 70 series, along with the rest of the range. Like the 1200, the new 1470 Traction King used hydrostatic steering for the front wheels and independent hydraulic power steering for the rear pair. This allowed the choice of crab steering, combined front and rear steering, and front or rear alone. It also had a disc brake operating on the main drive line. The biggest news though, was Case's new direct-injection diesel, here in 504 cu. in. form, with turbocharging. Another major update came in 1972, when Case's biggest tractor was replaced by the even more powerful 2470. that offered 176 hp, while the intercooled 2670 shown here was the most powerful Case yet, with 221 PTO hp.

LEFT: *Instead of a massive Cummins or Caterpillar V8, Case designed its own 504 cu. in. six, which was new for the 1470 Traction King, and later upgraded with intercooling for this 2670, with 219 hp at the PTO. Six years later, in the updated 2870, it was producing 250 hp. A comfortable cab with rollover protection was standard, as was the case with many of the two-wheel-drive Cases, such as the 1270. The latter was the first major new Case of the 1970s, and with 127 hp was the most powerful two-wheel-drive machine it had ever offered. More power soon followed, with the 143 hp 1370 and in 1975 the 180 hp 1570.*

CASE 2670 DIESEL

Engine: Water-cooled, six-cylinder, turbo intercooled
Bore x stroke: 4.62 x 5.0 in.
Capacity: 504 cu. in.
PTO Power: 219 hp @ 2,200 rpm
Drawbar Power: 189 hp @ 2,200 rpm
Transmission: Twelve-speed
Speeds: 2.0–14.5 mph
Fuel Consumption: 15.3 hp/hr per gallon
Weight: 20,810 lb.

JOHN DEERE 4430
[1972]

The 1970s saw a new emphasis on driver safety and comfort. And not before time. Over the years, hundreds of drivers had been killed or seriously injured when a tractor overturned. The answer was ROPS (rollover protection system) and John Deere's Roll Gard was available from 1966.

The company had offered its patents to the rest of the industry, but it was several years before ROPS became standard equipment on all machines.

In 1972, "Generation II" 30 series arrived, complete with the new Sound-Gard cab. As well as built-in ROPS, the emphasis was firmly on pampering the driver. With its large curved windshield and tinted glass, this new cab looked luxurious, and it was quiet enough to even allow the option of a stereo radio/cassette player. Other options were a pressurizer to keep dust and dirt out of the cab, or air-conditioning. Underslung pedals, a seat belt, and adjustable steering wheel were part of the 30 series package and over half of buyers paid extra for the Sound-Gard cab as well.

This was a real step forward in making life safer, quieter, and more comfortable for the driver, who was often the tractor's owner as well—maybe one reason why so many of them went for the Sound-Gard.

Even if the tractor's owner never actually used it, but paid someone else to, there was a purely economic benefit to paying extra for a quiet, comfortable cab. Research had shown that in noisy, unpleasant cabs drivers were disinclined to make use of full power, so all that expensive horsepower was failing to pay for itself. Only the refined tractors, it seemed, were being used to their full potential.

The 4430 shown here was the most popular 30 series, with a turbocharged version of JD's six-cylinder diesel, to give

LEFT: *A dozen years on from the New Generation, 1972 saw the Generation II John Deeres. Not as revolutionary a change as that in 1960, but the Sound-Gard cab was a genuine advance.*

JOHN DEERE 4430 DIESEL

Engine: Water-cooled, six-cylinder, turbo
Bore x stroke: 4.25 x 4.75 in.
Capacity: 404 cu. in.
PTO Power: 126 hp @ 2,200 rpm
Drawbar Power: 105 hp @ 2,200 rpm
Transmission: Sixteen-speed
  (eight-speed standard)
Speeds: 2.0–17.8 mph
Fuel Consumption: 15.6 hp/hr per gallon
Weight: 11,350 lb.

125 hp. If that wasn't enough, the inter-cooled 4630 offered 150 hp. There were new transmission features as well, including Perma-Clutch, with oil cooling to maximize clutch plate life, and a sixteen-speed Quad Range transmission.

BELOW: *The farmer's office—in terms of comfort, that was what the tractor cab had become. It still might not be as comfy as the average executive suite, but with air-conditioning and in-cab entertainment it was close. And in those pre-cell-phone days, no one could bother you either!*

LEFT: *There had been cabs before, but the John Deere Sound-Gard was a huge step forward. Four-post ROPS was standard (as it was if the full cab wasn't specified), and it was pressurized to keep out dust—that in turn made air-conditioning possible, and the cab was quiet enough to allow the use of a stereo. Remember the Minneapolis-Moline Comfortractor of 1938? This is what its designers were aiming for—but it took the industry thirty-four years to get there.*

RIGHT: *The 4430 was the best-selling of the American-built 30 series tractors, a natural successor to the 4320, 70 Diesel, and, for that matter, the Model D. A huge glass area ensured that the rollover protection didn't interfere with all-around visibility, and although this cab came at an extra cost, three out of four 30 series customers opted for it.*

ABOVE: *The familiar John Deere logo added the finishing touches to their latest model—an extra reminder just in case you didn't recognize the green and yellow machine at first glance.*

RIGHT: *On the 4430, it was possible to control the speed with which the hydraulics acted. This was a useful tool, given their extra power and flow compared to previous and much simpler systems.*

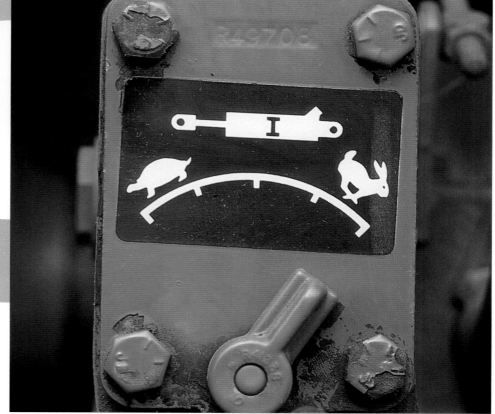

ALLIS-CHALMERS 7000 SERIES

[1973]

ALLIS-CHALMERS 7020

Engine: Water-cooled, six-cylinder, turbo/intercooled

Capacity: 301 cu. in.

PTO Power: 124 hp

Drawbar Power: 102 hp

Fuel Consumption: 13.1 hp/hr per gallon

Transmission: Twelve-speed

Speeds: 1.9–19 mph

Weight: 15,610 lb.

It was nearly ten years since the square-hooded One Ninety Allis had been unveiled. Its smaller brothers were only slightly younger, and all borrowed heavily from older A-C tractors. So it was a probably relieved audience of A-C dealers that witnessed the unveiling of a new range in 1973—the 7000 series. With its distinctive forward-sloping nose, this would be A-C's backbone through the 1970s. A new range perhaps, but most of it still depended on A-C's familiar 426 cu. in. diesel, now in 130 hp turbo and 156 hp intercooled forms. Power Director was still there, but now uprated to twenty forward speeds—rivals had long since eclipsed the original with twelve or sixteen speeds. The hydraulic system was load-sensitive, in that pressure and flow automatically adjusted to the work in hand—another Allis first. To counter John Deere's Sound-Gard cab of the previous year, A-C came up with the Acousta Cab, which it claimed was the quietest in the business.

As launched, the 7000 series kicked off with the 7030, using A-C's own 426 cu. in. six-cylinder turbo-diesel, producing 131 hp at the PTO. The twenty-speed Power Director transmission was standard (as it was across the range), and all the 7000s were built on a new computer-controlled Flexible Manufacturing System. Next up was the 7050, with an intercooled version of the same engine and 156 PTO hp, which in the Nebraska test proved marginally more fuel efficient than the plain turbo 7030. It was over a year before Nebraska tested the biggest 7000s: the 161 hp 7060 and 180 hp 7080, both equipped with dual rear wheels.

In the A-C tradition, the higher-powered 7000s went on sale first, but an entry-level version, the 7000, was unveiled in 1975, to replace the 200. It actually carried over many parts, although it was uprated to 106 hp and had the Acousta Cab and a twelve-speed power-shift transmission. Over 36,000 7000 series A-Cs were built during the 1970s, though the company was turning to rebadged Fiats to fill out its smaller tractor line.

LEFT: *The 7020 was produced from 1977 to 1981. Based on the larger 7000s, it came with a twelve-speed power-shift transmission, or Power Director.*

CASE 970
[1973]

Alongside the horsepower race of the 1950s and 1960s, transmission development had progressed as well. From a conventional four-, five-, or six-speed transmission, many manufacturers added a two-speed epicyclic gear between the clutch and transmission, effectively doubling the number of ratios available. Better still, changes between these two ratios could be made on the move, without using the clutch. Case didn't do this. Instead, its Case-o-matic used a torque converter which allowed an infinite variation of speed, and clutchless starts.

By the 1970s, power shift was the way to go. It was just another name for the ability to change ratio, under power, on the move. It was an option right across the Case 70 series range, and was an extension of the old two-speed epicyclic principle. In this case there were four mechanical gear ratios and three power-shift speeds, giving twelve forward speeds in all, and four reverse. The power shift consisted of a planetary gear train and four wet disc clutches, which could shift on the move, though there was an interlock preventing forward-reverse selection unless the foot clutch was disengaged. In other respects, too, the 70 series brought Case up-to-date. Self-adjusting disc brakes were standard, with power assistance as an option. A two-speed PTO—540 and 1,000 rpm—was available as well, thanks to a double-ended output shaft. To change speeds, you removed the shaft, turned it around and reinserted it.

CASE 970
POWER-SHIFT DIESEL

Engine: Water-cooled, six-cylinder
Bore x stroke: 4.125 x 5.0 in.
Capacity: 401 cu. in.
PTO Power: 93.4 hp @ 2,000 rpm
Drawbar Power: 79.9 hp @ 2,000 rpm
Transmission: Twelve-speed
Speeds: 1.8–17.0 mph
Fuel Consumption: 15.1 hp/hr per gallon
Weight: 11,190 lb.

BELOW: *The 870 and 970 were Case's mid-sized tractors. Old Abe, the bald eagle, was dropped in favor of the simple, strong "CASE" logo.*

MASSEY-FERGUSON 1135

[1973]

With its production bases in England and France, and the legacy of Massey-Harris, Massey-Ferguson had always been strong on small and mid-sized tractors. But the Red Giants (40–70 hp) were still puny by American standards. M-F needed to produce 100 hp+ machines to sell within the U.S. and Canada. In the early 1970s, it began making such tractors itself, in the U.S. The new 1100 and 1130 didn't have four-wheel drive or articulation (though M-F's contender for that market was already on the drawing board), but were high-power conventional machines.

Both were powered by the familiar 354 cu. in. Perkins six-cylinder diesel, giving 90 hp in the 1100, 120 hp in the turbocharged 1130—the first turbocharged Massey-Ferguson.

Pictured here is the 1135, a slightly updated version of the 1130, with the same engine. Both 1100 and 1130 boasted an Advanced Ferguson system with more sophisticated hydraulics, finer control, and the ability to handle larger, heavier implements. And in keeping with the times, driver comfort was given new priority, so the new tractors were offered with new well-appointed cabs.

Though big by Massey-Ferguson standards, the 1135 lacked something for the ultimate high-horsepower class. Next up was the 135 hp 1150, powered by a turbo-diesel V8. A super-tractor followed, the Canadian-built 1200, first with the Perkins 354, later (as the 1500 and 1800) with Caterpillar V8 power.

LEFT: *The 1135 was one of M-F's new generation of high-horsepower tractors. The Perkins V8-powered 1150 soon followed, which in updated 1155 form (in 1973) produced 141 hp at the PTO, 118 hp at the drawbar. Rated at 2,000 rpm, the Perkins measured 540 cu. in. and ran through just over forty-five hours of work at Nebraska. There was partial power-shifting on the twelve-speed transmission, as used on the 1135, but the bigger tractor proved more efficient, with 16.18 hp/hr per gallon (1135, 12.56 hp/hr per gallon) at a 75 percent drawbar pull.*

MASSEY-FERGUSON 1135 DIESEL

Engine: Water-cooled, six-cylinder, turbo
Bore x stroke: 3.88 x 5.0 in.
Capacity: 354 cu. in.
PTO Power: 120.8 hp @ 2,200rpm
Drawbar Power: 102.4 hp
Transmission: Twelve-speed
Speeds: 2.2–16.9 mph
Fuel Consumption: 16.18 hp/hr per gallon
Weight: 13,550 lb.

OLIVER 2255
[1973]

The Oliver 2255 tractor marks the end of three different eras. First, it's an Oliver. Over 31,000 Oliver 2255s were built from 1971 to 1976. This long-established name, in the tractor business for over forty years, was to finally lie down and die in 1976, a victim of corporate rationalization. In fact, a 2255 was the last Oliver to be produced. Second, it has two-wheel drive. Even today, there are plenty of two-wheel-drive tractors around, but all of the higher horsepower models have either mechanical four-wheel drive or front-wheel assist—it's simply the most efficient means of transmitting 100+ hp without too much wasteful wheel spin. But in the early 1970s, when four-wheel drive was still the preserve of massive super-tractors, like the Steiger or Big Bud, there were some conventional tractors sporting 120-150 hp and just two-wheel drive. The Oliver 2255 was one of them.

Just two wheels often weren't enough to transmit well over 100 hp, and when the 2255 was tested at Nebraska in September 1973, dual rear wheels were fitted to reduce wheel spin to an acceptable minimum, while nearly 1,600 lb. of ballast was added. Using the maximum 124 drawbar hp over two hours, they recorded a 5.98 percent slippage—that was in eleventh gear out of eighteen forward speeds, which allowed partial power shifting over the three ranges.

Finally, the 2255 was one of the last big tractors to do without a turbo. By the early 1970s, these were increasingly common (if not downright necessary) to extract big power figures from diesel engines. But Oliver followed the more traditional American adage—there's no substitute for cubic inches. Its 573 cu. in. V8 was bought in from Caterpillar, the crawler manufacturer. This gave 145 hp, not much less than the rival turbo-intercooled Allis-Chalmers six.

Although the 2255 Oliver was first built with the 3150 Caterpillar V8, many of the later models came equipped with the 3208 Caterpillar V8.

LEFT: *Oliver's 2255 relied on a big V8.*

OLIVER 2255 DIESEL

Engine: Water-cooled, V8
Bore x stroke: 4.5 x 4.5 in.
Capacity: 573 cu. in.
PTO Power: 147 hp @ 2,600 rpm
Drawbar Power: 124 hp
Transmission: Eighteen-speed
Fuel Consumption: 13.4 hp/hr per gallon
Weight: 16,407 lb.

STEIGER PANTHER ST310
[1974]

The Steiger brothers—Douglas and Maurice—had a big 4,000-acre farm in Minnesota, but couldn't find a tractor big enough to work it. So over the winter of 1957/58 they built their own.

Steiger No1 had all the features now associated with not just Steiger, but all giant super-tractors: a massive diesel engine, four-wheel drive, and articulated steering. Soon neighbors were asking for replicas, and the Steigers went on to build 120 big tractors between 1963 and 1969.

By the time this ST310 rolled out of the factory in 1974, Steiger was very well established as the U.S.'s (if not the world's) leading manufacturer of super-tractors. The brothers liked to name their tractors after big cats, for their association with agility and strength. So the ST310 was also known as the Panther—there were also Bearcats, Pumas, Cougars, Lions, and Tigers as well. Marketing flannel? Maybe not, as Steigers were certainly big, tough machines—the most powerful tractors of their day, with up to 525 hp available.

This Panther ST310 is in the traditional Steiger lime green, and powered by a six-cylinder Cummins of 855 cu. in. The engine was later upgraded to 893 cu. in. and 270 hp for the ST325. Economic problems lead to a takeover by Case-IH in 1987, but Steiger carries on as part of the CNH Global.

LEFT: *Panther, a typical lime-green Steiger of the 1970s, with well over 200 hp. The early Steigers had less power, though by the standards of the day they were horsepower-rich, and steadily gained more and more hp as the years went by. In 1963, the new lineup comprised the 125 hp 1200, 216 hp 1700, 265 hp 2200, and 350 hp 3300. These were followed in the 1970s by the Wildcat with 175–120 hp, and the Bearcat around 225 hp. Biggest of all at this time was the Tiger, powered by a 320 hp Cummins V8, which grew into the 450 hp Tiger II in 1978, this one with a 1099 cu. in. Caterpillar. Caterpillar actually built its own wheeled super-tractor, but it didn't match the success of the Steiger.*

STEIGER PANTHER III ST325

Engine: Water-cooled, six-cylinder, turbo-intercooled
Bore x stroke: 5.4 x 6.5 in.
Capacity: 893 cu. in.
Power: 270 hp @ 2,100 rpm
Transmission: Ten-speed
Speeds: 2.3–19.9 mph
Fuel Consumption: 14.82 hp/hr per gallon
Weight: 31,080 lb.

WHITE 4-150
[1974]

WHITE 4-180

Engine: Water-cooled V8 diesel
Bore x stroke: 4.5 x 5.0 in.
Capacity: 636 cu. in.
PTO Power: 181 hp @ 2,800 rpm
Drawbar Power: 157 hp
Transmission: Twelve-speed
Speeds: 1.9–18.9 mph
Fuel Consumption: 11.56 hp/hr
per gallon
Weight: 20,600 lb.

For over a decade, White Motors tried to rationalize its three tractor acquisitions —Cockshutt, Oliver, and Minneapolis-Moline—while making the most of the long-established names. In economic terms, it made sense, but White would

have done better to drop the old names right away rather than dilute their appeal with ten years of badge engineering. It wasn't until 1974 that White consolidated all its tractor lines under the White Farm Equipment name. A new tractor badge was born, using the additional brand of Field Boss. The first machine to bear these badges, in the new corporate colors of silver and white, was the big four-wheel-drive 4-150 Field Boss—"4" related to the number of driven wheels, "150" to the approximate PTO horsepower.

It might seem like a fresh start, but the first Field Boss made good use of White's existing parts inventory. Aimed at the articulated tractor market, it consisted of two Oliver transmission sets, and was hinged in the middle with power steering. None of the engines inherited from M-M or Oliver were suitable, so White bought in a

636 cu. in. Caterpillar V8 diesel. To improve visibility and engine access, the 4-150 had a low profile, made possible by having the engine crankshaft in line with, and at the same height as, the transmission input shaft. It soon had more power as well, as the 4-180. The 4-180 was powered by the same 636 cu. in. Caterpillar V8, now delivering just over 150 hp at the drawbar and 180 hp at the PTO. The transmission remained a 12-speed, without power shift. That was upgraded into an 18-speed with partial power shift for the 4-210 of 1979. This still used the Caterpillar V8, though now it wasn't able to live up to the badge, with a maximum of 182 PTO hp.

BELOW: Using existing parts, the White 4-150 matched two Oliver transmission sets with a Caterpillar V8 diesel, to produce a relatively small, articulated tractor for the sub-Steiger market.

WHITE 2-60
[1974]

In the mid-1970s, many of the American tractor manufacturers found themselves unable to build smaller tractors at home at a competitive price. The only answer (apart from pulling out of the lower end of the market altogether) was to import machines from abroad.

That's what White did. Its 2-60 of 1976, which replaced the mid-range Olivers, was really a four-cylinder Fiat, sold initially in the Oliver colors but soon changing to the new corporate silver color scheme. Not that this was a new thing—White had done the same in 1965 with the Fiat-based Oliver 1250. Now there was also a 47 hp 2-50 alongside the 63 hp 2-60. During the same period, Allis-Chalmers turned to Fiat as well for its 5040.

But the Fiat deal didn't last very long, and White soon transferred its allegiance to Iseki of Japan. The 2-50 and 2-60 were dropped, replaced by a range of four utility tractors spanning 28-61 hp, which were all built by Iseki.

However, the bigger Whites were still American-made. The 2-105 offered eighteen forward gears, a spacious glassy cab, and a turbocharged Perkins six-cylinder diesel of 354 cu. in. with 105 hp at the PTO. There was a naturally aspirated version as well, the 2-85, while the big 2-150 was an updated version of the Minneapolis-Moline 1355.

The new regime of White tractors (having dropped the older marques of Oliver, Minneapolis-Moline, and Cockshutt) didn't last long. The machines were outsold by every other mainstream manufacturer and, after six years, White sold its tractor-making arm (White Farm Equipment) to a group of investors. The new owners continued the business for five years before filing for bankruptcy, but White was revived as White-New Idea. That survived until 1993, when it was taken over by AGCO.

So against all the odds—bankruptcies, mergers, and takeovers—White had survived as a tractor marque.

BELOW: *This is White's replacement for the mid-range Olivers, the 2-60. This new model was really a Fiat tractor, repainted and rebadged to suit their range. Along with most of its American rivals, the company found it uneconomic to manufacture small tractors, with their correspondingly narrow profit margins, in the U.S.*

WHITE 2-60	
Engine:	Water-cooled four-cylinder
Bore x stroke:	3.9 x 4.3 in.
Capacity:	211 cu. in.
PTO Power:	63 hp @ 2,400 rpm
Drawbar Power:	40.4 hp
Transmission:	Eight-speed
Speeds:	1.5–15.5 mph
Fuel Consumption:	14.4 hp/hr per gallon
Weight:	5,160 lb.

ALLIS-CHALMERS
FOUR-WHEEL DRIVES

Allis-Chalmers produced several big four-wheel-drive tractors in the 1970s and early 1980s, making up for its relative lateness to this sector. It had actually built a few in the early 1960s—the T16 Sugar Babe (intended for use in sugar plantations) was really an Allis-engined version of Deerfield's existing TL16 loader. There were other attempts to design a big four-by-four in-house, but finally A-C gave up and bought the proven Steiger Bearcat, renaming it the Allis-Chalmers 440.

In 1976, A-C unveiled its very own four-wheel-drive tractor to replace the 440. The 7580 was very much a four-by-four version of the existing 7000 series, using the same 426 cu. in. six-cylinder diesel with turbo and intercooling. It was rated at 186 hp at the PTO, and also used the 7080's twenty-speed transmission and disc brakes. An even bigger 8550 used the massive 844 cu. in. engine from one of A-C's crawlers. It had twin turbos (though no intercooler) and produced 254 hp.

By now, A-C was well established in the four-by-four market, though its new announcements for 1982—the 4W220 and 4W305 (pictured here)—appeared only a few years before the factory closed its doors. They featured slightly derated engines compared to the 7580, but with the latest 8000 series cab. The 220 used A-C's own 670-HI diesel (426 cu. in. turbo intercooled) and the 305 the 731 cu. in. 6120T. But in 1985 Deutz took over A-C and closed it down, so that was that.

Although the Allis name survived as Deutz-Allis (and later AGCO-Allis) it would never appear on a four-wheel-drive super-tractor again, so it looks like the big A-Cs of the 1970s and early 1980s remain unique.

LEFT: *Starting in 1976, after selling the Steiger Bearcat, A-C designed its own super-tractors, at first derived from the more conventional 7000 series machines. This is a later 4W305. In the days before rubber-tracked crawlers, twin, or triple wheels, four-wheel drive was the best compromise between traction and road capability for bigger tractors.*

ALLIS-CHALMERS 7580

Engine: Water-cooled, six-cylinder, turbo/intercooled
Capacity: 426 cu. in.
PTO Power: 186 hp
Drawbar Power: 127 hp
Transmission: Twenty-speed
Speeds: 1.5–17.6 mph
Fuel Consumption: 14.81 hp/hr per gallon
Weight: 23,520 lb.

CASE 1570 "SPIRIT OF '76"
[1976]

Tractor manufacturers don't often go in for special editions. It's not like selling a car or a motorcycle, where buying decisions are usually subjective, based on image, color, and attractiveness as much any practical considerations. But tractors are working tools. Aren't they?

The Case "Spirit of '76" was probably the exception to this rule. It was America's bicentennial, and '76 special editions were seen everywhere, in patriotic red, white, and blue stars and stripes. Case was the only tractor maker to get sucked into this celebration of national pride. In fact, for Case it was a double celebration, as 1976 saw the unveiling of its most powerful two-wheel-drive tractor yet, the 1570. It used a turbocharged version of Case's 504 cu. in. six-cylinder direct injection diesel, with 180 bhp at 2,100 rpm. In fact, it had almost as much drawbar pull as the four-wheel-drive 2470 Traction King. A twelve-speed transmission was standard, as was a cab with tinted windows.

Part of the Agri King lineup, the 1570 was in production for two years. But it wasn't the only special edition Case ever made. The "Black Knights" were elegant black, silver, and red versions of the 870, specifically built as dealer demonstrators and carefully tuned and weighted to give optimum performance.

It was the culmination of a line of high-horsepower two-wheel-drive machines. Through the 1950s and 1960s, Case had not been at the forefront of the horsepower race—at 85 hp, the two-wheel-drive 930GP was powerful, but broke no records. But in the early 1970s, Case appeared to be striving to make up for lost time, with the 127 hp 1270 soon followed by the 143 hp 1370, and in 1975, by this, its most powerful two-wheel-drive machine to date. At 180 hp, the 1570 was at the limit of conventional two-wheel-drive technology.

LEFT: *Whatever farmers may have thought of it at the time, the "Spirit of '76" makes a good collector's item a quarter-century later, but still, the special-edition tractor doesn't seem to have caught on.*

CASE 1570 DIESEL

Engine: Water-cooled six-cylinder
Bore x stroke: 4.625 x 5.0 in.
Capacity: 504 cu. in.
PTO Power: 180 bhp @ 2,100 rpm
Drawbar Power: 148 hp
Transmission: Twelve-speed
Speeds: 1.9–19.5 mph
Fuel Consumption: 12.72 hp/hr per gallon
Weight: 16,290 lb.

WHITE 2-70
[1976]

Not all of the smaller Whites were imported. The mid-range 2-70 was really a rebadged, repainted version of the old Oliver 1655. So White's range was a real mixture in the late 1970s: rebadged old tractors (2-70, 2-150), imports (2-50, 2-60), and the substantially new (4-180).

Most of the 2-70 was very familiar. It still came with Oliver's 70 hp gasoline engine of 265 cu. in. and was in fact the last gasoline tractor offered by White. However, there was a new diesel option, a 283 cu. in. direct injection six-cylinder. Transmission options were the same as for the 1655:

Hydra-Power Drive, Over/ Under Hydraul-Shift, or Creeper Drive.

The 2-70, which like all Whites of the period was officially known as a White "Field Boss," was tested by Nebraska in May 1976. Like most of the later tractors tested, it needed no special attention during the test. As ever, the Nebraska engineers made sure to add ballast, to optimize traction, and 1,000 lb. was added to the 2-70's bare weight of 8,630 lb. Alongside it, they tested the upgraded 2-85, which used a 354 cu. in. Perkins in place of White's new diesel, giving slightly over 85 hp at the PTO, 71 hp at the drawbar. The more powerful 2-105 used a turbocharged version of the Perkins, while the 2-150 (White's biggest two-wheel-drive machine) was still equipped with the ex-Minneapolis-Moline big six of 585 cu. in.

By 1980, trading conditions had been increasingly tough in the late 1970s, and White's policy of importing and rationalization wasn't enough to maintain sales against the giants of the industry: John Deere, IHC, Case, and Allis-Chalmers. So in that year, it sold its White Farm Equipment arm to the Texas Investment Group, and with it went the Oliver, Cockshutt, and Minneapolis-Moline marques until, in 1993, White found a haven with AGCO.

LEFT: *The White 2-70 was the last gasp for gasoline. Diesel power was now the dominant choice in all sizes, makes, and models of tractor.*

WHITE 2-70 DIESEL

Engine: Water-cooled six-cylinder
Bore x stroke: 3.875 x 4.0 in.
Capacity: 283 cu. in.
PTO Power: 71 hp @ 2,200 rpm
Drawbar Power: 57 hp
Transmission: Eighteen-speed
Speeds: 2.1–16.6 mph
Fuel Consumption: 11.92 hp/hr
　per gallon
Weight: 8,630 lb.

INTERNATIONAL 1486
[1976]

In an affluent society, there seemed no reason why farmers should be exposed to a cold, uncomfortable ride. Plus research was showing that comfortable drivers were more alert, less liable to make mistakes, and more inclined to use maximum performance. Many tractor buyers were owner-drivers, and self-interest in driver welfare was high. Hence the new generation of quieter, more comfy cabs in the early to mid-1970s. John Deere's Sound-Gard was one of the first, while the Allis-Chalmers Acousta-Cab was claimed to be the quietest in the business. International Harvester responded with this, the Pro Ag 86 series line unveiled in September 1976. Its cab was all new, still with two doors (one each side) but a larger glass area of 43.2 square feet. ROPS was built in, and it exceeded the minimum legal requirements of the time. Placing the driver's seat eighteen inches further forward compared to the old 66 series made for a smoother ride, not to mention easier entry and exit. The doors were of double-wall construction, with heavy rubber seals on them to keep dust out. When the doors were shut, an air filter self-cleaned the cab of any dust. Air-conditioning was standard, and a radio, tape player, and hydraulically mounted seat were all options.

With all this attention on the new cab, the 86 series actually saw few mechanical changes. However, there was an optional (later standard) digital control center, which gave read-outs of engine rpm, PTO speed, exhaust gas temperature, and ground speed. The range spanned the 85 hp 886 to the 160 hp 1586. Since the 86 series was very similar to the 66 series that preceded it, specifications for the 1466 are given below.

LEFT AND BELOW: *The 145 hp 1486. The 86 series was International's "Pro-Ag" lineup for 1976, mechanically very similar to the 66 series it replaced. Cabs were still mostly optional, though many chose to spend the extra money for them.*

INTERNATIONAL 1466
TURBO DIESEL

Engine: Water-cooled, six-cylinder, turbo
Bore x stroke: 4.3 x 5.0 in.
Capacity: 436 cu. in.
PTO Power: 145.9 hp @ 2,600 rpm
Drawbar Power: 123.2 hp
Transmission: Sixteen-speed
Speeds: 1.5–22.3 mph
Fuel Consumption: 13.03 hp/hr per gallon
Weight: 13,670 lb.

INTERNATIONAL 784
[1978]

International's 84 series, unveiled in 1978, was designed to slot in underneath the 86 series. It was a new range of small row-crop and utility tractors, built in England. There were six 84s, starting with the 36 hp 384 Utility, powered by a 154 cu. in. four-cylinder diesel. Then came the 484, whose 179 cu. in. three-cylinder diesel offered 42 hp, and came with a three-point hitch, adjustable wide front axle, and 20-gallon fuel tank. Next up, the 52 hp 584 and 62 hp 684 used 206 and 239 cu. in. diesels respectively, both with eight forward and four reverse speeds. There was also a hydrostatic drive model, built to the same specification as the 684 but with a hydrostatic transmission replacing the gearbox. Top of the range was the 784 pictured here, which in diesel form used International's own 246 cu. in. diesel, offering 65 hp—as you can read in the specifications, a gasoline version was still optional, though by now most farmers were opting for diesel power.

All the 84 series diesel engines, both three- and four-cylinder, were built at International's factory at Neuss in Germany. But the 84 series was still similar to the 74 series it replaced. Like the 86, it used "split deck" control consoles (left-hand for the transmission, hitch, and PTO, and hydraulic controls on the right), and like its big brother really needed a driver with more than two hands to operate easily! One advance was hydraulic wet disc brakes, hydrostatic power steering, and a seat adjustable for both height and the driver's weight. Mounting the fuel tank between the rear wheels helped traction, by concentrating weight there, and maintenance was eased with easily accessible fuel and oil filters, and a maintenance-free battery.

The 84 series did well for International, so well that the basic design was in production right into the 1990s.

LEFT: *Like Massey-Ferguson, International had factories on both sides of the Atlantic. The 84 series was built in England, the bigger 86 series in the U.S.*

INTERNATIONAL 784

Engine: Water-cooled, four-cylinder
Bore x stroke: 3.9 x 5.0 in.
Capacity: 246 cu. in.
PTO Power: 65.5 hp @ 2,400 rpm
Drawbar Power: 56.8 hp
Transmission: Eight-speed
Speeds: 1.7–15.6 mph
Fuel Consumption: 15.34 hp/hr per gallon
Weight: 6,090 lb.

CASE 2590 POWERSHIFT
[1978]

In 1978, Case decided that the 70 series should be replaced by the 90s. The smallest Case 90 series was the 1190, powered by the company's own three-cylinder diesel of 165 cu. in. for 43 hp at the PTO, 35 hp at the drawbar. Front-wheel assist was an option on the bigger 1290,

again Case powered, this time by a 195 cu. in. four-cylinder unit giving 54 PTO hp. Like the 1190, it drove through a twelve-speed transmission without power shift. The 1390's diesel engine was a four-cylinder version of the 1190's triple, producing 61 PTO hp and 50 hp at the

drawbar from its 219 cu. in. The Case 1490 offered a turbocharged version of this unit, which according to Nebraska pushed out almost 71 hp at the PTO, 60 hp at the drawbar. Just as significant, it had a power shift option, giving on-the-go shifting between four ranges in the twelve-speed transmission. A six-cylinder version of the 1390's diesel powered the 1690, for 90 PTO hp, 73 hp at the drawbar, from 329 cu. in. Case's high-power range, most of them powered by the big 504 cu. in. six, were the 2090, 2390, and the 2590 pictured here.

Although most of the big Cases used the 504 six, this was unable to keep up with the highest power demands. From the mid-1970s, the 2870 Traction King used a 300 bhp Scania engine. But the smaller (less large) super-tractors carried on using in-house power units. There was also a bigger 4690 developed for the Canadian market. All these super-tractors made first use of micro-electronic controls, which later trickled down to cheaper models.

The 90 series lasted five years, though when it was replaced by the 94 series in 1983, it was the smaller two-wheel-drive Cases that got the update treatment first. But four-wheel-drive 94s soon followed, as the 4494 to 4994, the latter powered by a 400 bhp (gross) V8 turbo diesel.

LEFT: *This 2590 used Case's biggest 504 cu. in. six-cylinder diesel, in turbocharged 180 hp form. But for ultra-high horsepower applications, the company was forced to buy in power units.*

CASE 2590 POWERSHIFT

Engine: Water-cooled, six-cylinder, turbo
Bore x stroke: 4.625 x 5.0 in.
Capacity: 504 cu. in.
PTO Power: 180 hp @ 2,100 rpm
Drawbar Power: 153 hp @ 2,100rpm
Transmission: Twelve-speed
Speeds: 2.0–20.0 mph
Fuel Consumption: 13.3 hp/hr per gallon
Weight: 15,740 lb.

FORD 7810
[1978]

Through the 1960s, following its decision to go global, Ford's tractor division came up with ever more powerful machines. The 6000 of 1961, with 66 hp, was its biggest yet—it also used the troublesome Select-O-Matic transmission, but that's another story. It was followed by the 106 hp 8000 in 1968, powered by a 401 cu. in. diesel, and then the turbocharged 131 hp 9000.

But Ford never lost sight of the fact that it needed to offer a complete range of machines. There was never any question of just concentrating on bigger machines. Take 1976, when the range kicked off with the 1600 (really a Japanese mini-tractor with Ford badges); the smallest domestic tractor was the 32 hp 2600, then the 40 hp 3600, and 45 hp 4100. A 52 hp 4600 was next up, then a 60 hp 5600 and 70 hp 7600, while the high-horsepower tractors were the 8600 and 9600.

The 7810 shown here is another two years down the line from that, a highly successful mid-range machine that underlined Ford's commitment to no-nonsense mid-range machines. It used the same 401 cu. in. six-cylinder diesel as the original 8000, though here detuned to produce 86 hp—perhaps it was a more reliable route than turbocharging a smaller four-cylinder engine. An eight-speed transmission was standard, and sixteen-speed optional—front-wheel assist was on the options list as well. The latter was a popular option at this time, offering some of the benefits of four-wheel drive without the cost of a full four-by-four system.

At the beginning of the decade, comfortable, well-insulated cabs were just starting to come in as optional extras, and the John Deere Sound-Gard and Allis-Chalmers Acousta-Cab set new standards. Ford couldn't afford to be left behind, and all of its bigger machines were soon available with modern cabs.

BELOW AND LEFT: *Shown here, a 7810 model. Specifications are for the American-spec turbocharged four-cylinder 7700, which produced almost identical power to the 7810. But that went the same way as the non-turbo six-cylinder route, with more cubes—Ford actually detuned the 401 cu. in. six for this application. Both tractors could have a sixteen-speed transmission, though eight-speed was standard on the 7810.*

FORD 7700 DIESEL

Engine: Water-cooled four-cylinder turbo
Bore x stroke: 4.4 x 4.2 in.
Capacity: 255 cu. in.
PTO Power: 84 hp @ 2,100 rpm
Drawbar Power: 68 hp @ 2,100 rpm
Transmission: Sixteen-speed
Speeds: 1.4–18.6 mph
Weight: 8,400 lb.

VERSATILE 895
[1979]

The Steiger brothers may have pioneered four-wheel-drive super-tractors, but just as they were getting into their stride, a Canadian company was moving in the same direction. The first Versatile tractors had exactly the same key features: four-wheel drive through four equal-sized wheels, articulated steering, and a big diesel engine with more power and torque than any conventional tractor.

Versatile started life as the Hydraulic Engineering Company in Toronto in 1947, moving to Winnipeg three years later. At first, it made small agricultural implements, moving up to a big self-propelled swather in 1954. By 1963, Hydraulic had grown sufficiently to go public. To celebrate, it gave itself a new name—Versatile.

The first Versatiles were not in the Steiger class. They were big by conventional tractor standards, but not monsters of the prairies. The D100, launched in 1966, was powered by a 125 hp British Ford industrial engine, a six-cylinder diesel. Only one hundred of this type were made before it was replaced by the D145.

By 1977, Versatile had a complete range of big tractors, many of which were revised that year. One new model was the 500, which had four-wheel drive (of course), a live PTO, and adjustable wheel tread. Power derived from a Cummins V8 which produced 160 hp at the PTO, 192 hp at the crankshaft. But that wasn't the biggest Versatile by any means—the 825 promised 250 hp, and biggest of all was the 950, a new model for 1977. Once again, it was Cummins V8 powered, though this one measured 903 cu. in. for a formidable 348 hp at the crankshaft. The 950 turned out to be one of the largest-engined Versatiles ever, and the 555 of 1980 took its name from the capacity of its 555 cu. in. Cummins V8 engine. Like Steiger, Versatile tractors were designed for the big open spaces of the Midwest and Canada.

LEFT: *The 895 pictured here was typical of the machines of the late 1970s.*

VERSATILE 895

Engine: Water-cooled, six-cylinder, turbo-intercooled
Bore x stroke: 5.5 x 6.0 in.
Capacity: 855 cu. in.
Drawbar Power: 252 hp @ 2,100 rpm
Transmission: Twelve-speed
Speeds: 2.6–14.3 mph
Fuel Consumption: 15.15 hp hr per gallon
Weight: 24,620 lb.

The 1980s:
ONLY THE BIG SURVIVE

The American farm equipment business, according to conventional wisdom, went in seven-year cycles. Sales peaks in 1959, 1966, 1973, and (admittedly a year early) 1979 seemed to bear this out. But the 1980s blew that apart, with a sustained slump in tractor sales that was to last fifteen years. From that 1979 high of 188,000 tractors sold, sales slumped to 119,000 in three years. They then bumped along the bottom of a long-term recession, reaching a new low of just 87,000 tractors in 1992, less than half the 1979 figure.

There were several reasons for this slump. There were the global repercussions of the second oil crisis. And for farmers, the killer combination of low crop prices and high interest rates made expensive machinery purchases the first cutback. It's probably no coincidence that for much of the 1980s, sales of four-by-four and the more high-power tractors suffered more than the utility types.

Such a disastrous decade forced the American tractor industry into serious restructuring. In the short-term, many responded with lay-offs and redundancies, closing factories for weeks at a time. The longer term effect was that some long-established names were taken over, though all the big names survived the 1980s in one form or another. PIK—"payment in kind" —helped American farmers beginning in 1983, paying them for keeping acreage idle, but of course this didn't help the tractor makers, as fewer acres were being farmed. Tractor sales continued to fall, and financial analysts were now predicting that the entire American tractor industry

needed only two or three factories to fully satisfy this newly shrunken market.

From the middle of the decade, a wave of buy-outs and mergers began as the industry attempted to cope with the longest agricultural recession since the 1920s. International Harvester was the first casualty, its Farm Equipment division being sold to the Tenneco Corporation. Tenneco was no stranger to the tractor business, having owned J. I. Case since 1970. So the two rivals were merged into Case-International, which soon rationalized a complex range of fifty different models to just twelve. In fact, Case IH seemed to weather the rest of the 1980s pretty well, thanks to that rapid rationalization, and the corporate muscle of Tenneco behind it. In 1986, it bought the Steiger concern— expensive super-tractors were even less saleable than conventional machines, and Steiger wasn't big enough to survive on its own. After a loss of $8 million in 1985, the takeover came as a relief.

Allis-Chalmers survived the 1980s in name only. Soon after the Case IH merger, it was revealed that A-C was talking to Massey-Ferguson about a joint venture. That never happened, and later in 1985 a more ignominious deal was struck with Deutz of Germany. The tractor business was sold to Deutz, but not the old West Allis works, which closed at the end of the year. Allis-Chalmers were now given Deutz-Allis

RIGHT: *Tough times, but Case came out of the 1980s well, as the dominant partner in the newly merged Case-International. The addition of Steiger in 1986 produced a wide, strong range of tractors.*

The Largest 4WD Tractor Line In The Industry

If your operation calls for the size and power of 4WD, why not call on the leading 4WD family: the 9300 Series from Case IH. These ten workhorses bring substantially more power, performance and flexibility to the 4WD category. Ranging in size from 205 to 425 horsepower, the 9300 Series includes three Row Crop Special models and the revolutionary new QUADTRAC tractor, which features four unique, independent tracks for unsurpassed ground contact and reduced compaction. 9300 Series tractors from Case IH. The biggest name in four wheel drive.

tractors to sell, either rebadged old stock, or imported direct from Germany. A new line of larger Deutz-Allis badged tractors was announced for 1989, built for the company by White and powered by Deutz air-cooled diesel engines. White itself was having an eventful decade, bought up by new owners in 1981 and again in 1985, before finding a home with AGCO in 1993.

Nor was Ford exempt. In 1985 it announced it was planning to stop producing tractors in the U.S. altogether. But it also unveiled a more far-reaching move, which proved to be less of a distress purchase than the other takeovers. It bought New Holland, the well established maker of farm equipment. This put Ford in a strong position, with a full lineup of both tractors

ABOVE: *Steiger nearly went bust in the 1980s, but new ownership gave it new impetus, new bodywork, and a refreshed range. Early plans to drop the hallowed badge were later abandoned.*

BELOW: *Case's Quadtrac sought to combine the new technology of reinforced rubber tracks with an articulated chassis, for both traction and maneuverability.*

and implements from the renamed Ford–New Holland concern. It underlined that strength by adding Versatile to its stable two years later. In fact, once the dust had settled from all the mergers, closures and sell-offs, it was very clear that only one company had been able to come through independently—John Deere.

But in the midst of all this turmoil, some businesses evidently thought tractors were still worth investing in. For instance, Long Manufacturing, the company that had begun importing East European tractors in the 1970s, and modifying them for the American market, actually filed for bankruptcy at one point, but later bounced back. And a new name appeared in 1981— Hesston was an established maker of hay and forage equipment, now controlled by Fiat of Italy. From 1981, it began importing Fiat tractors, badged and painted as Hesstons. A complete range was available, from the 42 hp three-cylinder 480-8 to the 160 hp 1880. Interestingly, the mid-range 880-5 also had a five-cylinder diesel engine.

During the 1970s, manufacturers had finally begun to give serious attention to driver comfort, with safer, quieter cabs being fitted. This trend now gathered pace, though there was still some way to go. In Britain, the Silsoe Research Institute (SRI) developed a cab with full suspension. The idea was to keep the driver isolated from most the tractor's vibration, thereby enabling higher work rates. Not all the industry was impressed, but the SRI cab helped Renault develop its own cab with suspension, the Hydrostable.

Announced in 1987, it had taken ten years to develop and went into production on Renault's flagship TZ tractors. A combination of coil springs, anti-roll bars, shock absorbers, and locating rods were claimed to tame the pitching and rolling movements, as well as up and down bouncing and lateral swaying. At first, Renault faced the same problem Allis-Chalmers had faced all those years ago with rubber tires—the apparent high cost of the Hydrostable option put farmers off, and

ABOVE: *As Case-International had bagged Steiger, Ford snapped up Versatile, ensuring its dealers of a supply of well-proven super-tractors. This Ford 946 still carries the Versatile badge.*

there were not many takers. It wasn't until the mid 1990s when the message finally got through, and by the end of that decade, eighty percent of Renault Ares tractors sold in Britain came with Hydrostable.

Cabs themselves were changing in the 1980s. In consultation with ergonomics experts, designers strove to make cabs more spacious and uncluttered, with a greater glass area for better visibility, the latter particularly important for all sorts of tractor work. Also to improve visibility was the distinctive forward sloping hood, which many manufacturers adopted in the 1990s, though Deutz was first with its Agratron in 1989. As well as transforming the usual square-rigged tractor look into something more futuristic, the sloping nose was a great help when using front-mounted implements.

ABOVE: *The White name had three different owners in the 1980s, but survived. By the end of the decade they were building machines for Deutz-Allis.*

BELOW: *From Beauvais in France, the 3000-series was Massey-Ferguson's 1980s mid-size tractor, adopting many high-tech touches from the 2000.*

maneuverability and of course more road speed than any steel tracked crawler.

Caterpillar—the crawler pioneer and long-time world leader in the field—saved the day. In 1986 it unveiled the revolutionary new Challenger 65, aimed specifically at farmers. Instead of steel, its tracks were made of rubber reinforced with steel cables, promising to combine the traction and weight distribution of a crawler with performance close to a wheeled tractor on the road. And it did. The Mobil-trac system allowed road speeds up to 18 mph and its 24.5-in. wide belts didn't induce soil compaction as heavy four-by-four wheeled tractors could do. Each belt was driven by large steel wheels covered in a two-inch layer of rubber, with pneumatic rubber idler wheels at the front and four smaller bogies. Success didn't come immediately, but once it was clear that the Mobil-trac system was both tough and durable, Caterpillar had a success on its hands. It later followed up the Challenger 65 with smaller 45 and 55 models, and—the ultimate compliment—tractor producers

While wheeled tractors were forging ahead with cabs and convenience, crawlers were in decline for agricultural work. Big four-wheel-drive tractors, with twin or even triple wheel attachments, were taking over the role of the big crawlers, having excellent traction, but with reasonable

LEFT: *Revolution? Caterpillar created a new type of tractor in 1986 with the Challenger, which used reinforced rubber tracks in place of wheels—for track levels of traction with the versatility of wheels.*

such as John Deere and Case IH brought out their own rubber-tracked machines. The Challenger had an enormous impact, and in terms of crawler technology, it was as big a leap forward as pneumatic rubber tires had been for wheeled tractors way back in 1932.

Just as significant, though more of a gradual revolution than a sudden leap, was the use of electronics in tractors. Computer technology found its way into almost every facet of life in the 1980s and 1990s, and tractors were no exception. Combine harvesters had actually used electronic monitoring systems in the previous decade, using sensors to note things like ground speed, acreage worked, and fuel used. The next step forward was to use this mass of information to control, as well as monitor, all these various functions.

It came in 1987 when Massey-Ferguson, a pioneer of electronics in tractors, announced the Datatronic system as an option on its 3000 series machines. Datatronic measured and reported on sixteen lines of data, from engine speed and fuel reserve (in hours) to wheel slip and acres worked per hour. It also included a limited amount of electronic control, notably of the rear linkage, and automatic traction control. It was a big technological step forward, allowing the driver to adjust to an optimum work rate, based on what Datatronic told him. As was the way with all the significant breakthroughs in tractor technology, other manufacturers soon followed suit, and electronics became increasingly common, and far more sophisticated, in the 1990s.

BELOW: *Massey-Ferguson pioneered the use of electronics in tractors, for the control of everything from hydraulics to diesel injection to driver information systems.*

INTERNATIONAL 956XL
[1980]

Not the most famous tractor in the U.S., but the International 956XL, together with its bigger brother the 1056XL, was something of a legend in its native Europe. and was in production for ten years.

It originated in the 946 and 1046 of 1975, which were built in IHC's German factory.

Two years later they were replaced by the French-built 955 and 1055. Both series were powered by the same D358 six-cylinder diesel as the 956/1056, a robust unit that could withstand 10,000 hours of hard work without needing major attention. In 1979, the famous "XL" cab was unveiled. This—

also dubbed the "Control Center"—was a big step forward in cab design. Built at IH's plant in Croix, France, it was first fitted to the new "Fieldforce" range of tractors. It had a one-piece frame and being isolated from the chassis gave a high level of comfort. It was quiet, too, at 82 Db(A).

A year later, the 956 and 1056 came along as updates, both fitted with the XL cab as standard. Power was up by 5 hp and torque increased as well, while the four-wheel-drive versions incorporated a ZF self-locking limited-slip differential. Few big changes took place in the 956/1056's decade of production: the Sens-O-Draulic system was added in September 1983, and a center-drive ZF front axle in 1986—giving a much improved turning circle of just 176 in. The 956/1056 six-cylinder diesel was also used in some American-spec Internationals. Until 1980, it powered the 886, which then switched to the American-built D360 unit, The D358 carried on in the lower-spec 786, which came in as a budget machine to fight the John Deere 2840 and Ford 7700. In 1981, many Internationals were updated. The new American equivalents of the 956/1056 were the 3488 and 3688, the former available with hydrostatic transmission. But nothing lasts forever, and the two 1956 tractors were dropped by Case IH in 1992.

LEFT: *This later 956XL carries the Case badge, marking it as a postmerger machine, after which all Case and International tractors were badged Case-International. Eventually, "International" was dropped, and Case is now part of CNH Global.*

INTERNATIONAL 956XL

Engine: Water-cooled, six-cylinder diesel
Bore x stroke: 3.9 x 5.1 in.
Capacity: 365 cu. in.
Power: 95 hp
Torque: 364 Nm
Transmission: Sixteen-speed
Weight: 10,274 lb.

JOHN DEERE 8850
[1982]

The Steigers could never have known what they'd started. Their first articulated four-wheel drives of the 1960s bred a new generation of super-tractors. This market was so important that most of the major tractor manufacturers tried to grab a slice as super-tractors made eco-nomic sense. Big expensive tractors could still do the work on big farms faster and cheaper than smaller ones.

So these tractors got ever bigger, until a turbocharged six-cylinder engine wasn't enough any more. John Deere's answer was this 8850, a new top-of-the-range V8 which ran alongside the existing six-cylinder 8450 and 8650. Instead of buying in a Cummins or Caterpillar, Deere designed its own, a turbocharged and intercooled diesel with 300 hp at the PTO. This was the biggest, most powerful tractor John Deere had ever built and it was all done in-house, with the turbo-intercooled V8 designed and put together at Deere's famous Waterloo factory, in Iowa. Reflecting the difficult times, the new tractor (and its updated six-cylinder cousins) were advertised as, "Three new ways to tighten your belt." Along with its smaller brothers, the 8850 was given improved visibility (exhaust pipe and air cleaner intake were moved to the right-hand side) and new ISO remote hydraulic couplers. A sixteen-speed Quad-Range transmission was standard, controlled by a single lever, and just to prove that fuel economy was an issue as well as power, the 8850 had a viscous fan drive that reduced fan speed in cooler temperatures. Finally, just to make abso-lutely clear to the world that the 8850's owner had bought the most expensive John Deere available, the 8850 was given six headlights instead of the 8650's four. Recession? What recession?

LEFT: *Never mind that the American tractor industry was facing its worst recession in years, or that super-tractor sales were suffering more than most, John Deere still chose 1982 to launch its all-new 8850 V8—it paid off, though.*

JOHN DEERE 8850 DIESEL

Engine: Water-cooled V8,
  turbo intercooled
Bore x stroke: 5.5 x 5.0 in.
Capacity: 955 cu. in.
PTO Power: 304 hp @ 2,100 rpm
Drawbar Power: 270 hp @ 2,100 rpm
Transmission: Sixteen-speed
Speeds: 2.1–20.2 mph
Fuel Consumption: 14 hp/hr per gallon
Weight: 37,700 lb.

VERSATILE 256
[1983]

Not all Versatiles were super-tractors, monsters of the prairies. This Versatile 256 was a baby by the standards of Steiger, Big Bud, or indeed Versatile itself. Instead of six or eight cylinders, it had only four, which between them measured only a paltry 239 cu. in. It was turbocharged, but the power output of 84 hp at the PTO was nothing special in the early 1980s, even by conventional tractor standards. It weighed little more than 9,000 lb., making it a flyweight by super-tractor standards.

But that didn't matter, because the 256 was a bidirectional tractor—its purpose lay not in sheer sod-breaking power, but in its versatility. Developed from the original 150 bidirectional, the 256 could operate equally well in either direction, with the driver's station able to swivel through 180 degrees to face front or rear as required. Like the 150, this latest two-way tractor had four-wheel drive through equal-sized wheels, driving through a hydrostatic transmission. This was fully automatic, giving infinitely variable ratios from zero to 19.9 mph. An auxiliary three-speed manual transmission gave three distinct ranges of stepless automatic drive.

Power came from a four-cylinder 239 cu. in. diesel producing 84 hp at the PTO and 61 hp at the drawbar. It was built by Consolidated Diesel Corporation (CDC), a joint venture between Case and Cummins, though CDC was happy to supply engines to rival tractor manufacturers. In 1985, a turbocharged version of this unit was added to create the Versatile 276, which was available alongside the 256, until that was dropped in 1987. The turbo CDC engine pushed out just over 100 hp at the PTO, 71 hp at the drawbar, and used the same hydrostatic transmission as the 256. From 1988, after the Ford takeover, the tractor was named the Ford-Versatile 276.

LEFT: *The Versatile 256 was a new type of tractor, the first of the modern bidirectional machines that could operate equally well in either direction.*

VERSATILE 256

Engine: Water-cooled, four-cylinder, turbo
Bore x stroke: 4.0 x 4.7 in.
Capacity: 239 cu. in.
PTO Power: 84 hp @ 2,500 rpm
Drawbar Power: 61 hp @ 2,500 rpm
Transmission: Auto hydrostatic + three-speed range
Speeds: 0–19.9 mph
Fuel Consumption: 16.9 hp/hr per gallon
Weight: 9,150 lb.

WHITE 4-225
[1984]

In 1980, White Farm Equipment was taken over by Texas Investment, a group of financiers with no experience of the tractor industry. The next few years saw less investment in producing new tractors.

A range of five new Iseki machines were imported from Japan to fill out the lower end of the range. Offering 28 to 75 hp, they made up a substantial part of the WFE line. However, this was an expensive way to do business and WFE was becoming dangerously dependent on Iseki.

There were some new homegrown Whites under the Texas regime, notably two new four-wheel-drive machines launched in 1984, the 225 hp 4-225 and the 270 hp 4-270. Both were designed to slot in above the existing 4-210. This shows just how fast the power race was moving—a decade earlier, White had launched the 4-150 as its top tractor and now the biggest machines needed close to 300 hp to remain competitive. Both the 4-225 and 270 were built along the same lines as the 210, with four-wheel drive, an articulated chassis, and bought-in V8 diesel engine.

These were the last of a long line of White articulated four-wheel drives. It was a mix of existing and bought-in components, with Oliver transmissions married to a Caterpillar diesel. It worked, keeping White in the high-horsepower four-by-four market after it had abandoned the sub-75 hp arena to bought-in, rebadged Isekis. But only a year after the 4-225 was launched, the Texas Investment Group sold White to the Allied Products Corporation of Chicago. Unlike Texas, Allied did have some agricultural experience—but would that bode well for the future of White?

In the meantime, White's success depended on tractors like the 4-225. Its 4-210 predecessor used the same layout, and specifications for this are given below.

LEFT: *A silver hood stripe denoted the White Motors era, which lasted up to 1980. A red stripe appeared in 1981, to commemorate White Farm Equipment, now owned by Texas Investment.*

WHITE 4-210 (1979)

Engine: Water-cooled V8 diesel
Bore x stroke: 4.5 x 5.0 in.
Capacity: 636 cu. in.
PTO Power: 159 hp @ 2,800 rpm
Drawbar Power: 127 hp
Transmission: Eighteen-speed
Speeds: 2.2–18.3 mph
Fuel Consumption: 12.34 hp/hr
  per gallon
Weight: 23,735 lb.

STEIGER PANTHER KP1360

[1982]

STEIGER PANTHER KP1360 DIESEL

Engine: Water-cooled, six-cylinder, turbo-intercooled

Bore x stroke: 5.5 x 6.0 in.

Capacity: 855 cu. in.

PTO Power: 326 hp @ 2,100 rpm

Drawbar Power: 289 hp

Transmission: Twelve-speed

Speeds: 2.4–16.5 mph

Fuel Consumption: 15.45 hp/hr per gallon

Weight: 35,480 lb.

The early 1980s were tough times for Steiger. It was hard for a small independent manufacturer to survive, and sales of big super-tractors were hit hard by the slump.

But they carried on and the early 1980s saw a new range of Panthers, the 1325, 1360, and 1400—all powered by Cummins or Caterpillar six-cylinder diesels. The "baby" 1325 used a Caterpillar 893 cu. in. unit, which fell just short of 300 PTO hp when tested at Nebraska and covered a speed range of 2.4 to 16.5 mph in its twelve forward ratios.

The Cummins six which powered the 1400 was actually smaller at 855 cu. in. but produced twenty-seven percent more horsepower at the drawbar. It also was much more fuel-efficient than the smaller 1325. This was probably due to the Cummins, which proved more economical in the midrange 1360 too. This tractor was available with either power unit, the 893 cu. in. Caterpillar or 855 cu. in. Cummins. These gave identical drawbar power in the tests and similar PTO power. However, the Cummins proved again more efficient, with 15.45 hp/hr per gallon in the drawbar test.

BELOW: *One of the last independently built lime-green Steigers, before the company was taken over by Case-International in 1986.*

ZETOR 7540
[1985]

During the Cold War, certain Eastern Bloc products gained a reputation in the West for being well engineered and relatively cheap.

Zetor was such a postwar creation, its first prototype tractor being built in 1945. The company moved fast, and was soon accounting for most of Czechoslovakia's entire tractor output. From the beginning, exports were a key to their success and 1,000 of the first 25 hp twin-cylinder diesel were sent abroad in 1947. It was soon joined by a higher-powered 30. A 42 hp

BELOW: *Zetor of Czechoslovakia was probably the most respected of the former Eastern Bloc manufacturers. It survived the political and social upheavals of early 1990s eastern Europe, and today offers a full range of machines up to 104 hp.*

four-cylinder machine which arrived in 1954, in both wheeled and crawler form. By that time, Zetor was building 10,000 tractors a year, a production rate which had doubled by the early 1960s.

Zetor launched a new unified range in the early 1960s, with two-, three-, and four-cylinder machines. In fact, the factory seemed determined to keep up with Western tractor technology. The unified range—initially the 2011, 3011, and 4011 —had Zetor-matic hydraulic lifts and ten-speed transmissions, while four-wheel-drive versions followed. Zetors were also fitted with quiet safety cabs before many Western European manufacturers got around to doing so. Higher-powered Zetors, such as the six-cylinder turbocharged 12011, followed.

ZETOR 7321 (2002)
Engine: Water-cooled, four-cylinder turbo-diesel
Power: 78 hp @ 2,200 rpm
Transmission: Ten-speed
Speeds: 1.1–18.4 mph

By the late 1970s, Zetor had built half a million tractors, by combining a relatively advanced specification and a low price. The 7540 shown here is a typical Zetor of the mid-1980s, using the company's own four-cylinder diesel. By 2002, Zetor could claim to have built over a million tractors, and was offering a full range of two- and four-wheel-drive machines of 42 to 104 hp.

MASSEY-FERGUSON 3095
[1986]

Throughout the late twentieth century, Massey-Ferguson had two major European factories at Beauvais in France and Coventry, England. The Banner Lane plant in Coventry could trace its tractor roots right back to the Ferguson TE20 of 1946. Now it concentrated on the smaller, simpler tractors, while Beauvais specialized in high-tech mid-range machines. The biggest machines were still built in the U.S.

This 3095 was a Beauvais tractor, part of the new 3000 series announced in 1986. It wasn't actually part of the initial range, which stretched from the 71 hp 3050 to the 107 hp 3090, but joined soon afterward. All had electronic control of the three-point linkage, while higher-spec versions like this one added Autotronic, which gave automatic operation of the differential lock, front-wheel assist, and PTO.

Above the 3000 series was the 2000, launched back in 1979. The 2640, 2680, and 2720 covered the 110–150 hp range, with all three machines using a variant of the faithful Perkins six-cylinder diesel. All had a high-tech push-button transmission which allowed full-power range changes, and offered sixteen forward speeds and twelve reverse. This didn't help the Banner Lane plant, as AGCO announced that its Coventry factory would close in 2002.

Still, the 3000 series proved to be a popular tractor. In 1996, *Profi* magazine tested a secondhand example, and declared the ten-year-old design to be up to 1990s standards in its comfort and electronics. They didn't like the slow gear change and steering, but praised the reliability and ease of use of the Datatronic system, the robust, low-maintenance Perkins diesel, and general easy maintenance. A higher-horsepower version of the 3000—the 3600—replaced the 2000 in 1987. As for the 1980s 3000, American customers had their own version before the Europeans—specifications for the American-spec 3505 are given below.

LEFT: *The 3000 series was Massey-Ferguson's mid-range tractor of the 1980s, all Perkins powered.*

MASSEY-FERGUSON 3505 (U.S. SPEC, 1984)

Engine: Water-cooled, six-cylinder, turbo
Bore x stroke: 3.875 x 5.0 in.
Capacity: 354 cu. in.
PTO Power: 91.5 hp
Drawbar Power: 73.4 hp
Transmission: Sixteen-speed
Speeds: 1.3–18.2 mph
Fuel Consumption: 14.3 hp/hr per gallon
Weight: 12,935 lb.

MASSEY-FERGUSON 3630
[1987]

By 1987, Massey-Ferguson's 2000 series was eight years old—elderly for a modern tractor. It was replaced by the 3600, which was really a high-powered version of the 3000. There was slightly more power from the Perkins sixes as well, with 113 hp, 130 hp (turbo), and 150 hp (intercooler). Three years later, the 3000s too became part of the 3600 family, replaced by new versions with a lower specification.

Valmet agreed to have their tractor built for them by M-F at its Beauvais plant in France. There was already a link, as Valmet was supplying engines for the 180 hp M-F 3680. Introduced in 1989, the new Mega 8300 and 8600 were a mix of components: Valmet engines, M-F transaxle, and hydraulics, while the cab and driven front axle came from Italy, with assembly at Beauvais. With 140 hp (non-turbo) and 170 hp (turbo) from its six-cylinder diesel, it was the most powerful Finnish tractor yet.

This 3630 was one of the lower-powered 3600s, though it used Perkins latest 1000 series six-cylinder direct injection diesel. Perkins's new idea was the Quadram bowl-in-chamber system, a combustion bowl in the piston crown, with four lobes cast into it to optimize mixing of the fuel/air charge. This made combustion faster and evened out combustion pressure peaks, which it said improved torque at low speeds.

Perkins was part of the Massey-Ferguson family, so all 3600s used a variation on the six-cylinder diesel. Power was boosted for the 3645 (142 hp) and 3655 (155 hp) in 1990, while two years later, the 3600 series benefited from the Dynashift transmission, which married a four-speed epicyclic gear system to the basic eight-speed gearbox. The 3600s were replaced by the 6100/8100 tractors in the mid 1990s.

LEFT: *All 3600s were Perkins powered, using the latest direct injection 1000 series, which had superseded the faithful 354 cu. in. six. The exception was the 180 hp top range 3680, which used a Valmet power unit—by the end of 1995, 6,000 Valmet-powered M-Fs had left the production line.*

MASSEY-FERGUSON 3525 (U.S. SPEC, 1984)

Engine: Water-cooled, six-cylinder, turbo
Bore x stroke: 3.875 x 5.0 in.
Capacity: 354 cu. in.
PTO Power: 108 hp @ 2,400 rpm
Drawbar Power: 90 hp
Transmission: Sixteen-speed
Speeds: 1.3–18.2 mph
Fuel Consumption: 16.7 hp/hr per gallon
Weight: 13,100 lb.

FORD NEW HOLLAND 946
[1987]

Versatile came close to closure in 1986, thanks to financial problems with its parent company, Coronet Industries. But things weren't as black as they seemed. The company now had long experience and expertise in the field of super-tractors, which made it very attractive to established makers of conventional machines. So just as Case IH took over Steiger in 1986, it wasn't long before a savior appeared for Versatile.

In fact, in late 1985, just as Ford was in the process of taking over New Holland, John Deere had announced their intention to buy the Canadian company. The plan was to use the Canadian factory, with its long experience of building big tractors, to assemble both Versatile and John Deere four-wheel-drive machines, with parts shipped in from John Deere's main plant based in Waterloo, Iowa. But the John Deere deal fell through, and it was Ford, fresh from its takeover of New Holland, that stepped in to save Versatile from extinction. Within a few months, tractors were rolling out of the Winnipeg plant once again.

The colors and badges changed of course. Versatiles now came in Ford New Holland blue, while the Versatile name was retained as small print only. The 946 (pictured here) was launched in the same year as the Ford takeover, and was part of the range up to 1993. It was the second-largest machine on offer within the range—the 846 and 876 were lower powered, the 976 higher—and it was the only six-series machine to be exported to Britain, proving these giant super-tractors weren't just restricted to the Midwest.

Like most Versatiles, the 946 was powered by a Cummins six-cylinder diesel, the 855 cu. in. in this case, turbocharged and aftercooled to produced 325 hp. And according to one British farmer, it used little more than a gallon of diesel per acre—not bad from 855 cu. in.

LEFT: *The 946 was one of four Versatile super-tractors on offer in the late 1980s. After the merger, they all adopted Ford colors and the Ford badge, although the Versatile name was still there in the small print (just visible in this picture), if you cared to look hard enough.*

FORD NEW HOLLAND 946

Engine: Water-cooled, six-cylinder, turbo-diesel
Capacity: 855 cu. in.
Power: 325 hp @ 2,100 rpm
Transmission: Twenty-four-speed
Weight: 31,900 lb.

CASE IH 9250
[1988]

This Case IH 9250 isn't really a Case at all, but a Steiger. When Case took over the Dakota-based maker of super-tractors in 1986, it probably intended to drop the Steiger name altogether and to close the Steiger plant to cut costs. Sure enough, the new 9100 series (and the 9200 series, including the mid-range 9250 pictured here) was painted in Case colors, and the Steiger name didn't appear, though the tractor was still built in Steiger's factory and continued the Steiger tradition of a four-wheel-drive super-tractor with articulated chassis. There were five Case-IH 9100s for 1987, and each one replaced a corresponding Steiger model. The 9110 (190 hp) replaced the Steiger Puma 1000; the 9130, with 235 hp, did the same for the Wildcat 1000. With a 280 hp engine (specifications show PTO and drawbar power), the 9150 took over from the Cougar 1000 and the 9170 (335 hp) replaced the Panther 1000. The range-topping 9180, with 375 hp, replaced the equivalent Steiger Lion 1000.

All these were badged as Case IHs, as were the 9200s that replaced them, but the Steiger name soon reappeared and the famous super-tractors continued to be built at Fargo, North Dakota. After three decades, Steiger was an immensely well-respected name among American farmers and still is.

The 9300 used the same basic layout as the 9250, though the range soon included ten machines. Power outputs ranged from the 240 hp 9330 to the 425 hp 9390, and there were even two row-crop models. Engines were a choice of Case's own 532 cu. in. and the Cummins N14 or M11. A twelve-speed transmission was standard, with twenty-four-speed SynchroShift and twelve-speed Powershift options. The future of Steiger looked secure.

LEFT: *Taking over Steiger brought Case IH a ready-made range of four-wheel-drive super-tractors, which would act as corporate flagships for years to come, even wearing a Steiger badge.*

CASE IH 9150 (1987)

Engine: Water-cooled six-cylinder turbo-intercooled Cummins
Bore x stroke: 4.92 x 5.35 in.
Capacity: 611 cu. in.
PTO Power: 246 hp @ 2,100 rpm
Drawbar Power: 230 hp @ 2,100 rpm
Transmission: Twelve-speed full power shift
Speeds: 2.3–19.1 mph
Weight: 26,000 lb.

CASE MAGNUM 7130

[1988]

CASE MAGNUM 7130

Engine: Water-cooled,
six-cylinder turbo

Bore x stroke: 4.49 x 5.32 in.

Capacity: 505 cu. in.

PTO Power: 173 hp @ 2,200 rpm

Drawbar Power: 155 hp

Transmission: Eighteen-speed

Speeds: 1.8–19.2 mph

Weight: 17,090 lb.

BELOW: *It cost Case $450 million to research, develop, and put the Magnum into production. The first fruit of the recently merged Case IH, it repaid that investment in spades.*

In 1985, Case merged with International Harvest and became Case IH, the second-largest American manufacturer of tractors. It had a huge range of around fifty models, many of which competed with each other.

The first joint Case IH tractor, the Magnum, came out in 1988. It came in two-wheel-drive only at first, to replace the existing 2294, 2594, 3394, and 3594. The new range had the 7110 (130 PTO hp) and the 7120 (150hp), 7130 (170 hp), and the range topping 7140 (195 hp). All four used an engine from CDC. It was a six-cylinder turbocharged diesel, with intercooler on the 7140. Standard transmission was an eighteen-speed with full powershift and an optional creeper which gave an extra six speeds, for twenty-four speeds in all. Other

options were front wheel assist and a true ground speed sensor.

The Magnum was new from the ground up, including a new Silent Guardian II cab, which reduced noise to as little as 72 dB(A) and gave good visibility. To make the Magnum, a 700,000 square feet portion of the old Racine factory was completely revamped, and with production costs, the total bill came to $450 million. But it was money well spent, as the Magnum formed the backbone of its range during the 1990s.

As merged, Case IH was subject to serious rationalization, which meant the loss of jobs and factories as well as tractor models. The Meltham plant in England was closed, jobs lost, and production was concentrated in Doncaster.

CASE MAGNUM 7140
[1988]

The Case 7140 pictured here was the top tractor in the first Magnum range. The range was updated as the 7210/20/30/40 in 1994, but power output was unchanged—the 7240 still offered 198 hp, though it was no longer the flagship. In 1992, the Magnums were topped by a 215 hp 7150, which became a 7250 for the same power.

For 1997, the Magnums did get a power increase, covering the range 155–264 hp. Comparing those 1997 Magnums to the 2002 versions, it's interesting to note that the latest machines are no more powerful, and in some cases less. Instead, tractors are making better use of the power they have, thanks to more sophisticated transmissions, hydraulics, electronics, and information systems.

The latest Magnums offer 145 hp to 235 hp against the 1997 range of 155–264 hp. Four models were listed in 2002, the MX180, 200, 220, and 270. The top-range MX270 uses a four-valves per cylinder, with turbocharging and intercooling. It offers a eighteen speeds, but again, electronic control makes up the difference.

Nevertheless, the Magnum remains Case IH's (or CNH Global, as it is now called) second-largest tractor to the STX Steiger range. Case bought Steiger sixteen years ago, but the name lives on. All the Steigers are four-wheel drive, of course, and the power range now covers 275 to 450 hp. They're also available with Quadtrac, four caterpillar tracks in place of the double or triple wheel options used on this size of machine.

CASE MAGNUM 7140

Engine: Water-cooled, six-cylinder, turbo-intercooled
Bore x stroke: 4.49 x 5.32 in.
Capacity: 505 cu. in.
PTO Power: 198 hp @ 2,200 rpm
Drawbar Power: 181 hp
Transmission: Eighteen-speed
Speeds: 1.9–20.4 mph
Weight: 17,565 lb.

BELOW: *The 195 hp 7140 was the flagship Magnum for four years, from the 1988 launch until 1992—this was when Case unveiled the new 215 hp 7150 model.*

WHITE 60
[1989]

WHITE 60

Engine: Water-cooled, four-cylinder

Bore x stroke: 4.02 x 4.72 in.

Capacity: 239 cu. in.

PTO Power: 61 hp

Drawbar Power: 52 hp

Transmission: Six-speed (eighteen-speed optional)

Speeds: 2.1–24.2 mph

Fuel Consumption: 14.58 hp/hr per gallon

Under its latest new ownership, things looked better for White. It already owned the New Idea name, and would shortly combine its two lines to form White-New Idea.

Allied also seemed more serious about investing in new machines. Only a year after the takeover, big changes were announced for the American-made part of the range. Four new machines were unveiled, ranging from 94 to 188 hp. The Field Boss name was dropped, and the new machines were known as plain Whites: 100, 120, 140, and 160. All had an eighteen-speed transmission, with the option of front-wheel assist, an increasingly popular option in the 1980s, offering as it did some of the traction benefits of four-wheel drive without the cost and complication of a full mechanical system. Power units for all White's domestically produced tractors now came from CDC, a joint venture between Case and Cummins.

With everyone from John Deere to Allis-Chalmers importing their smaller tractors from Europe, it seemed accepted that nobody could profitably make small- to mid-size tractors in the U.S. any more. Then, in 1989, White announced the new 60 and 80, the smallest tractors sold and made in the U.S. The 60 shown here offered 61 hp, and a basic six-speed transmission was offered as standard, with a three-speed power shift as an option.

BELOW: *In 1989 White defied the accepted industry norm that it wasn't economical to produce American-made sub-90 hp tractors, unveiling the "American" 60 and 80.*

WHITE 80

[1989]

Remember how White Motors bought its way into the tractor business in the early 1960s? First by calling itself Oliver, then Cockshutt, then Minneapolis-Moline. After ten years of dilution through badge engineering, all three famous names were dropped in favor of White itself.

Moving on twenty years, and White, under its second new owner, has designed and is about to launch two new row-crop tractors, the 60 and 80. One of their biggest selling points is that they're actually made in the U.S.—not rebadged European or Japanese imports. In fact, the "American" 60 and 80, as they were badged, actually replaced a range of Japanese imports. The White 2-55, 2-65, and 2-75 were rebadged Isekis tractors, as the company had become dependent on Iseki for all its smaller machines. The Japanese machines were undoubtedly good quality and up-to-date, but in the long term this strategy made little financial sense. It was cheaper in the short term, by saving design and development costs, but in the final analysis, it cost more to buy someone else's tractor and sell it as your own.

The 80, powered by a turbocharged CDC four-cylinder diesel, was actually the first sub-90 hp tractor to be built in the U.S. for a decade. White was able to use the CDC power unit, another product of the joint venture between Cummins and Case, which concentrated on big six-cylinder diesels, but also made this smaller four.

How do they capitalize on the fact that these were the first all-American smaller tractors for ten years? The answer was simple: badge them as the "American" 60 and 80, and resurrect the old corporate colors of Oliver, Cockshutt, and Minneapolis-Moline. So the new 60 and 80 came in

Oliver green, Cockshutt red, Minneapolis gold, or White's classic silver.

Sadly, the company's revivalist optimism didn't last long. The new "Americans" just couldn't compete with cheaper imports and were dropped from the lineup barely three years into their production run, in 1991.

BELOW: *A brave attempt, but the new White "Americans" lasted only three years, before being replaced by imports from Lamborghini of Italy— which no doubt were still cheaper, even after being shipped across the Atlantic.*

WHITE 80
Engine: Water-cooled, four-cylinder turbo diesel
Bore x stroke: 4.02 x 4.72 in.
Capacity: 239 cu. in.
PTO Power: 81 hp
Drawbar Power: 71 hp
Transmission: Six-speed (eighteen-speed optional)
Speeds: 2.1–16.7 mph

The 1990s:
HIGH-TECH RECOVERY

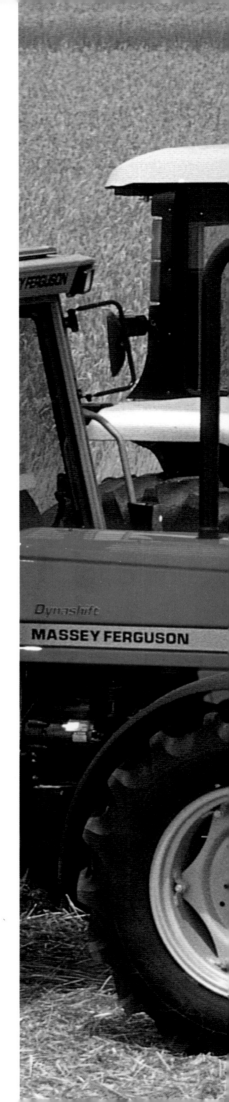

In 1993, American tractor sales finally began the long haul back. Sales of big machines and four-by-fours had recovered slightly in the late 1980s, but the sub-40 hp class went into decline. This, coupled with a slowdown in Europe and uncertainty over the Gulf War conspired to force overall sales down even further. From 108,000 tractors in 1990, they fell to 94,000 the following year, and 87,000 the year after. When sales rose eleven percent in 1993, it was the first increase in fourteen years.

Nor were the mergers over yet. The Ford-New Holland agricultural arm was bought by Fiat, while Deutz-Allis found another new home with AGCO. AGCO, which stood for the Allis-Gleaner Corporation, was an American success story of the 1990s. Originating in management buy-outs of both Gleaner and Deutz-Allis, the company bought Massey-Ferguson U.S.A., White in 1993, and McConnell Tractors two years later. Other acquisitions soon followed, rapidly transforming AGCO into a major world player. Not until early in the twenty-first century were the cracks beginning to show—in 2002, AGCO announced it was to close the famous Ferguson Banner Lane factory in England.

But ten years earlier, that was all in the future, and AGCO wasn't the only company doing well out of the tractor revival—John Deere and Case IH both posted big profits in 1993. In fact, optimism about the future seemed rife, with a whole strong of technical developments in the 1990s that made tractors more efficient, comfortable, and easier to use than ever. Take the JCB Fastrac of 1991. JCB was a British manu-

facturer of construction equipment, but jumped into agriculture with an innovative high-speed tractor of unusual design. Powered by Perkins diesels, the Fastrac could reach 45 mph on the road: full-time four-wheel drive, four-wheel braking, and all-around suspension (coil springs at the front, self-leveling hydro-pneumatic at the rear) were the Fastrac's high spots. Here at last was a spiritual successor to Minneapolis-Moline's 1938 Comfortractor. The difference was, the Fastrac was a great success and inspired a new generation of high-speed tractors.

It also inspired a flood of new front-suspension systems, mostly based on hydraulics rather than steel springs. For instance, John Deere's TripleLink of 1997 used double-acting hydraulic rams to give 3.9 in. of vertical travel; Massey-Ferguson's Quadlink used one ram; Same-Deutz-Fahr followed a similar path, while New Holland's Terraglide automatically locked out under 1 mph; the Aires system, used by Valtra, relied on compressed air rather than hydraulics, using an engine-driven compressor. All these systems suspended the tractor's front axle as one unit, but the system adopted by some Case and Steyr machines provided independent front suspension, with separate hydraulics for each front wheel, allowing each to act independently of the other.

RIGHT: *The three faces of AGCO in the early 1990s—bright red Massey-Ferguson, silver White, and orange Allis. AGCO's growth through the decade, from management buy-out to major world force, was phenomenal.*

Cab suspension moved on from Renault's pioneering work as well—SAME designed a self-leveling cab, in which sensors continuously measured the distance between the cab and the tractor's chassis, using compressed air to correct any tilting. Case/

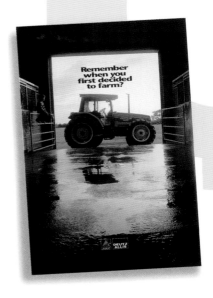

ABOVE: *Familiar orange tractor, familiar farmyard setting, and a good dose of nostalgia were the selling points for a newly independent Deutz-Allis.*

Steyr meanwhile, used a combination of springs, hydraulic cylinders, and gas struts as their cab suspension medium.

The use of electronics in tractors, from its first beginnings in the 1980s, really took off in the 1990s. Remember how Massey-Ferguson pioneered the field with its Datatronic system in 1987? The updated Datatronic II illustrated well how electronics had developed in the meantime. Instead of just monitoring how the tractor was doing, Datatronic II could be programmed to "remember" certain setups that the driver might want for a particular crop or conditions. Data from the monitoring could be printed out or saved onto a smart card, then transferred to the farmer's office computer. Automatic traction control and implement depth control were part of the package, the tractor's "brain" raising the implement if wheelspin increased.

Massey-Ferguson continued to play a leading role in the development of tractor electronics in the 1990s. Take GPS (global positioning systems), which can pinpoint the exact position of a tractor, within about

ABOVE: *Caterpillar followed up the rubber-tracked Challenger with smaller versions, which competed directly with conventional big row-crop tractors.*

a meter, by bouncing signals off a satellite. That enables accurate yield maps of each field to be built up, which in turn can be used to pinpoint problems areas (such as poor drainage), to adjust the application of seed or fertilizer more precisely.

Yet another area of electronics application is in tractor transmissions, especially for CVT (continuously variable transmissions). Multispeed power shift, with fast, clutchless changes between fixed ratios, had become the standard transmission on most tractors apart from the low-power class. CVT was different. It was an automatic transmission, allowing an infinite spread of ratios up to maximum speed, with the engine running at a constant (most efficient) speed. There were plenty of advantages over a conventional power shift: CVT is smoother and easier to use, is more efficient than a pure hydrostatic system, and its electronics can be integrated with those of the engine. Claas, Fendt, and transmission specialist ZF—all of them German companies—independently came up with similar tractor CVTs in the late 1990s. In the early twenty-first century, the arrival of CVT looked like a major step forward in tractor technology.

Electronic control of engine systems is now very common, apart from in budget and low-power tractors. As in the world of cars, buses, and trucks, this has greatly improved the power, smoothness, and "cleanliness" of diesel engines. Emissions in particular have been an increasing pre-occupation for manufacturers in the 1990s, as legal standards are tightened up. More efficient combustion through electronics and turbochargers brings cleaner emissions and less fuel used, a vital development in a world whose resources are finite.

But not all tractor developments of the 1990s related to electronics. Caterpillar's rubber-tracked Challenger had been a huge success, spawning a renewed interest in the use of crawlers on farms. The company followed it up with smaller, cheaper versions of the Challenger, in more direct competition with the high-power row-crop tractors. John Deere, Case, and the rest could do little but respond in kind. Deere announced a rubber-track version of its 8000 and later of the pivot steer 9000. Case IH unveiled the dramatic Quadtrac, which for the first time replaced four wheels with four rubber tracks. So great was the new interest in tracks, that conversion kits came onto the market, enabling farmers to convert their existing wheeled tractors to rubber tracks, and back again as the conditions dictated.

But as ever, the background to all these technical developments is ever-changing market conditions. The Western-based manufacturers now look likely to come under low-cost competition from the Far East—simple, cheap tractors from India or South Korea could make serious inroads into Western markets, given sufficient technology transfer from companies like AGCO and CNH Global. It might seem odd that Western companies are investing in potential competitors, but from their point of view it makes profitable sense. It gives them part-ownership of a range of budget tractors that could not be made for such a low price domestically and the possibility of using these factories as a source of cheaper components for American- or European-made tractors.

The tractor business, like just about every other form of manufacturing, is becoming more worldwide than ever before, with low-cost production counting for more than tariffs, political considerations, and brand loyalty. As a poignant signifier to this changing outlook, the new company formed in 1999 by a merger between Case IH and New Holland was given the name "CNH Global." We've come a long way since those first tractors of 110 years ago.

BELOW: *Under the protective umbrella of AGCO, Massey-Ferguson has been able to consolidate its position as the maker of small and mid-sized tractors, and has in turn brought its electronics expertise to the group.*

MASSEY-FERGUSON 3690
[1992]

M-F's 3600 series, with its roots in the original 3000 of 1986, was replaced by the 6100/8100 in the mid-1990s. But before then, it had one final major update. It was Dynashift, an electronically controlled transmission, which appeared in 1992. Tractor transmissions were getting more sophisticated, partly to cope with the higher power of modern tractors, partly because of the ever more specialized roles they were taking on, and partly because electronic control had made it all possible. M-F's latest take on transmissions offered thirty-two speeds, forward or reverse. It did this by coupling a four-speed epicyclic gear system to the standard eight-speed transmission. Twenty-four of the thirty-two could be selected without the clutch, but there was no danger of the driver wrecking the transmission by pressing the wrong button. If he did, the electronics would block it, thus protecting the engine and transmission.

In fact, this last incarnation of the 3600 positively bristled with electronics. As well as the existing Autotronic, which allowed automatic operation of front-wheel assist, the PTO, and differential lock, Datatronic added a digital display of all vital functions in the cab. It also had wheel-slip control, whereby the driver could limit the degree of slip to maximize traction. For tractors, the 1990s was the decade of electronic control. As ever, the top 3600, the 3690 shown here, used a turbo-diesel six supplied by Valmet of Finland. Tested at Nebraska in April 1992, this produced 169 hp at the PTO, 148 hp at the drawbar, with a top fuel efficiency of 17.1 hp/hr per gallon. Interestingly, the slightly smaller Valmet in the MF 3670 gave slightly better figures. (Specifications are given for the 8200 series, which is the 2002 equivalent of the 3690.)

LEFT: *The hood extension hints at the extra power of this top-of-the-range 3690, which, along with the 3670, used a Valmet turbo-diesel—402 cu. in. in the 3670, 442 cu. in. for the top tractor.*

MASSEY-FERGUSON 8245 (2002)

Engine: Water-cooled, six-cylinder, turbo-diesel
Bore x stroke: 4.3 x 5.3 in.
Capacity: 452 cu. in.
PTO Power: 160 hp @ 2,000 rpm
Torque: 600 lb. ft. (443 Nm)
Transmission: Sixteen-speed
Speeds: 1.5–24.9 mph
Weight: 18,500 lb.

JOHN DEERE 6400

[1993]

JOHN DEERE 6420
(2002 MODEL)

Engine: Water-cooled, four-cylinder, turbo

Bore x stroke: 4.2 x 5.1 in.

Capacity: 282 cu. in.

Power: 120 hp @ 2,200 rpm

Torque: 337 lb. ft. @ 1,495 rpm

Transmission: Twenty-four-speed

Speeds: 1.0–25 mph

Weight: 10,350 lb.

BELOW: *As revolutionary as the New Generation of 1960? They might not look so different from the tractors they replaced, but the 6000-series of 1993 were practically all new. Together with the three-cylinder 5000s (signaling a return to small tractor production in the U.S.) and six-cylinder 7000s.*

John Deere was busy in the early 1990s. In 1992, it surprised everyone by unveiling an all-new range of small and mid-range tractors, built in a brand-new factory in Atlanta, Georgia. The three-cylinder 5000 series covered the 40–60 hp class, and all had hydrostatic power steering, nine-speed transmission, and optional four-wheel drive.

Meanwhile, the European arm of John Deere hadn't been snoozing either. The following year it launched the new 6000 and 7000 series. According to author Don Macmillan, this was "the most revolutionary development in John Deere tractor models since the New Generation multicylinder models replaced the two-cylinder line in 1960." The company claimed that just nine components had been carried over from the old 60 series. Engines, transmissions, hydraulics, cab,

PTO, and electro-hydraulic hitch were all fresh out of the design department.

The 6000/7000s were actually a joint project. The four-cylinder 6000s were built at the Mannheim plant in Germany. This range comprised a 75 hp 6100, 84 hp 6200, 90 hp 6300, and 100 hp 6400, the latter three all turbocharged. But custom and practice dictated that the bigger six-cylinder 7000s would be built in the U.S.

The new cab fitted to all these machines was claimed to be the quietest in the world—JD evidently wanted to repeat the impact of the Sound-Gard cab of twenty years before. This one had twenty-nine percent more glass area than its 1970s predecessor, and forty percent more space. Together, the 75–140 hp 6000/7000 formed the backbone of John Deere's range through the 1990s. JD certainly didn't do things by halves.

JOHN DEERE 6900

[1993]

If there was a gap in the new 6000/7000 series, it was between the two ranges. The power gap between the 100 hp 6400 and 110 hp 7600 wasn't very big, but there was a bigger gulf in price and sophistication. No manufacturer could afford to leave gaps like that unplugged, which was the surest way to lose sales.

John Deere responded by taking the 6000 upmarket, fitting the smaller six-cylinder engine from the 7000. It was a canny example of mix and match components—using existing parts to create a new model. There were three of them, all using the 435 cu. in. diesel which hitherto had only seen service in the 7600. The 113 hp 6600, 120 hp 6800, and the 130 hp 6900 pictured here—all three were turbocharged.

The transmission specification reflected Deere's determination to move the 6000 upmarket. PowrQuad gave four ranges (changeable under load, without declutching) for twenty speeds in all. The clutch was the oil-cooled Perma-Clutch II. One interesting point about the 6000 John Deeres was that they reverted to chassis construction. For decades, most tractors had used unit-construction, which was lighter and cheaper than a traditional chassis—the tractor was built around the engine and transmission as load-bearing members rather than on a separate frame. However, unit construction didn't have the ultimate strength for high-horsepower applications. In the early 1990s, JD was the only mainstream manufacturer to revert to this format—it might be stronger, but the extra weight of a separate frame would reduce a tractor's work capacity for a given power output. Chassis or no, the upper 6000 series effectively overlapped the lower end of the 7000 series.

JOHN DEERE 6920
(2002 MODEL)

Engine: Water-cooled, six-cylinder, turbo
Bore x stroke: 4.2 x 5.1 in.
Capacity: 435 cu. in.
Power: 150 hp @ 2,100 rpm
Torque: 499 lb. ft. @ 1,365 rpm
Transmission: Twenty-speed
Speeds: 1.6–31 mph
Weight: 12,936 lb.

BELOW: *John Deere plugged the gap between the 6000 and 7000 by simply slotting the latter's six-cylinder engine into the former. Shown here is the 2002 version, but this was still powered by the company's 435 cu. in. turbocharged six, putting out 150 hp—in 1993 the choices were between 113 hp, 120 hp, or 130 hp.*

JOHN DEERE 7800

[1993]

Those 6000s—especially the four-cylinder ones—might represent the European arm of John Deere, but the 7000s represented the U.S. All had six-cylinder turbocharged diesels, and all were built at the Waterloo factory where John Deeres had been made since 1918.

Initially, there were three of the new generation 7000s: the 110 hp 435 cu. in. 7600, 125 hp 487 cu. in. 7700, and 140 hp 7800 (also 487 cu. in.). The top of the range 7800 (the one pictured here) had four-wheel drive and a nineteen-speed power-shift transmission, plus dual-stage braking and

wet discs. As with the 6000 series, every major component was brand new, with only a few parts carried over from the 60 series it replaced.

So the 7000s were a complete break from the 60 series, which itself was more of a gradual development, an update of the 1987 55 series. That in turn was an improvement on the 1982 50 series, the 40 of 1977, and 30 series of the early 1970s. All were developments of the original New Generation 10 series of 1960. Of course, those John Deeres of the 1980s had few, if any, components in common with their 1960 ancestors, but there was certainly a direct line of development between them. And that was the point of the new 6000 and 7000 tractors—they were almost completely new, owing very little to any previous John Deeres.

All the 7000s had the same new quiet cab as the 6000s. John Deere hoped that this one would set new standards, just as the Sound Gard had done two decades earlier. As well as greater space and glass area than the old cab, it had an air-cushioned seat. The instrument panel tilted with the steering wheel, so whatever shape or size you were, the view was the same.

The success of this 1990s generation of John Deeres is reflected in the fact that nearly ten years later, they are still the mainstay of the range.

LEFT: *The John Deere 7000s were a success story of the 1990s, in production right through the decade and a playing a key role in JD's range for a decade.*

JOHN DEERE 7800

Engine: Water-cooled, six-cylinder, turbo
Bore x stroke: 4.56 x 4.75 in.
Capacity: 487 cu. in.
PTO Power: 147 hp
Drawbar Power: 136 hp
Transmission: Nineteen-speed
Speeds: 1.0–24.2 mph
Weight: 15,560 lb.

JOHN DEERE 8100
[1995]

One trend of the 1990s was toward ever-bigger row-crop tractors. Power outputs that were once only the preserve of big super-tractors—the Steigers and Versatiles—now came off the shelf.

John Deere's contribution was the 8000 series, launched in 1995. It claimed that this was the first tractor ever to have its design concept patented. The key element was what they called "integrated chassis design." This mounted the engine over the front axle, which JD said improved weight distribution and allowed a "wasp-waisted" shape that provided excellent visibility for the driver. There were four 8000s initially: the 8100 (185 hp, pictured here), 8200 (210 hp), and 8300 (230 hp) all used a 464 cu. in. turbocharged six-cylinder diesel. The range-topping 8400 boasted a larger 494 cu. in. unit with 260 hp. A year into production, all three smaller 8000s graduated to versions of the 494 cu. in. engine. A new sixteen-speed power-shift transmission was standard across the range, and front-wheel assist was an option, though standard on the 8400. A rubber track option was added in 1997. To avoid confusion, the articulated four-wheel-drive super-tractors were renamed the 9000 series, culminating in the 425 hp 9400T.

The 8000s got a major update in late 1999, as the 8010. As well as power increases across the range (up to 270 hp for the 8410), there was a host of other changes, such as the electronic Implement Management System and hydraulic damping for the three-point hitch. By late 2001 power was up to 295 hp for the 8520 top tractor, while independent front suspension and Starfire GPS positioning were other high-tech advances.

But a few years down the line, how did this big, complex, high-tech tractor stack up as a secondhand machine? In 2002 *Profi* magazine reckoned it was a good buy, recommending the later 494 cu. in. engine over the earlier 455 cu. in. unit.

LEFT: *Row-crop tractors just kept on getting bigger, matching the power of specialist super-tractors like the Steiger and Versatile from the 1960s and 1970s.*

JOHN DEERE 8120 (2002 MODEL)

Engine: Water-cooled, six-cylinder, turbo
Bore x stroke: 4.6 x 5.2 in.
Capacity: 494 cu. in.
Power: 200 hp @ 2,200 rpm
Transmission: Sixteen-speed
Speeds: 1.2–26 mph
Weight: 19,800 lb.

RENAULT 180.94

[1995]

RENAULT ATLES 935 (2001)

Engine: Water-cooled, six-cylinder,
turbo-intercooled

Capacity: 462 cu. in.

Power: 250 hp

Transmission: Eighteen-speed F/
nine-speed R

Renault isn't always thought of as a technology leader in the tractor industry, but it has an impressive track record for innovation. Through the 1960s, it introduced features like torque converters and four-wheel drive. It was also at the forefront of cab design, offering heaters

BELOW: Renault has been at the forefront of technical advance since the Second World War. A shuttle transmission and suspended cab were just two of its many innovations.

and anti-vibration cabs before they became common. Renault was also one of the first manufacturers to offer electronic information displays.

In 1974 it unveiled an innovative forward/reverse shuttle transmission, for quick and easy changes of direction. This was part of a completely new range of tractors that went all the way from 30 hp to 115 hp. There were more cab advances in the 1980s: a passenger seat, roof hatch, and better visibility in the TX cab of 1981, and the TZ in 1987, which was mounted on springs and shock absorbers to isolate the driver from bumps and vibration—it won a Gold Medal from RASE (the Royal Agricultural Society of England).

Fast forward to the mid-1990s, and the 180.94 was the top of Renault's tractor range. As well as that TZ cab, it used a multishift transmission with twenty-seven speeds in forward or reverse, thanks to shuttle. You could also power shift (that

is, under power without declutching) between nine ratios in each of three ranges. By 1999, it had been replaced by the 185 hp Ares, complete with new RZ Hydrostable hydraulically leveled cab. But in 2001 that too was surpassed by the Atles, Renault's most powerful tractor yet which saw them move up to the super-tractor class. Their rather belated launch of a super-tractor (whose specifications are given here) reflected Renault's concentration on the European market.

In 2003, the complete range kicked off with the Pales and Dionis Fructus, (the latter a vineyard tractor), both covering 52–76 hp. Next up was the Ceres (67–97 hp), Cergos/Ergos (77–97 hp), and Temis (102–154 hp). Three separate Ares tractors offered 90–194 hp between them, while the Atles came with up to 250 hp.

Early that year, it was announced that Renault's tractor division was being taken over by Claas.

SAME SILVER 90

[1995]

SAME—Societa Anonima Motori Endotermici—was a manufacturer that had its roots in the early 1920s. Francesco Cassani was something of a tractor pioneer. He was a very early user of diesel power, in 1927 building the first diesel tractor outside Germany. He was also selling a four-wheel-drive machine in 1952, years before this became a mainstream idea, and in the 1930s offered a 10 hp three-wheeler with reversible seat, so that the driver could check on rear-mounted implements. Most

BELOW: *SAME's Silver was designed by Guigiaro, the famous car stylist—a rerun of the 1930s, when American tractor manufacturers brought in designers to stylize their machines.*

of these tractors were badged as Cassanis, as SAME wasn't established until the late 1930s. After the Second World War, full production didn't restart until 1950, when SAME launched a new range of twin-cylinder machines, and the following year a complete range was on sale, with single-, twin-, three-, and four-cylinder air-cooled diesel engines all manufactured on the modular principle.

SAME took over Lamborghini tractors in 1972, the Swiss concern Hurlimann in 1977, and Deutz-Fahr in 1995. Now the company produces a range of up-to-the-minute machines. SAME announced its new 1000 series diesel in the mid-1990s. This used the same modular principle as its

SAME SILVER 90

Engine: Air-cooled, four-cylinder turbo
Capacity: 256 cu. in.
Power: 90 hp @ 2,500 rpm
Transmission: Sixty-speed Agroshift

1950s diesels: that is, a whole range of engines sharing many components, to reduce costs. And unusually for modern tractors, SAME's 1990s machines were still air-cooled. The Silver pictured here covered the 80–100 hp class, with 256 cu. in. four-cylinder or 385 cu. in. six-cylinder versions of that modular range.

WHITE 6105
[1992]

White tractors have to be the takeover veterans of the tractor industry. Formed in the 1960s when the parent company took over Oliver, Cockshutt, and Minneapolis-Moline, they were then sold off to the Texas Investment Group in 1980. Five years later, another new owner came along—Allied Products Corporation. Finally, in 1993 White became part of the burgeoning AGCO empire. Writing this nine years on, it looks as though White may have finally found its corporate haven.

AGCO was the American tractor phenomenon of the 1990s. It was a new name to the business, just as White had been twenty years before, formed in 1990 as a management buy-out of the American end of Deutz-Allis. AGCO began selling a range of tractors using Deutz and Allis parts—the machines themselves were built for AGCO by White, so there was already a link before White was taken over in 1993. They were not alone as in that same year, AGCO also bought up the American arm of Massey-Ferguson. And a couple of years after that, McConnell (manufacturers of articulated four-by-four tractors) was taken over and added to the stable.

So in a few short years, AGCO had become the biggest tractor manufacturer in the United States, making use of famous names to sell different lines of tractors that shared common components.

Top of the AGCO-White range (the big 6215 apart) in the mid-1990s was the 6100-series, a range of six-cylinder turbo diesel machines. The 6105 (pictured here) was the lead-in model, though that was later uprated into the 6125, which used a 359 cu. in. Cummins engine—also demonstrating that White has remained faithful to its long-time engine supplier.

But it was a gradual process, and in its early years AGCO remained dependent on Deutz air-cooled diesels for its engine supply. A new generation of Whites were imported Lamborghini, rebadged, and painted in White silver.

LEFT: *White has survived takeover, merger, and bankruptcy in order to make it into the twenty-first century as an established tractor marque.*

WHITE 6125 (1993)

Engine: Water-cooled six-cylinder turbo-diesel
Bore x stroke: 4.02 x 4.72 in.
Capacity: 359 cu. in.
PTO Power: 124 hp
Transmission: Thirty-two-speed power shift

NEW HOLLAND 8340
[1992]

It's hard to believe now, but New Holland—a common badge on modern tractors—never started out to build tractors at all—the badge didn't even appear on a tractor until the 1990s.

The company, founded in 1895 in Pennsylvania, specialized in non-powered implements. It was taken over in 1940 and again in 1947, in between times producing one of the first successful automatic pick-up hay balers. In 1964 its then-owner, the Sperry Corporation, took a major interest in Claas, then one of the largest combine manufacturers in Europe. That led to Sperry New Holland concentrating on combines as well as implements until 1986, when it was taken over by Ford. Soon, all Ford tractors wore the New Holland badge, even after the tractor arm was sold to Fiat in 1991. By the late 1990s, many New Hollands came in Fiat colors as well.

That 60 series featured a sloping hood, which became a key styling feature of modern 1990s tractors. But the earlier 40 series, of which the 8340 pictured here was the top of the range, betrayed its older design with a bluff, squared-off hood. Unlike the smaller four-cylinder 40s, this one used a turbocharged six of 456 cu. in. and 125 hp. The standard transmission was a twelve-speed (forward and reverse) syncromesh unit, or twenty-four speed if you opted for the dual-range power shift. NH Geotech, the Fiat/New Holland combine, merged with Case IH in 1999 to form CNH Global, which instantly became one of the four biggest tractor makers on the planet. The others were John Deere, AGCO, and the SAME Deutz-Fahr group of Italy/Germany, reflecting how the American tractor industry was still a dominant world force. CNH Global was in fact so big that anti-trust authorities dictated that two of its plants had to be sold off, to prevent it becoming overdominant in the market.

LEFT: *New Holland's popular 40 series range was topped by the turbo-diesel 8340. It had a turbocharged six of 458 cu. in. with 125 hp.*

NEW HOLLAND 8340

Engine: Water-cooled, six-cylinder turbo-diesel
Bore x stroke: 4.4 x 5.0 in.
Capacity: 458 cu. in.
PTO Power: 125 hp
Drawbar Power: 97 hp
Transmission: Sixteen-speed power shift
Speeds: 1.5–19.6 mph
Weight: 18,150 lb.

NEW HOLLAND 7840
[1996]

New Holland might have been owned by Fiat, but it was still sold in Ford blue as well as Fiat red, through the appropriate dealer network.

This styling split meant that the New Holland 40 series was sold as the Fiat S Series in some parts of Europe, just as the big 70 series New Holland was sometimes a Fiat G. No matter what badge it wore, the 40 series was highly successful, and in 1996, the year this particular 7840 was built, the 7,500th example rolled off the production line at the Basildon factory, in England. The 7840 was the best-seller of the 40 series range, and for a time it was also Britain's best-selling tractor of any type.

It was actually a busy year for New Holland Geotech, as the Fiat/New Holland group was now named. A new smaller tractor, the 35 series, was announced. This was an Italian-built machine, and was produced to cover the 65–95 hp range—as a Fiat, it was styled and marketed as the L series, and as a New Holland, the 35.

As if that weren't enough, 1996 also saw the launch of the 100–160 hp 60 series range, this one was built at the Basildon plant. Once again, it came with either Fiat or New Holland badges, and was sold as the 60 or M-series. Significantly, style-wise, it also came with the modern low-nose look that many tractors adopted in the late 1990s, most notably the dramatic looking Deutz Agrotron.

All the 60 series were powered by a six-cylinder 464 cu. in. diesel which was capable of meeting the latest EPA emissions regulations—pollution control was now extending from road vehicles into the field. At launch, there were four 60-series tractors: the 100 hp 8160, 115 hp 8260, 135 hp 8360, and 160 hp 8560.

"Everything you ever wanted in a tractor," boasted New Holland's confident full-page ad of the time, which featured the a smiling, plaid-shirted farmer, "(but never dared ask for)."

LEFT: *Built at New Holland's (once Ford's) plant in Basildon, England, the 7840 was the latest addition to what was a long line of practical, hardworking British tractors.*

BELOW: *The square-rigged 7840 was a typical 1970s/1980s tractor, which now looks very dated compared to the low-nose designs that started to appear in the 1990s.*

NEW HOLLAND 7840

(Specifications for 1992 Ford 7840)
Engine: Water-cooled, six-cylinder
Bore x stroke: 4.4 x 4.4 in.
Capacity: 401 cu. in.
PTO Power: 90 hp
Drawbar Power: 75 hp
Transmission: Sixteen-speed power shift
Speeds: 1.4–18.8 mph

NEW HOLLAND 7740

[1997]

The mid-size 40 series was a new tractor from Ford New Holland in 1992. There were six of them, named the PowerStar series. Cheapest was the 5640 (66 PTO hp), followed by the 6640 (76 hp), the 7740 shown here (82 hp), the six-cylinder 7840 on the previous page (90 hp), the 96 hp 8240, and top of the range 8340 at 106 hp. A new engine range to suit, the Genesis, was announced, in four- and six-cylinder form, with or without turbo. Straightforward and up to date, with a wide range of transmission options, the Basildon-built 40 series was a success.

By 1997, the 40 series was nearing the end of its life. This 7740 was from the middle of the range, and was powered by a 95 hp turbocharged four-cylinder diesel. The engine was part of Ford/New Holland's "Genesis" family, a four-cylinder version of the 401 cu. in. six that powered the 7840, with exactly the same bore and stroke dimensions.

But popular and adaptable though it was, the 40 series would sooner or later have to be replaced. It happened in 1998, with the new TS range. There were three of them, all with a choice of two- or four-wheel drive, and all with the low rounded hood line already seen on the smaller 35 and 60 series. The 305 cu. in. Powerstar four-cylinder diesel came in 80 hp non-turbo and 90 or 100 hp turbo forms: these were the TS90, TS100, and TS110 respectively.

The following year, a higher-powered six-cylinder TS115 (though rated at 100 hp) was announced to take over from the 7840. It used New Holland's own Powerstar 458 cu. in. engine and a sixteen-speed transmission. A twenty-four-speed "Dual Command" unit was optional, and four wheel-drive was standard on the TS115. In 2000, NH Geotech merged with Case IH to form CNH Global. Within months it was closing plants in the U.S., Canada, Britain, and Italy. The future looked uncertain.

LEFT: *New Holland became a tractor marque almost by default. The name appeared on tractors only after the takeover by Ford.*

NEW HOLLAND 7740

(Specifications for 1992 Ford 7740)

Engine: Water-cooled, four-cylinder turbo-diesel

Bore x stroke: 4.4 x 5.0 in.

Capacity: 304 cu. in.

PTO Power: 87 hp

Drawbar Power: 77 hp

Transmission: Sixteen-speed power shift

Speeds: 1.4–19.8 mph

MATBRO TR250

[1997]

Utility tractors have always had to do the odd piece of yard work, but it was only in the 1990s that specialist yard shunters came onto the market. It was the perfect illustration of how farm machinery has become much more specialized over the years, not least because modern capital-intensive farms can now afford to invest in one special machine for each job.

The Matbro—built in England—was one of the first specialist shunters. You wouldn't use it for plowing, but that's not what it was designed for—this was a yard shunter, pure and simple. To give it the maneuver-ability essential for doing yard work, the little machine was articulated to allow a tight turning circle in confined spaces. The front loader could manage up to 2.5 tons at a time, underlining the Matbro's role as a sort of super-forklift.

The transmission needs of a yard tractor are obviously different from those in the field, and the top of the range TR250 had a Clark power-shift transmission with four forward speeds and three reverse, with electronic selection. Perkins supplied the 256 cu. in. four-cylinder diesel, in 75, 96, 106, and 114 hp forms. Matbro was taken over by the U.S. Terex Corporation in 2001, and production of the renamed Terex TM200R and 250R moved to England.

But despite its pivot steering, the Matbro or Terex wasn't the ultimate in yard tractors. In 1996, there was news of the Master Mate, made in the Czech Republic. It weighed 5.4 tons, could lift to a height of 4.2 meters and was powered by its 71 hp engine—so far, so normal. It also had four-wheel steering, which isn't unusual in yard tractors, but its unique point was a pivot above each of the four wheels, which allowed the Poclain wheel motors to swivel—thus equipped, the Master Mate could spin around in a perfect circle of just 3.2 meters, making it one of the tightest-turning yard tractors you could buy.

LEFT: *Pictured at Glastonbury on the scenic Somerset levels in southwest England, this pristine Matbro looks ready for a lifetime of hard work.*

MATBRO TR250

Engine: Water-cooled, four-cylinder, turbo
Capacity: 256 cu. in.
Power: 106 hp @ 2,200 rpm
Torque: 298 lb. ft. (220 Nm) @ 1,400 rpm
Transmission: Four forward, three reverse
Lifting weight: 2.5 tons
Unladen weight: 13,750 lb.

JCB FASTRAC 2150
[1998]

JCB FASTRAC 2150

Engine: Water-cooled turbo diesel
Power: 150 hp
PTO power: 133 hp
Torque: 467 lb. ft. @ 1,400 rpm
Transmission: Fifty-four forward,
  eighteen reverse speeds
Weight: 14,032 lb.

The concept of a farm tractor capable of high road speeds is not new, and there have been sporadic attempts to produce one over the years, notably the Minneapolis-Moline UDLX and 1970s Trantor. But the JCB Fastrac will go down in history as the first successful high-speed tractor.

JCB's research showed than in Europe road hauling made up a large part of each tractor's work, sometimes as much as seventy percent. So a fully capable agricultural tractor capable of up to 40 mph could be ideal. As it turned out, the Fastrac was. Launched in 1991, it combined four-wheel drive with all-around suspension and disc brakes. It could pull a five-bottom plow in the field and haul up to 14 tons at 40 mph. The sophisticated suspension was far more comfortable for the driver than conventional live axle suspension. It was also self-leveling at the back, to cope with implements and heavy towing loads.

JCB is a British company, so naturally enough the Fastrac is powered by the Perkins 1000 turbo diesel engine, with power choices ranging from 115–170 bhp. The transmission is a particularly complex 54 speed forward, 18 reverse setup, needed to cope with everything from a slow crawl in the field to 40 mph on the road. A four-wheel steering system (termed Quadtronic by its maker) automatically switches between two- and four-wheel drive for quicker turns at the end of the field. As well as self-leveling for loads, the suspension levels laterally, which is useful for traversing steep hillsides.

However, if the early Fastrac had a flaw, it was its thirteen-meter-plus turning circle, which restricted its usefulness as a field tractor. This was cured in 1995 with the four-wheel-steered Quadronic, powered by 115 hp or 135 hp Perkins power units, and with a turning circle cut down to ten meters, which JCB claimed was better than that of some conventional tractors.

The JCB Fastrac was one of the most significant tractors of the later twentieth century. Not bad for a company that started out making simple two-wheel trailers!

BELOW: *Like Caterpillar, JCB wasn't an established tractor manufacturer, but this helped it apply a fresh approach to the concept—the Fastrac was the result.*

TERRA GATOR

[1999]

The Terra Gator is another good example of more specialized equipment, like the Matbro loader. There comes a point where it makes economic sense to use specialized machines that can do the job faster and more efficiently than a conventional tractor. Terra Gators are just that kind of machine, specialist high-capacity spreaders, with massive low pressure tires designed to minimize soil compaction by reducing ground pressure to as little as possible.

All are built on a big scale—the 1664 (pictured here) is an earlier Terra Gator, but in September 1998 the company announced the new John Deere–powered 8103. This was a 320 hp machine, thanks to its turbocharged six-cylinder diesel that measured 519 cu. in. John Deere also

supplied the Mate 2 1400 axle, allegedly to increase axle life and improve reliability. The transmission (an Ag Chem Terra-Shift) gave eleven very close gear ratios, with gaps of as little as 14.5 percent. As with most modern tractor transmissions, it also allowed clutch-free changes on the move. Other changes on the 8103 included a new cab with better visibility, improved ergonomics, and less noise. Plus its new chassis used a rectangular tube frame for greater strength.

But the 8103 wasn't the biggest Terra Gator by any means. The 1903 used a 400 bhp Caterpillar diesel, and was later joined by a four-wheel-drive version, the 8144, in 2000. Terra Gators aren't the most common pieces of farm machinery, but 10,000 have been built so far.

TERRA GATOR 8103

Engine: Water-cooled, six-cylinder Cummins
Capacity: 519 cu. in.
Power: 320 hp @ 2,400 rpm
Torque: 634 lb. ft. @ 1,500 rpm
Transmission: JD Funk 2000 Powershift, six-speed
Axles/Brakes: John Deere
Fuel capacity: 78 gallons

BELOW: *Produced by Ag Chem of Holland, using many John Deere parts, the Terra Gator has proved itself adaptable to a number of uses, from oil field work to tourist transports. The exact specification varies according to model and use.*

NEW HOLLAND TV140
[1998]

Bidirectional tractors, as the name suggests, can work equally well running forward or backward, with the driver's seat and controls swiveled 180 degrees to suit. On some bidirectional machines, a duplicate set of controls is provided, and certain implements, such as harvesting machinery or an industrial loader, are much easier to use in this way.

Versatile was a pioneer of the modern bidirectional tractor, with the 150 Push-Pull of 1977. Far smaller than Versatile's usual four-wheel-drive super-tractors, it could operate in "pull" mode like a conventional tractor, or in "push" with the driver and seat swiveled around 180 degrees. Without an engine hood to obscure the view, this gave perfect visibility of implements like swathers and loaders, while an articulated chassis made the 150 very maneuverable for yard work. The transmission was hydrostatic, allowing for a rapid switch between forward and reverse, with three ranges in either direction. This bidirectional technology was part of the Versatile legacy for New Holland, the company's eventual owner. NH's current bidirectional (the TV140 shown here) was launched in 1998 to replace the elderly 9030. On the TV140, the driver faces either directly out of the cab or over the hood, depending on which way the tractor is being used. The Turnabout console swivels by 180 degrees, taking all the controls and instrumentation with it, in less than five seconds. Articulated steering gives the TV140 a best-in-class turning radius of 142.5 in.

The 140 was first powered by a 135 hp six-cylinder diesel, but a municipal Utility version introduced in early 1999 offered a 105 hp version of the same engine. All TV140s now use this lower powered unit, albeit with higher PTO torque rise (sixty percent against forty-two percent).

LEFT: *You might think that this was a conventional tractor. The giveaway is the rear-mounted (though "front" and "rear" have little relevance here) loader. Look closer, and you see the gap between cab and engine hood, allowing for the articulated chassis.*

NEW HOLLAND TV140

Engine: Water-cooled, six-cylinder turbo
Capacity: 456 cu. in.
Power: 105 hp @ 2,100 rpm
Transmission: Auto hydrostatic + three-speed range
Speeds: 0–18 mph
Weight: 18,000 lb. (max operating weight)

VALMET 6300

[1998]

VALTRA S SERIES (2002)

Engine: Water-cooled, six-cylinder turbo-diesel

Capacity: 538 cu. in.

Power: 260 hp @ 2,200 rpm

Torque: 1,050 Nm @ 1,400 rpm

Transmission: Forty-speed forward/reverse

Speeds: Up to 31 mph

Weight: 19,360 lb.

BELOW: *From its humble beginnings, Valmet has now become a significant European manufacturer.*

Valmet of Finland—now sold as the Valtra brand—began producing tractors back in 1952. Its original name was a shortened version of Valtion Metallitehtaat—the company had been in existence since before the start of the Second World War.

Valmet's first tractors were small, and the original Valmet 15 was powered by a 15 hp power unit of less than 100 cu. in. However, a more powerful version followed and within a few years, Valmet's first diesel was unveiled. The company designed its own three-cylinder diesel, an advanced water-cooled unit with direct injection, which powered the 33D tractor. Four-cylinder versions followed later, and in the late 1960s they began to pay attention to ergonomics and produced the 900 tractor of 1967 which had a rubber mounted cab, with a built-in safety cage.

There were plenty of other milestones as well. Bigger, more powerful Valmets came along, such as the T470 Bison, while the six-cylinder T800 of 1966 was the company's first 100 hp machine. Trac Trol (Valmet's version of power shift) came in 1969, with turbocharging and four-wheel drive at around the same time.

Ten years later, an agreement was signed with Volvo BM to jointly produce the Nordic, an all-new tractor aimed at both the agricultural and timber markets. This was the Valmet 04-series, and by 1985 the Finns had bought out Volvo's share of the project. Soon afterward, Valmet made history by being the first tractor company to offer a choice of colors! Red, yellow, white, green, and blue . . . but their revolutionary idea didn't catch on.

By the 1990s, Valmet/Valtra was a well-established manufacturer, and produced a wide range of machines. The 6300–8000 Mezzo range sold especially well in Britain—the 6300 model is pictured here. Most of these tractors came with a thirty-six-speed Delta Power shift transmission (forward or reverse) with the option of a HiTrol turbine clutch. The HiTrol was a system designed to protect the transmission from shock overloads and to prolong the life of the clutch. Also bulking up the extras list was Autocontrol 4, which was an automatic gear shifting system combined with engine monitoring. In 2002, the equivalent Valmet was the 260 hp S Series, and specifications for this are given above.

LANDINI LEGEND 130
[1999]

From near collapse in the late 1950s, with an outdated range of single-cylinder diesels, Landini has revived to become a major manufacturer. It was taken over by Massey-Ferguson in 1960, and is now Italian owned, building tractors under the McCormick brand.

Landini announced a major new range of tractors in 1973, the 6/7/8500 lineup with 12+4 transmission. Four years later, it unveiled Europe's first 100 hp four-wheel-drive tractor with a conventional layout. Orchard and vineyard tractors were a Landini specialty, thanks to the nature of the home market. A new range of orchard machines was launched in 1982, with a vineyard lineup following in 1986. Landini

has also tended to concentrate on smaller tractors, and while under the Massey-Ferguson wing, it sold these in some markets with M-F badges. Similarly, the bigger Masseys were marketed in some areas as Landinis.

In the late 1990s, Landini's top-of-the-range tractor was this, the Legend, which came in 110, 123, or 138 hp form. All three were powered by a 385 cu. in. Perkins six-cylinder turbo-diesel. Four-wheel drive was standard, with air-conditioning on the top two tractors. By 2002, the range had extended up to 160 hp, while the Landini lineup was extensive, including 35 hp compact tractors, the Atlas field machine, Rex orchard tractor, and Trekker crawler.

LANDINI LEGEND 130 (2002 MODEL)

Engine: Water-cooled, six-cylinder turbo-diesel

Capacity: 385 cu. in.

Power: 126 hp @ 2,200 rpm

Transmission: Thirty-six-speed forward/reverse

Wheelbase: 112 in.

Weight: 12,760 lb.

BELOW: *The Legend was a modern tractor, with turbocharged six-cylinder diesel, four-wheel drive, and up to 138 hp.*

CASE 9380 QUADTRAC
[1999]

Caterpillar revolutionized crawler tractors in 1986 with the rubber-tracked Challenger. With its air-suspended rubber tracks, it had crawler levels of traction on soil, but more speed and comfort than steel tracks on the road. Soon other manufacturers were rushing to follow suit. Claas of Germany sold the Challenger in Europe under its own name, while John Deere soon developed rubber crawler versions of its wheeled machines.

Case IH's take on the new crawler technology was slightly different. As its name suggested, the Case Quadtrac used four rubber tracks, one at each corner. Each of them was 30 inches wide and could pivot up and down by ten degrees, allowing them to follow ground contours more easily, and each of the four worked independently, having a better chance of keeping in contact with the ground. Twenty-six degrees of oscillation between the front and rear of the Quadtrac helped as well.

Case claimed that the Quadtrac—unlike a two-tracked crawler, which steers by braking one or the other track—would steer just like a conventional four-wheel-drive tractor, with a turning radius of less than twenty feet. Compared to a two-track unit, it was able to keep the tractor's articulation, so you could still turn under load. Otherwise, much of the Quadtrac was the same as the conventional 9300 series tractor on which it was based.

Case IH, like every other manufacturer, had been suffering from the decade-long downturn in sales, but for the 1990s a new strategy emerged. Instead of building tractors for stock, and pursuing market share ahead of profitability, the company would concentrate on meeting what demand there was, and making a profit. So stocks were cut back radically, with only common subassemblies kept in large numbers. This was a move focused on the American tractor market, where brand loyalty was extremely strong.

LEFT: *The Case 9380 Quadtrac had both wheels and tracks—the best of both worlds, perhaps?*

CASE 9380 QUADTRAC (2002 MODEL)

Engine: Water-cooled, six-cylinder, turbo-intercooled
Bore x stroke: 5.6 x 6.1 in.
Capacity: 855 cu. in.
Power: 360 hp
Transmission: Twelve-speed SyncroShift
Track Width: 30 in.
Weight: 43,750 lb.

MASSEY-FERGUSON 4300
[2002]

Could this possibly be the last of the new Massey-Ferguson machines to roll out of the old Banner Lane factory in Coventry, England? It looked likely, as only months after the 4300 model was launched, AGCO announced that the factory would close in 2003. It was a sad end, after over

ABOVE: *End of an era perhaps, but the 4300 was a neat mid-size tractor, and a useful update on the 4200, with lower emission engines, more torque, and other changes.*

LEFT: *The end of a long history of British production. This 4300 series was the last tractor to come off the production line at Banner Lane, which had been making tractors since the 1940s.*

half a century of production at the Banner Lane plant.

Not that it would be any consolation to the 1,000 workers who lost their jobs, but the 4300 was a good note to go out on, a straightforward mid-range tractor, the sort of thing Banner Lane had been turning out since the first little gray Fergies rolled off the line. It was an evolution of the 4200 series, which in turn had replaced the 300 series in the 50–120 hp market in 1998.

There were no radical changes, and the most significant difference was the adoption of Perkins's latest lower-emission diesels, in three-, four-, or six-cylinder form, with or without turbocharger. The new engines provided a wide power range for the new tractors, with eight choices: from the 52 hp non-turbo triple in the 4315 base model, through the 85 hp 1000 series four-cylinder turbo (powering the 4345), and topped out by the 110 hp six-cylinder

turbo (4370). As well as lower emissions, the revised engines offered more torque backup, by 2–14 percent, depending on the model.

The transmission did not change very much, still ranging from an eight-speed forward/reverse with manual shuttle to a twenty-four-speed job, again forward or reverse with power shuttle. One change was in the optional Supercreep, which now allowed speeds down to 0.1 mph, half of what was available previously. There were many minor changes introduced as well, such as repositioned controls, upgraded seat options, a side mounted exhaust, telescopic/tilting steering wheel, and a rather bigger, front-mounted toolbox.

MASSEY-FERGUSON 4370

Engine: Water-cooled, six-cylinder
  turbocharged
Capacity: 366 cu. in.
Power: 110 hp @ 2,200 rpm
Torque: 335 lb. ft. (454 Nm)
  @ 1,400 rpm
Transmission: Eighteen-speed
  (twenty-four-speed optional)
Brakes: Wet disc brakes
PTO: Two-speed (540/1000 rpm)

JOHN DEERE 8020

[2002]

When it was launched in early 2002, the 8020 was John Deere's new flagship tractor, replacing the 8010. However, within a few months it was eclipsed by the pivot-steer 9020 series, which offered up to 450 bhp—the most powerful tractors JD had ever made. But

LEFT: *Air suspension, hydraulics, and electronic control—and that was just the seat! John Deere's 8120 was a real state-of-the-art, high-horsepower tractor for the twenty-first century.*

ABOVE: *For the first time the 8520 offered ILS as an option, increasing traction and comfort.*

the 8020 remained a formidable tool, with nearly 300 rated bhp on the top model, and the choice of wheeled or rubber-tracked models—Deere had taken the Caterpillar Challenger lesson to heart, and now offered several rubber tracked tractors.

The biggest news about the new 8020 was ILS (independent link suspension). For many years, tractor suspension systems had changed little. Only in the late 1990s did front independent systems, and hydraulics, make big inroads. ILS was the logical progression of all this, using a combination of mechanical suspension, hydraulics, and electronics to keep the front wheels vertical to the ground, and in contact with it, with obvious benefits for traction and comfort. A rear-suspension version came later. Hydraulic rams controlled the movement of mechanical upper and lower arms, with the electronics acting as an overall "brain" keeping the system on an even keel. Wheel travel at the front was 3.9 in., more than twice that of JD's Triple Link suspension, which had been new only five years earlier! ILS was standard on the top 8520 and optional on

the others, though even 8520 owners had to pay extra for the Active Seat. Perhaps the most sophisticated tractor seat to date, this combined air suspension with hydraulics and electronic control—the seat's position was monitored many times a second, and the hydraulics brought into action accordingly, to provide a smooth, comfortable ride. No wonder the Active Seat cost the equivalent of an extra $5,210 in Britain! But for many operators it was worth it, allowing longer hours and higher speeds before the driver was tired. All 8020 tractors used Deere's latest six-cylinder diesel with electronic common-rail injection, with a turbo and air/air intercooler. Johnny Popper, it was not!

JOHN DEERE 8520

Engine: Water-cooled, six-cylinder turbocharged/intercooled
Capacity: 494 cu. in.
Power: 295 hp rated, 325 hp max
Transmission: Sixteen-speed power shift
Suspension: Optional ILS front
Range: 8120 (200 hp)–8520 (295 hp)

1889   1892   1898   1901   1902   1907   1910   1912   1914–15

•1889

John Charter mounts a single-cylinder engine in a Rumely steam traction engine chassis. World's first gasoline tractor.

•1892

John Froelich fits a Van Duzen engine to his own wooden chassis. It's successfully demonstrated, and four are made.

•1898

Huber enters tractor production after buying Van Duzen. A batch of thirty machines make it the leading U.S. tractor manufacturer.

•1901

In England, Daniel Albone builds the first practical lightweight tractor, patents it in1902 ,and goes into production.

•1902

Charles Hart and Charles Parr build their first tractor, a 30 hp twin.

•1907

French Gousi tractor pioneers the power takeoff for towed implements. Deutz builds the first bidirectional machine. Henry Ford begins experimenting with tractors.

•1910

Motor plows increasingly popular. Much cheaper than full-size machines, and compatible with horse-drawn implements, they enjoy a brief boom, until killed off by the Fordson.

•1912

Waterloo Boy, the forerunner of John Deere tractors, goes into production. J. I. Case builds its first production gasoline tractor.

•1914–15

International introduces its first successful small tractors, the 8-16 Mogul and 10-20 Titan. Ditto Allis-Chalmers with the 6-12.

1929   1930   1930–32   1932   1934   1935   1936   1938

•1929

Two significant mergers: Minneapolis Steel & Machinery joins with the Minneapolis Threshing Co. and Moline Plow, to form Minneapolis-Moline. Oliver merges with Hart-Parr. And Case replaces its famous Crossmotor line.

•1930

Caterpillar pioneers diesel power, and its Diesel 60 sets a new economy record at Nebraska. Massey-Harris launches the four-wheel-drive GP.

•1930–32

Disastrous slump in U.S. tractor sales, from over 200,000 in 1930 to just 19,000 in 1932. Many small manufacturers collapse, and by 1936 nine big companies control most U.S. tractor production.

•1932

Allis-Chalmers U is the first tractor with pneumatic rubber tires—higher road speeds, more comfort, and better economy. By 1940, ninety-five percent of new tractors are air-equipped.

•1934

John Deere offers a hydraulic lift for implements.

•1935

Oliver 70 is the first high-compression gasoline tractor using high-octane fuel, giving good power from a relatively small six-cylinder engine. International shows the first American wheeled diesel tractor.

•1936

U.S. tractor production finally recovers to match that of 1929. Over a million tractors are now in use on U.S. farms—this has doubled in 11 years. Ferguson-Brown is the first production tractor with the Ferguson hydraulic three-point hitch.

•1938

Minneapolis-Moline UDLX "Comfortractor," first machine with an integral steel cab. Heater, radio, passenger seat, and 40 mph on the road. High price puts the buyers off though.

1917   1919   1920   1923   1924   1925   1928

• 1917

Fordson F enters production, at the behest of the British government. Thanks to mass production and clever design, this full-size four-cylinder tractor is cheaper than a motor plow. The single most important tractor of all time.

• 1919

Minneapolis Steel & Machinery unveils the 12-20, with four-cylinder 16-valve engine, pressure lubrication, and enclosed oil bath transmission.

• 1920

Tractor testing begins at the University of Nebraska—a set of standard tests that are soon recognized as a de facto national standard across the U.S.

• 1923

John Deere introduces the Model D, the first of its own long line of Johnny Poppers. It sticks with this twin-cylinder format for over forty years.

• 1924

International Farmall is the first genuine all-purpose tractor, combining both power (for belt work) and agility (for row crops). Within a few years, all major manufacturers have a "general purpose" model.

• 1925

Bitter rivals Best and Holt, the two leading U.S. crawler manufacturers decide to merge. The result? Caterpillar.

• 1928

Ford moves Model F production to Cork in Ireland, from where it emerges as the Model N (now outdated).

1939   1940   1941   1942   1945   1946

• 1939

Henry Ford and Harry Ferguson's infamous "handshake agreement" results in the Ford 9N, an all-new modern lightweight with Ferguson three-point hitch. It's a huge success.

• 1940

U.S. tractor production reaches a new record—250,000.

• 1941

Wartime material shortages begin to bite. Austere 2N replaces Ford 9N, with no pneumatic tires, electric starter, or battery. Other manufacturers make similar moves, or cease production altogether.

• 1942

Tractor testing at Nebraska suspended for the duration of the war, and production falls to 105,000 the following year.

• 1945

Willys designs an agricultural version of the military Jeep.

• 1946

Belarus tractor production starts in Russia—and becomes the biggest manufacturer in the world. Harry Ferguson starts building his own tractors in Coventry, England.

• 1947

Cockshutt of Canada introduces the live PTO and live hydraulics, an industry first. Ford ends its agreement with Harry Ferguson.

• 1948

U.S. production recovery complete, with a new record of half a million tractors built.

• 1949

John Deere R is the first postwar diesel from a U.S. manufacturer. Sets a new record for fuel efficiency.

1952   1953   1954   1955   1957   1958   1959   1961   1963   1964   1965

● **1952**
Case 500 marries old chain-drive LA tractor with a modern six-cylinder diesel.

● **1955**
Oliver Super 99 is the most powerful tractor of its time: 72 hp from GM supercharged two-stroke diesel.

● **1960**
John Deere replaces its entire two-cylinder line with an all-new four- and six-cylinder range. Also leads U.S. in fitting ROPS (rollover protection system).

● **1965**
Comfort King cab from Case is mounted on rubber to help isolate vibration.

● **1953**
Massey-Harris and Ferguson merge to form Massey-Harris-Ferguson (later Massey-Ferguson).

● **1957**
Case-O-Matic transmission replaces clutch with a torque converter. Mercedes introduces the Unimog.

● **1961**
First production turbocharged diesel tractor, the Allis-Chalmers D19. International 4300 has 300 hp and four-wheel steering.

● **1963**
First production 100 hp two-wheel-drive tractor, the Allis-Chalmers D21.

● **1954**
International unveils Torque Amplifier, a dual-range transmission which allows on-the-go shifting. Other manufacturers follow suit.

● **1959**
The Steiger brothers begin building four-wheel-drive super-tractors.

● **1964**
Massey-Ferguson unveils the Red Giants 100-series, renewing its entire lineup.

1978   1979–82   1981   1982   1983   1984   1985   1986   1987   1988

● **1978**
Steiger Tiger III typical super-tractor of the 1970s: 1,150 cu. in. Cummins, over 350 hp, and 20,000 lb. of drawbar pull.

● **1982**
John Deere announces its biggest tractor yet, the 300 hp V8 8850.

● **1984**
Tenneco Inc. takes over International, to form Case-International. It closes the Farmall Illinois factory, cutting U.S. production capacity by one-third.

● **1986**
Caterpillar Challenger 65 is the first modern crawler with rubber tracks—one of the most significant crawlers ever made. Case IH buys Steiger.

● **1988**
Case launches the 130–195 hp Magnum, the first joint Case IH tractor.

● **1979–82**
U.S. tractor sales slump from 188,000 to 119,000.

● **1985**
Deutz of Germany buys Allis-Chalmers, Allis West Works closed. Ford buys New Holland.

● **1983**
Ford TW range offers radar-operated monitor of ground speed and wheel slip.

● **1981**
Knudson self-leveling tractor, for hillside working, returns to production.

● **1987**
Massey-Ferguson announces the Datatronic electronic monitoring system.

1967   1968   1969   1970   1971   1972   1973   1974   1975   1977

●**1970**
Reducing cab noise now a priority, and Nebraska introduces a noise test.

●**1967**
First production hydrostatic drive, from International, using a hydraulic drive system in place of gearbox.

●**1972**

●**1975**
In U.S., sales of 100hp+ tractors exceed those in 40–99 hp class.

●**1971**
First production intercoolers on turbodiesel tractors—John Deere 4620 produces 136 hp.

●**1968**
Ford 8000 is the first Ford tractor of more than 100hp.

New John Deere cab, the Sound-Gard, first of a new generation of quiet, rubber mounted cabs. Systems tractors, able to operate implements at both ends simultaneously, introduced by Mercedes and Deutz.

●**1977**
Versatile 150 is a modern bidirectional tractor which swivels driver's platform 180 degrees to allow easy operation in either direction.

●**1969**
John Deere and Ford introduce their first turbocharged tractors, the 122 hp Deere 4520 and 130 hp Ford 9000. Tenneco Inc. takes over Case.

●**1973**
Allis-Chalmers introduces a twenty-speed Power Director transmission.

●**1974**
White begins selling tractors under its own name, dropping the Oliver, Minneapolis-Moline, and Cockshutt brands.

1990 1991   1992   1993   1994   1996   1997   1999   2000   2001

●**1990**
AGCO is formed out of a management buy-out by the U.S. management of Deutz-Allis.

●**1992**
U.S. tractor sales fall to 87,000, less than half sold in 1979. Massey-Ferguson Dynashift thirty-two-speed transmission combines eight-speed gearbox with 4-range epicyclic system.

●**1994**

John Deere launches the all-new 6000 and 7000, a joint U.S./German project.

●**1997**
Matbro TR250 typifies new breed of specialist yard shunter.

●**2000**
NH Geotech merges with Case IH to produce CNH Global.

●**2001**
GPS satellite positioning systems now common on high-tech tractors.

●**1991**
JCB Fastrac heralds a new generation of high-speed tractors—40 mph on the road with four-wheel drive, four-wheel steering, four-wheel suspension, four-wheel braking. Ford sells its tractor arm to Fiat, which forms NH Geotech.

●**1993**
U.S. tractor sales up eleven percent, the first increase for eleven years. John Deere and Case IH post big profits.

●**1996**
All major manufacturers now offer full power shift, with on-the-go shifting through all ratios.

●**1999**
Claas, Fendt, and ZF all produce CVT—continuously variable auto transmission—for tractors. Case IH Quadtrac uses four independent rubber tracks.

INDEX